D0906309

Mormon Odyssey

Ida Hunt Udall.

Mormon Odyssey

The Story of
Ida Hunt Udall, Plural Wife

EDITED BY

Maria S. Ellsworth

UNIVERSITY OF ILLINOIS PRESS

Urbana and Chicago

1992

© 1992 by the Board of Trustees of the University of Illinois
Manufactured in the United States of America
C 5 4 3 2 1

This book is printed on acid-free paper.

Library of Congress Cataloging-in-Publication Data
Udall, Ida Hunt, d. 1915.
    Mormon odyssey : the story of Ida Hunt Udall, plural wife / edited
by Maria S. Ellsworth.
        p.   cm.
    Includes bibliographical references and index.
    ISBN 0-252-01875-3 (alk. paper)
    1. Udall, Ida Hunt, d. 1915.   2. Mormons—United States—
Biography.   3. Pioneers—Arizona—Biography.   4. Women pioneers—
Arizona—Biography.   I. Ellsworth, Maria S. (Maria Smith), 1918–
II. Title.
BX8695.U33A3 1992
289.3′092—dc20
    [B]   91-27152
                                                              CIP

I would like to take you on a trip down to Arizona, in the St. Johns country. I preached faith there once, but I want to tell you I haven't got enough faith to stay in such an undesirable country. You talk about good people; you talk about righteous people; I tell you there are people in this city who are not worthy to unlatch their shoestrings. That hard country, and their obedience to the priesthood of God, has made those men great characters. You can't discourage them. They will build a dam across the Colorado River every five years, if it washes out the next day, and live on dry bread and molasses. Yet that is their home; that is their country; there they worship God.

—J. Golden Kimball
General Conference Address, April 1908
Salt Lake City, Utah

CONTENTS

INTRODUCTION

"The history of the Mormon community reads like a tragic poem," wrote Mormon historian Orson F. Whitney, "and the heart and soul of that poem is in the lives, labors and sacrifices of the heroic women." [1] This statement is certainly true of my grandmother Ida Hunt Udall, a devout Latter-day Saint and a socially gifted woman, who chose marriage as the plural wife of Mormon church leader David K. Udall and spent much of her married life away from her husband and his first wife, on farms and ranches in eastern Arizona's plateau country.

Accounts of heroic men and women fill the history of the pioneer settlement of Mormon country and the American West. Crossing the plains and settling in the central valleys of Utah, though difficult, was easy compared with pioneering in southern Utah and in Arizona. Only those who lived there could tell what an unremitting struggle it was. Eastern Arizona pioneers had to contend with limited arable land, an irregular water supply (variable from drought to floods), and the contested meeting of Mormon and non-Mormon settlers. The drama of personal sacrifice and triumph over great obstacles, natural and personal, was enacted on that stage.

Born in a wagon, Ida Hunt Udall was never far from the ever-necessary wagon to convey her on her many moves. Her journal, which constitutes the core of *Mormon Odyssey*, begins on 6 May 1882, the day she left on her wedding trip from her home in Snowflake, Arizona, to St. George, Utah, along the Honeymoon Trail with David K. Udall, her husband-to-be, who was bishop of St. Johns, Arizona; his wife Ella; and their two-year-old daughter, Pearl.

In choosing to become a second wife, Ida took a difficult road that never smoothed out over the years. The marriage had an ominous beginning when Ida was obliged to leave home and family two years

after the wedding and spend over two years "on the underground" in
Utah, avoiding arrest by federal marshals who wanted her testimony
against her husband for "polygamy" or "unlawful cohabitation." Her
underground journal is a major contribution to Mormon pioneer literature. Written over a four-and-a-half-year period, it gives keen in-
sights into the lives of those engaged in "celestial marriage," particularly the intimate feelings of a second wife living among strangers. It
contains many observations on the institution of polygamy as practiced among the Mormons. It also has much to say about life in
Mormon towns and pioneering in Arizona. The journal is a valuable
source of information on David's court trials and prison experiences
as well. Letters he wrote her from prison, faithfully copied into her
journal, give an intimate view of the emotional impact of those experiences on the whole Udall family. They may also help explain why
for two generations so many Udalls were interested in the law as a
profession.

Ida's story after her return from exile in 1887 is a contribution to
the history of the Udall clan in Arizona. Her happy, lovable disposition was pitted against the harsh realities of pioneering, poverty,
religious persecution, and bankruptcy. The Udalls always seemed to
live in the wrong place at the wrong time, where extremes of drought
or excessive rain ruined the best-laid plans for financial success, in
spite of much hard work.

That Ida did not get a fair deal in her marriage was the opinion
of her Hunt family, friends, and especially her daughter. Though all
of the Udalls suffered because of financial stress, Ida gave up more
than the rest. When David became president of the St. Johns Stake
and Ella became stake president of the Relief Society, Ella needed a
home where she could entertain church leaders from Salt Lake City.
For this reason she always had better living conditions. It was also
the case that Ida was by nature generous, loving, and very loyal to
the Udalls, and she early learned to accept a lesser role. In my research of Ida's life, I have come to see her as a heroic figure, whose
life had aspects of tragedy. For most of her married life, she lived
under primitive conditions (at one time in a house with a dirt floor
covered by her hand-braided rug), isolated from any social life and
faced with never-ending hard work. It is little wonder that her health
broke when she was still in her forties. Surely the last seven years of
her life spent as a semi-invalid were tragic.

Our generation may regard certain aspects and some years of the
Udall experience as tragic; however, my grandparents did not. Indeed, they could have chosen a much easier life with more material

rewards. These were great and good people, caught up in times that produced most unusual trials. They knew life was difficult, but they did not pity themselves. They accepted every challenge, endured failures, and triumphed in the end.

For faithful Ida, her children were reward enough for her sacrifices. Because of them, it was all worthwhile. She believed her children were superior because of their family and religious heritage and because they had learned to work, to sacrifice, and to set goals. For Ida, all of the Udall children were "ours," not "mine" and "hers," and she took satisfaction in the accomplishments of each of them.

Her husband, David K. Udall, was one of the outstanding men in a generation of great leaders. He was characterized by Andrew Jenson, church historian, in these words: "He is industrious and very hopeful, even under the most adverse circumstances, showing discretion and forethought in his counsels. Humble and unassuming in nature, those who know him best cannot but appreciate his exemplary life, his temperate habits, his strict observance in keeping the commandments of God, and his justice in dealing with his fellow men. He is naturally spiritually minded. He has labored faithfully to promote the interest of the people over whom he has presided . . . a man of great faith. . . ."[2] His wife Ella was also loved and honored by everyone who knew her. This book, while telling Ida's story, should not detract from the lives and contributions of David K. Udall and his wife Ella.

Ida was considered by all who knew her to be a talented woman. She showed musical aptitude at an early age, later learning to play the guitar to accompany her singing. Her writing, both prose and poetry, showed ability and was beautifully inscribed. She was a bookkeeper, a teacher, and a seamstress. Her natural poise allowed her to sing or speak in public with ease, something she did often in her early years. During her lifetime, she made friends readily and kept them. Her friend from her youthful days in Beaver, Utah, Julia Murdock (Mrs. Philo T.) Farnsworth of Salt Lake City, who was one of the social elite of the city and a member of the General Board of the Relief Society, wrote the following tribute after Ida's death in 1915:

> Ida was a woman of refinement and information. Her education in school was as many of the pioneer children, gained only in the district or common schools of that period, but always pure and wholesome in quality. She was a great reader and a close observer, consequently well posted in the line of useful information. She was amiable and gentle and always loyal to her friends and family, patriotic to her church and people, generous to others' failings, loving and constant toward all.

She was courteous & thoughtful of strangers and possessed a cheerful, sunny disposition. No wonder she readily made friends and they were legion. Ida had blue eyes and an abundance of auburn hair; she was of medium height, and possessed a beautiful alto voice. She loved flowers, poetry, and music and played the guitar with ability. . . . Ida visited in Salt Lake nine years ago last October and became a Charter member of the Daughters of the Mormon Battalion. She was always interested in everything that would unite, harmonize, elevate, and ennoble man and womankind.

My mother Pauline, Ida's oldest child and only daughter, inherited Ida's journal, personal documents, and collection of letters. She then gathered other letters and documents. She bequeathed them all to me with the exhortation that I publish her mother's journal because her mother's story had never been told. These sources tell the family story. They also depict pioneer life in eastern Arizona and the struggle for existence in a harsh land.

Long before my mother promised to give me her mother's journal for publication, I was interested in the grandmother who died before I was born. I grew up in Snowflake, Arizona, where the family of Ida Hunt Udall lived. I admired her sisters and brothers, who told me many stories about her and their father, John Hunt, who was bishop of Snowflake for thirty-one years. My father, Asahel Henry Smith, had idolized his mother-in-law, and he and my mother told and retold stories about her.

Stories about Ida came to me from strangers as well. As a college student, I met Joseph Farr of St. Johns, who told me how my grandmother influenced his life. When he was a young man living at Hunt, he began to smoke. Ida talked earnestly with him about what he was doing. He credited her for getting him to stop.

Years later, in Logan, Utah, a friend brought LaPriel Crosby Nunnery to see me. She had grown up in Eagar, Arizona. At the time of her birth, she was given up for dead by the midwife, who then gave attention to her twin sister. Ida Hunt Udall came into the home and, seeing the lifeless baby, began working with her and got her to breathe. LaPriel said that she was always told that she owed her life to Ida.

Also in Logan I met Myrtle Farnsworth Christiansen, the daughter of Ida's friend Harriet Shepherd Farnsworth. She had met my grandmother during the summer of 1905. Ida had sung a song that Myrtle never heard again but never forgot. She sang it for me.

Hearing such stories increased my interest in Ida; however, it was not until I had spent years researching her life and reading and re-

reading her journal and letters that I came to know her. She has come alive to me. Knowing of her deep love for and loyalty to the Udall family, I hope that nothing I have written here will detract from the harmony in the Udall family she worked so hard to achieve.

Ida's *Mormon Odyssey* begins with her memoirs, which are presented in their entirety in part 1. The memoirs, written on the first nine pages of her journal, were not completed, but they do recount her ancestry and her early years in Beaver, Utah. From her fifteenth birthday in 1873 to 1905 she made annual entries in a birthday book, carefully recording what she did on her birthday. After 1885 she also used the birthday book to summarize important events of the year. Her birthday book is presented in part 2 to give the reader an overview of her life from her youth to her first stroke, when she stopped writing in her birthday book.

Since Ida wrote very little about her life between March 1874 and her marriage to David K. Udall in May 1882, I used the writings and recollections of others to describe that period in part 3. Ida's journal, published in its totality in part 4, is a vivid portrayal of her marriage and life on the underground from May 1882 to November 1886, which speaks for itself.

To round out the story of her life, I have written about the years she spent pioneering in eastern Arizona after she returned from Utah in 1887, the last years of her life, and the legacy she left when she died in 1915. Parts 5, 6, and 7 are again based primarily on the journals, letters, records, and recollections of others but also on her birthday book and her own letters. Appendices provide genealogies of her family and samples of her letters.

Ida's handwriting in the memoirs, birthday book, journal, and letters has been rendered in a literal manner. In general, she was an excellent writer and speller. Her word order, spelling, punctuation, and capitalization thus have not been changed here but have been transcribed as carefully as possible. I have occasionally added identifiers and other material to her work, which appear in square brackets or in the notes at the end of the book.

Acknowledgments

I am grateful to my mother, Pauline Udall Smith, for gathering materials on her mother's life and willing them to me. I wish to thank the people at the Historical Department Archives of the Church of Jesus Christ of Latter-day Saints in Salt Lake City for access to ward and stake records. I thank Alison Thorne for permission to use the journals of her grandmother, May Hunt Larson, and Thalia Kartchner for providing me with extensive extracts from the journals of her mother, Annie Hunt Kartchner. Thanks also to the family of Lois (Loie) Hunt West for the use of her journals; to Elma Udall for placing the extensive Udall family records and letters in the Special Collections of the Library of the University of Arizona, Tucson, at my disposal; to Keith and Gwen Udall for their helpfulness; and to Margaret Udall Warnock for the use of Ida's photograph in the frontispiece.

I deeply appreciate the help of my brothers Richard and Marion Smith and Marion's wife, Wanda, for reading an early draft of portions of the *Mormon Odyssey* and making comments. A special thanks to my son Mark for his suggestions and his interest in the project.

This publication would not have been possible without the extensive help of my husband, George, who typed the manuscript of my writings, made helpful suggestions, corrected errors, wrote historical information, and composed the bibliography and the endnotes.

PART 1

Ida's Memoirs: Early Life in Beaver, Utah, to March 1874

I AM THE ELDEST child of John Hunt, and Lois B. Pratt. My Father was the fifth child of Jefferson Hunt and Celia Mounts. My Mother the third daughter of Addison Pratt and Louisa Barnes. My Ancestors are American, dating back to the War of the Revolution on both sides of the house.

My father's parents are of good families, can trace their ancestors back to the old Puritan Stock.[1] My Grandmother's father, Mathias Mounts fought in the War of the Revolution. My Grandparents Jefferson and Celia Hunt were born in Kentucky. He in 1804. She in 1805. They joined the Church of Jesus Christ of Latter Day Saints in 1834. They were driven with the church from Missouri. Traveled in the "Mormon Battalion" where Grandfather was Captain of one of the Companies. They reached Salt Lake Valley three days after the Pioneers.[2] Shared in the famine and privation of the early days, living on roots, herbs and wild game for weeks, and months. My Grandfather was sent with the first company to California, for supplies. (My father a boy of 14 years accompanying him.) They suffered greatly for food. For fourteen days having nothing but the meat of their "give-out" mules to live upon. He afterward acted as Pilot to several Companies of emigrants, on what is called the north route to California. Was sent with his family in the year 1851 to help establish a branch of the Church in San Bernardino Cal. They remained there until 1858 when by order of the first Presidency they left their beautiful homes and returned to Utah. While in California, Grandpa was sent from San B. Co. as representative to the State Legislature held in Sacramento, for Seven years. He entered into the order of Celestial Marriage in Nauvoo, taking Matilda Neice for his second wife. Was the father of twenty-one children.

My mothers parents, Addison Pratt and Louisa Barnes were born in the year 1802.[3] He in Winchester New Hampshire, she in Dunham, Canada East. They were baptized into the Church in June 1838. Came to Nauvoo with their family of four daughters, in 1841. Grandpa was sent on a mission to the Society Islands, by the Prophet Joseph in 1843. He was gone over five years, during which time my Grandma by the aid of her needle as Tailoress built a neat frame house in Nauvoo, clothed and schooled her children as respectably as any of their playmates. Left her home to be sold by Uncle [Jonathan] Crosby, and went with the first Company to Winter Quarters. As Uncle could do no better, all the hard labor she had spent in building her home, was exchanged for one broadcloth overcoat. In the year 1848 she migrated to Salt Lake Valley in Prest B. Youngs Company, to which place Grandpa returned from the Islands via San Francisco. In the fall of 1849 Grandpa was again sent on a mission to the Islands, to continue the good work he had begun there. The following Spring 1850 his family my Grandma & her four daughters, (Ellen, Frances, Lois, & Louisa, aged respectively, 17, 15, 13 & 10 years,) were sent to him, accompanied by Grandma's sister & brotherinlaw, Jonathan & Caroline Crosby, and others. They remained on the island of Touboui, one of the Society Islands, one year & a half. Learned their language, taught the natives in the principles of the gospel etc. In 1852 the French Government to which these islands were subject, denied our elders the right to preach there longer, so they were forced to return to California. In Dec 1852 they reached San Bernardino Cal. and joined the colony of Saints located there. Here my parents became acquainted and spent many bright happy days of their youth.

My father was born March 9th 1833, in [Albion, Edwards] Co. Illinois. My mother was born March 6th 1837 in the town of Ripley, [Chautauqua] Co. New York. They were married in 1857 in San Bernardino Cal. The following year 1858, Johnson's Army visited Utah. The Saints were all requested to gather to Utah.[4] All who were alive to their obligations, as Saints prepared to obey immediately, sacrificing their beautiful homes for little or nothing. The faint hearted felt that the sacrifice was too great, & remained there, three of my fathers sisters and their husbands among the number. My father & mother joined their parents in the move to Utah. Made the weary Journey over deserts, sand & rocks.

[Birth and Early Years]

When they had reached what is now called Hamilton's Fort, Iron Co. Utah, I, their eldest child was born on the 8th of March 1858. I

John and Lois Pratt Hunt with daughter Ida Frances, San Bernardino,
California, about 1860.

was born in a wagon, and it seems to have fallen to my lot to be a
traveler ever since, much as I dislike that kind of life.

In attempting to keep a journal or record of the most important
events of my life, I earnestly desire the blessing of God to be upon my
labors. That what I may write may someday be a comfort and help to
my children if I should be blessed with any, and that nothing herein
recorded may cause aught but pride & pleasure to the peruser. I thank
God that I was privileged to be born among His chosen people. That
He blessed me with kind, loving and noble minded parents, and pray
that I may always prove myself worthy of these blessings.

My parents remained in Iron Co. Utah until I was a year old, then
returned to San B. Cal. My father bought a farm on the Santa Anna
River two miles below town. Here my Sister May Louise was born
May 5th 1860, also my sister Annella Feb 15th 1862. Soon after this
my Grandma Pratt came from Beaver, Utah to visit us, and remained
seven months, and as my parents felt ill-at-ease and unsettled in California, they determined to dispose of their property, and return with
Grandma to Utah, to her great delight. Grandpa also came from upper
Cal. [California,] Aunt Frances [Pratt Dyer's] home, and joined the

Company. He made his home with his daughters as he was greatly afflicted with rheumatism & other complaints. My very first recollections are of dear old Grandpa Pratt, holding sister May and I on each knee, trotting and singing to us. Although but five years of age when we left Cal. I had attended three different schools. Can remember each teacher, also the situation and surroundings of the old home, and many incidents that transpired on the journey. Grandpa drove the carriage drawn by a span of white horses, in which we always rode.

[Beaver, Utah]

We reached Beaver, Utah, in May 1863. My father bought a home within one block from Grandpa Pratt, where we spent many happy years. No girl has a happier childhood to look back upon, than I. Possessed of a father whose highest aim was to rear his children respectably educate and bring them up in the fear of the Lord. A mother who always welcomed us home from school, with the same cheerful smile, and made things so comfortable & pleasant for us, and a dear kind Grandma to whom we could always run when ma did not have time to attend to our wants. No matter whether it was a dress to make for some certain occasion, a lesson to learn, or an essay to write, we never applied to Grandma Pratt in vain. She was always equal to the occasion.

My mothers youngest Sister, Aunt Louisa was still unmarried, and she and Grandma taught school a good part of the time. Ephraim, (Grandma's Kanaka boy) lived with them.[5] My sister Christabell was born August 27th 1864, making four daughters to the Hunt family.

When I was eight years of age, through grandma's urgent request, my parents consented for me to take a trip to Ogden with her to visit my dear Aunt Ellen [Pratt] McGary who then resided there. We were gone all one summer. Many of the events of that trip are still fresh in my memory. We stayed several days at the Lion House, in Salt Lake as guests of Aunt Zina [wife of Brigham Young] who was a dear friend of Grandma's. I distinctly remember one circumstance, when we had assembled one evening, in the large family prayer room, President Young called me up to him, admired my long yellow hair, took me on his knee & kissed me, saying I was certainly his girl because he claimed all those with sandy hair.[6]

While I was in Ogden, Grandpa Hunt came down from Huntsville, and with Grandma's consent took me home with him to visit Aunt Matilda and her family.[7] I spent one week there, which is the only time I ever saw Grandpa Hunt to remember him. (Grandma Hunt was at that time visiting in Cal.)

Ida and her grandmother, Louisa Barnes Pratt, Salt Lake City, Utah, 1866.

The following year Aunt Frances Dyer came from California to visit us, bringing her only son, Addison, who was then eight years old. Grandpa Pratt who had returned to Cal. and was making his home with her, sent all his grandchildren, dolls, toy books, & dresses, which made Aunt Frances' visit one long to be remembered.

On the 14th day of November 1866, my brother Lewis was born. We were attending Miss Lucinda Lee's school[8] at the time and I well remember how proud we were to hasten to school and bear the joyful tidings of our first & only brother's arrival. A sweet brown-eyed baby he was and called "Boy Hunt" all over the neighborhood.

My Aunt Louisa at the age of twenty-six disappointed all her friends by marrying Thomas Willis, a man in no way worthy of her. She moved to a home of her own, and my poor Aunt Ellen, through the misbehavior of her husband was forced to separate from him, and came home to live with Grandma, bringing her three children.[9] Soon after she buried her only son Addison & her daughter Aurora, which left her only one child, my cousin Nellie McGary. Aunt Ellen and Grandma taught school together, which we children attended most of the time.

Soon after the Railroad was completed to Salt Lake Grandma disposed of some of her stock, & with the means went back to visit [in May 1871] the old home where she was born, in Dunham Canada East.[10] She had been absent thirty years, and with all the hardships she had endured in her life as a Mormon, she looked and felt younger than her playmates who had never been out of Canada. She stayed one whole summer returning in November. O! what a time of rejoicing that was for we children. The endless presents and cakes of Maple Sugar she brought us, made the occasion even brighter than Christmas with Santa Claus.

My second brother John Addison was born September 1st 1869.

The following winter my father went to California with a team to bring Grandma Hunt who had been visiting her daughter there. Uncle Sheldon Stoddard & Will Morse returned with him. In May 1870 my parents went to Salt Lake when they had their endowments and were sealed. They took Grandma Hunt to Ogden to visit Aunt Mary [Hunt Black].[11] They were gone some four weeks which seemed an endless length of time to me, as I had the responsibility of keeping house with Grandma's occasional overseeing. I was baptized by Bro Wm J. Flake, when 11 years of age, Nov. 1869, in the Beaver River.

When thirteen years of age, Bro Richard Horne[12] came to Beaver and opened his first term of school there. I attended the same regularly for three years, as did also my sisters May and Annie. My father having to pay $18.00 cash per term for our schooling. This was the best school I ever attended and those three years will always be remembered as among the happiest days of my life. My dear friend and playmate Hattie Shepherd[13] and I occupied the same desk for many terms. We also attended a term of night school during the winter of 1873 which will long be remembered. E. W. Thompson Jr. and Charley Shipp, were our respective boy admirers, and as the snow was very deep they used to take us to & from school in a sleigh, generally stealing a short ride before and after school. I fear our minds were more intent on the fun of getting there than the Book-keeping we professed to study, but all such innocent enjoyments tend to make youth the oasis of our lives.

When thirteen years of age I was invited by Bro Wm Robinson the leader of the Choir to become a member of the same which with the consent of my parents I did. My two near neighbors & dear friends Esther Barton & Jennie Harris joined the Choir at the same time, they as treble singers, I as alto, and oh what nice times we used to have going to practice every Saturday night, and taking such pride in always being at our post on Sunday. We also attended Theological Class taught by Bro Wm Fotheringham on Sunday afternoon.

In 1873 a Mutual Improvement Association was organized for the Young Ladies of Beaver.[14] I was chosen Secretary, which office I filled for some length of time.

I had failed to mention that in Nov 1872 another sister christened Nettie was born. Pa was away from home at the time of her birth, and I being the eldest, felt greatly the responsibility of having Ma sick in his absence. The baby was a little fair, blue-eyed sprite, and oh! how we all loved her.

For thirteen years my father served the public as the Sheriff of Beaver Co. being called to fill that office by Prest Murdock,[15] who told him he might consider it as a mission, for they would have no other man run for that office so long as he was able to act. His office required him to follow and arrest the most desperate men, and having soldiers and miners on all sides of Beaver he had a great deal of such business.[16] Had my mother not been a woman of great faith she would have had a miserable life on that account, but she felt that he was laboring for the Saints and had their faith and prayers, and the Lord would always preserve him which he certainly did.

On July 4th 1873. The Celebration was quite a grand affair. Gentiles and Mormons joining together to make the day memorable. Our school was called on by the Committee for a Special No. of the Friday Entertainer, our school paper, to be edited & read in the Celebration.

Ida Hunt, Beaver, Utah, age fifteen or sixteen.

Bro Horne, the teacher decided that the school should appoint the Editor by ballot, and to my great sorrow and surprise I received a large majority of votes. I felt that I could not perform any part before so vast an assemblage, but they all encouraged me and I made the attempt. My old school teacher Mr [George W.] Crouch afterward told me that Mrs [Elizabeth Cady] Stanton could not have been more self possessed nor read more distinctly. That same summer Aunt Martha Stoddard from Minersville, came to our house and was sick there 10 weeks. Dr. Elbry of Ft. Cameron attending her.

March 8th 1874. I was sixteen years of age. During that month I finished my last term of school as pupil. In April My Uncle Joseph Hunt with his wife Catherine or Aunt Kit as we always called her came from the north and settled down in Beaver. They had three daughters—Celia, Ina and Ida. Grandma Hunt also came down with them and lived part of the time with us. Although my cousin Celia was nearly two years my junior, she was a companion for me in every way and we immediately became fast friends. That [Memoirs end here.]

PART 2

Ida's Birthday Book: An Overview of Her Life, 1873 to 1905

Ida Frances Hunt's Book.
A present from her mother,
and Grandmother L. B. Pratt.
On her 14th birthday,
March 8th, 1872.

It is with little trouble,
That my crochet hook I lift,
To prepare this little tribute
For you a birthday gift.

I would wish that it were better.
But as its the best I have,
I am sure you will accept it
As a tribute of my love.

Accept this from your friend,
Harriet Shepherd,
Beaver
March 8th 1872.

My fifteenth birthday, March 8th 1873, was spent in Beaver. Was presented, by my father with a pocket derenger. Went horseback-riding, with Miss [Esther] Barton, and Miss [Hattie] Shepherd.

My 16th birthday, 1874, spent in Beaver. There were present, at my dinner, Meisses. Hamlin and Thrower from Minersville. Reced. nothing but small presents.

My Seventeenth birthday 1875 spent in Beaver. Attended Mrs [Lucinda Lee] Daltons school during the day, and went to the Theater in the evening with Mr J. M. Murdock. Had several small presents.

My eighteenth Birthday March 8th 1876. I spent at Loraine, Sevier Co. U.T. [Utah Territory] where my parents removed in Nov. 1875. Went visiting, in company with Mrs A. E. Levitt. Was presented by my father, with a brindle heifer. Also, by my Friend, Hattie Shepherd, with a bunch of hair flowers.

My ninteenth birthday, March 8 1877 I spent in driving team 20 miles, between Wolf Hole, and Link Spring, Arizona, while removing with my parents, to San Lorenzo New Mexico, where we arrived May 18th 1877.

My twentieth birthday March 8th 1878 I spent in Savoia Valley, New Mexico, where we removed May 29th 1877. Was presented, by my mother with a glass decanter, which was presented her on her 20th birthday, and by my father with a black and white heifer.

My 21st birthday, 1879 I passed with my Grandma Pratt, in Beaver, (with whom I had returned to live a few months,) Mrs H. E. Shepherd, and Aunts Louisa [Pratt Willis], and [Caroline Barnes] Crosby took dinner with us, and in the evening quite a number of friends and neighbors, gave me a pleasant little surprise by calling in to spend a few hours. We had music, games, songs, and refreshments. Reced some small keepsakes.

My 22nd Birthday, 1880, found me still with Grandma Pratt in Beaver, Utah, but anticipating a speedy return to my home in Arizona. During the day I taught school, and at 4 oclock partook of a bounteous dinner, which had been prepared in honor of the day, by Aunts Ellen [Pratt McGary], Louisa [Pratt Willis], Cousin Nellie [McGary], and friend Josephine Cox. In the evening, I first attended a Reunion, and took parts in Singing, dancing etc. until 10 oclock. Then escorted Mr. Will. M. Scow to a Leap Year Ball, which was quite a grand affair, gotten up by Misses Aggie Low, Ina Christian and Nellie Bettenson. Was presented by my escort, with a long-wished for volume of "Scotts Complete Poetical Works," beautifully bound in red-morocco and gilt.

My 23rd Birthday, March 8th 1881, I passed with my parents, brothers and sisters in Snowflake, Apache Co. Arizona, having returned from Utah, the preceding May. Many changes had taken place during the year. My Grandma Pratt died in Beaver, only four months after I left her, and my Grandma Hunt had come to live with us, and was present at my birthday dinner, as also Mrs. Sarah D. W. C. [Christopherson] of Round Valley. After dinner, we had cake, wine, toasts, etc. Grandma H. promising me every desire of my heart, beginning and ending the list with a good husband.

My 24th birthday, 1882, I passed in the schoolroom, and at the house of Bro and Sister Phillip Cardon, in Taylor, Apache Co. Arizona, where my sister Anna and myself were engaged in teaching a term of school. Nothing transpired worthy of note. In the preceding October, 1881 my sister May, younger than myself, was married; which was the first break in our happy home circle.

March 8th 1883 My 25th birthday was the first passed after my marriage to David King Udall, in the St. George Temple, May 25th 1882. I spent the day pleasantly, at his home in St. Johns A.T. [Arizona Territory] in company with other members of his family. Wife Ella & little daughters Pearl and Erma. Sister Anna Riggs took dinner with us, after which Pearl and I called on Sister [Henry] Knowles where we heard some beautiful music. Passed the evening in pleasant converse with my husband after his hard days work in the field, perfectly happy in the thought that I at once possessed the man of my choice and one whom I knew to be a sincere Latter Day Saint.

My 26th birthday 1884 found me visiting with my parents brothers and sisters in Snowflake. Sister Anna was married the preceding Oct. and happily settled down to housekeeping near home. During the day I attended the Stake Conference held at Taylor, and in company with my husband took dinner at the home of Bro and Sister Heber Perkins.

My 27th birthday, March 8th 1885, found me in Nephi, Juab Co. Utah, in the childhood's home of my husband, with Father Udall and Aunt Rebecca [Udall], where I had sought refuge, and found a hearty welcome, the preceding October, on account of the persecutions of our enemies in Arizona. This was the first birthday I ever passed away from all those with whom I had ever been associated before, a closely confined prisoner (my whereabouts known only to a few dear friends) to prevent being subpoenaed as a witness against David, in Polygamy Suit brought against him. After Sunday School, Bro Wm Paxman, Stake President, called in to see me, and at Auntie's suggestion he and Father U. gave me one of the greatest blessings I ever received, which was a great comfort to me, and served to make this birthday one never to be forgotten. My faithful friends, Kate Love and Mary Linton took dinner with us. Reced. presents from dear Aunty [Rebecca], and Sister [Emma?] Bryan.

March 8th 1886. Finds me in Nephi Utah, again, though I had traveled a great deal during the past year, which has been the most eventful of my life. My beloved mother was called to a better world on the 9th of March 1885, and only a few days after, my little Pauline was sent by a merciful Father to comfort me. Through the wicked persecutions of our enemies my husband was tried on a false charge of purgery and sentenced to three years in the Detroit House of Correction, but through the overruling Hand of Providence was pardoned by the President, after four months imprisonment. My sister Bell was married to Charles L. Flake in September. My 28th birthday finds baby nearly one year old. Her papa has never seen her but once, and that when she was but seven weeks old. Weather cold, snow deep. Friends Leonora Hartley and Mary Linton took birthday supper with Aunty and I, each made me small presents.

March 8th 1887. Finds us still in the old homestead with Father Udall and Aunty. Pauline has never seen her papa since he came from prison but the joyful news that he is now on the road to see us and take us back to Arizona to live, keeps our spirits from falling. His polygamy case was dismissed Dec 3rd 1886. The weather is like spring, with beautiful moonlight nights. My dear friends, Bessie Sparks, M. E. Neff, Nora Hartley, Mercy Wright and Mary Linton visited in the afternoon and took supper with us, after which we all took a moonlight stroll. With accompaniament on the guitar, serenaded some of the neighbors. Mercy presented me with beautiful crape kerchief. Mary with silk gloves & bracelets. Aunty with China bowles.

My 30th birthday 1888 will long be remembered. After living happily in Snowflake for nearly one year, I started the morning of

March 8th to remove from there to the farm and Mills owned by
Udall Bros in Round Valley, where David thought it advisable for
me to live so that he might get acquainted with his family without
having to leave his home and business. My brother John was engaged
to take me by team, and I was also accompanied by my sister Annie
and husband who were engaged to live at the mill for a few months.
I parted with the rest of my dear family not expecting to see brother
Lewis again until he returned from a mission to England, upon which
he started April 1st 1888. We left Snowflake at 9 a.m. traveled till
9 p.m. Were afflicted with every kind of storm the elements could
muster, besides a balky animal that hindered us on every hill. When
darkness came it found us stuck in a mud-hole, the rain pouring
down and the horses discouraged and refusing to pull together. But
the Lord blessed us, and we were enabled to get to the Tanks fifteen
miles from Snowflake to camp for the night. My little son, Grover
Cleveland, born Dec 28th 1887, was two months old; rather young
to travel, but was remarkably good the first day out.

My 31st birthday finds me again at Snowflake. I staid at the Mills
in Round Valley from March 10th until Christmas Eve 1888. Lived a
very secluded monotonous life, but had the pleasure of assisting my
husband in his labors by cooking for the many farm and mill hands
employed there. I also enjoyed more of his company than I had done
for years past, and was favored through the summer with two visits
from Aunt Ella and her children. During the harvest time Brother
Jos. Udall & wife [Emma] came up and lived with me two months,
which was a great help and company for me. I returned to Snowflake
for New Years, and as it was not thought safe for me to go back to
R.V. I accepted my father's kind offer to occupy Aunt Hap's house for
a season as she was absent in Utah. My birthday passed pleasantly.
In the evening a host of kind friends, led by Sister [Mary Jane] West,
bearing baskets of picnic, and hearts full of love and good will, gave
us a surprise by coming in to pa's to spend the evening. The party
was in honor of us both, as his birthday is the day following mine.
We had a very enjoyable time. I received a nice present from Sister
Bell, also a bundle of presents from dear friend Mary L. [Linton] and
others in Nephi.

March 8th 1890. Saturday. Finds me still in Snowflake living with
Aunt Hap. My little son John Hunt was born Aug 23rd 1889. He
is a fine large baby. Black hair and eyes. The exact opposite of his
brother in complection. I spent the day attending to the wants of my
three little ones, and very proud in their possession. My husband and
family reside in Round Valley. They have been sorely afflicted with

Lagrippe & pneumonia during the past two months, and I feel very grateful to my Heavenly Father that they are spared to us, and will be able to attend the Quarterly Conference now convened in St. Johns. Aunt Hap, sisters Annie & Nettie have also gone to attend it, which leaves us quite lonely at home.

My 33rd birthday 1891. Am again in Round Valley, at the Mill Farm, having come back the latter part of March the year before. Spent a happy summer living with Ella and family, until September when she went to St. Johns for the purpose of sending children to school. Winter at the farm was much more lonely, and in February my little John H. was stricken with pneumonia and came near to death. My birthday, a lonely Sunday, found him slowly recovering, and I spent the day attending him, and cooking for carpenters who were putting in Roller Mills. One of them Lyman Hamblin presented me with "Pearl of Great Price." Dear friend Sister [Emma] Coleman also wrote me a birthday poem. Jos & Emma Udall had moved to the Mill in January and we spent the day together. Our Mexican boy Pablo Perea and his newly made bride (arrayed in white satin and lace) taking dinner with us. David was in St. Johns attending conference.

March 8th 1892. Finds our family living under one roof again. Ella having moved back to the farm in Nov 1891. The preceeding April, my dear friend, Mary Linton Morgan from Nephi, with her baby boy came out and spent 4 months with me. Two months of that time we spent in Snowflake while keeping out of the way of Deputy Marshals who were again on our track. But the trouble blew over and I returned home in September, Bro [John] Morgan coming after Mary at the same time. My birthday came at Conference time as usual and David, Ella and three of their children were in St. Johns attending it. Erma and Luella were left with me. We had Joseph, Emma and family over to dinner, their son Joseph being seven years old on that same day.

My 35th birthday 1893 was one of the saddest I had ever spent. The wind blew a hurricane. I passed the day in packing up and removing my household goods from the Union Coop Store in Eagerville, back to our home on the Farm. I had lived there and looked after that Store from the preceding May until Nov. when with my Sister Loie I went to visit our family in Snowflake and to meet relatives from California. Dear old Grandma Hunt at the advanced age of 87 having returned to live with us. We were in the height of our reunion, when our beloved brother Charles L. Flake was shot and killed by a desperado whom he was assisting his brother James to arrest, and who was killed by the latter at the same instant Charles was. It was a sad blow to his entire family. I spent the remainder of the winter with my dear widowed Sister Bell and her three fatherless children, who had so suddenly been bereft of their best earthly friend, but who felt to acknowledge the Hand of God in their affliction. I returned with David via St. Johns the 1st of March, attended some of the Con. meetings being held there. B. H. Roberts in attendence, also Bros Cluff & Dalton from Utah. I arrived in Round Valley on the 7th. David, Ella & family, besides a large number from the Stake were making all preperations to attend the grand Dedication of the S L Temple to be held April 6th 1893.

My next birthday 1894 found me with another sturdy little son Jesse Addison by name. He was born June 24th 1893, while Ella and family were making a six months visit in Utah. For two months preceding his birth I was scarcely able to be out of bed and my dear sister Nettie spent most of the summer with me. My birthday found me in Snowflake where I had come to spend the Holidays, and remained for a few weeks after. My brother Lewis and family who were visiting from Utah, and myself lived together, and we all helped to look after our dear old Grandma Hunt through a long spell of sickness. I also attended Sister Ruth Hatche's "Reform Class." Was invited to a lecture by her, on the night of my birthday. Flake's Hall was packed on my entrance, and to my great surprise I found it was a birthday surprise on my father & myself.

March 8th 1895. I spent at the farm in Round Valley. David was attending the Quarterly Conference in St. Johns. I had Aunt Ella and family in to dinner, and in the afternoon Sister Emma [Udall] and friends Wilmirth DeWitt and Dora Rencher came over to spend a few hours. Sisters Loie and Bell who were attending Conference at St. Johns sent me some presents from there.

March 8th 1896. A lonely Sunday. Spent in Round Valley. David & daughter Pearl attending Conference at St. Johns. I spent the day helping to doctor our family and neighbors who were sick with lagrippe. Two weeks previous we had been called upon to bury our little baby Paul with that dread disease. He was fourteen months old while my little Gilbert Douglas was five months younger being born May 13th 1895.

My 39th birthday I spent in St. Johns attending the Quarterly Conference. Left Gus Gibbons to keep the house and look after Grover and John H. and brought Pauline and two babies with me. I had just recovered from a long seige of lagrip. I spent the morning with Sister [Mary] Anderson, noon at Rachel Berrys and the night with Sister [Mary E. B.] Farr. Had a most pleasant birthday. Pauline and her papa presented me with some nice picture frames for birthday presents. The preceding May I had moved back to the old Hall on the farm, where I first lived. Jos and Emma [Udall] having moved to a new home in Eagerville.

My 40th birthday 1898. At the old farm in Round Valley. It found me with another sweet little blue-eyed son, Don Taylor, born July 20th 1897 (Jubilee Day). I now have a family of six children to care for and was just emerging from a long winter of sickness, both baby and myself. The preceding May, my baby sister, Lois, was married to Jos. A. West, and moved to Salt Lake to live. On my birthday Sister Emma [Udall] and I took a ride to town in p.m. She made me a present of some silver spoons. Bro Jos Udall went on a mission to England the 1st of Jan.

My 41st birthday, 1899 spent at the Old Mill. My Sister Nettie who was married to Jos A. Rencher the Oct. previous, had come to live in Eagar in a home of her own. Our daughter Pearl had gone back to Provo to attend the B.Y. [Brigham Young] Academy the Oct. previous. We had just got through with our first "Old Folks Reunion," in Eagar, which was a great success. I was on the committee, and Nettie and I composed two songs for the occasion. My dear husband was in Phoenix, as a member of the 20th Legislative Council of Arizona, being a Republican Delegate from Apache Co. Nothing happened on my birthday.

My 42nd birthday 1900, I spent at the home of Sister Nettie in company with Sister Emma [Udall] and her sister Lell [Goldsbrough] who was visiting from Utah. I was living at the time in a little house belonging to Bp [George H.] Crosby in Eagar, where I removed six months before, when financial ruin overtook us as a family, brot about by Mr H. Huning forclosing the mortgage he had on the mill and farm together with other heavy obligations falling due at the same time. We had nothing left but ½ interest in a ranche at Lee Valley valued at $500.00 and team, wagon, cows etc valued at $500. and what cows and household goods I had. The cause of the failure being due to the many years of drouth our country had suffered and also heavy losses in sheep business. My poor husband was almost prostrate with sorrow and disappointment. Only the sustaining power of God helped him to bear this humiliation. We will remember with pleasure the kind and fatherly care of Apostle Heber J. Grant at this time, also Bro Jos B. Patterson.

My 43rd birthday found me living back at the old mill farm, alone with my family. We had leased the mill and a portion of land for one year, of the company who bought it. Aunt Ella and family moved to

St. Johns the previous April, and looked after Mail and Express business there, while I & boys looked after cows, mail horses, and cooked for mail driver at the mill. Daughter Pearl, after two years at Provo, was teaching the Primary Dept in the St. Johns Stake Academy, which beautiful building was dedicated Dec. 16th 1900, by the Prophet Jos F. Smith. Our family were nearly all present and had a glorious time. The Grist Mill shut down in Dec. and the balance of the winter was very lonely for me, my four older children going one mile away to school. My birthday was celebrated by an Arizona Blizzard, but I went through it to spend the day with sisters Nettie [Rencher] & Emma [Udall], in Eagar. And as the storm increased in fury, I spent the night there. Reced a nice present of fruit from Aunt Augusta Smith of Snowflake, sent by friend Susie Jarvis. I was expecting to leave Round Valley for good, and remove to St. Johns the following month.

My 44th birthday 1902 was a very happy one. It was the 2nd day of our Quarterly Con. held in St. Johns where I had lived for nearly one year. Sister Julia M. Brixen was our Y.L.M.I. missionary from S.L.C. and my brother Lewis, sister Bell, and Bashie Smith came from Snowflake to Con. They brought me kind words and presents from my father, Aunts [Sarah and Happalona], and sisters in Snowflake. Also loving letter from Nettie. Sisters Jensen and friends Susie & Wilmirth Greer took dinner with me, and we all went to Aunt Ellas to supper. We had come out from Bankruptcy. David had succeeded in getting a Patent on an Agricultural Machine. Our children were all attending the Academy in St. Johns and altogether our prospects were much brighter.

March 8th 1903   Found us on our Home stead in Sec. 18 Township 14 N. 26. E where we located the preceding April. Leaving Pauline, Jno H. and Jesse with Aunt Ella to attend school. Papa, Grover, Gilbert, Don and myself came and pitched our tent under a Cedar, making a corral for our cows from Cedar brush and a coop for our fowls, out of screen doors and horse blankets. Our only luxury being a well 15 ft deep, with plenty of water. Our only hope of obtaining water for irrigation was to reservoir the flood waters on the Little Colorado, 10 miles above us. St. Johns being 20 miles above us. Our nearest neighbor, Harris Greer and family living 1¼ miles from us. My husband and boys worked reservoir thro the winter and Spring to the Amt of about $600.00. Grover had sun-stroke and barely escaped with his life. We camped out 6 weeks then moved into a lumber house with good floor and roof. We tended the Mail Station and raised poultry. In Feb daughter Pearl had smallpox. Our family in St. Johns were quarentined but none but her took it. My birthday found me confined to bed with a three weeks sick spell. Bro G. H. Crosby visited us and gave me a Patriarchal Blessing.

My 46th birthday finds us on the homestead 50 acres of land fenced, and mostly plowed. Our house enlarged, good cellar built, comfortable stables yards etc for animals, and two good neighbors (Bros [Elijah] Freeman & [Willard] Farr) close by, with prospects of others soon. Reservoir proved a success and one crop of grain hay raised. A school District granted us and my daughter Pauline teaching the school with an attendance of 18 pupils. Taught part of the time in our own house. During the winter we were visited by dear Father Udall and Aunt Rebecca from Nephi and Sister Eliza [Udall Tenney] from Mexico, remaining with us some months. Sister Mary Linton Morgan with her three sons came with father arriving Dec 23rd 1903 where they expect to make their home, and share our fortunes as a family. This birthday found me toothless having had them all taken out in Feb. by Dr [Joseph S.] Woolford, preparatory to having some new ones.

My 47th birthday I spent in traveling from our ranche home (now a Post Office) called Hunt, to Snowflake, in company with brothers John,—also Taylor and Ross [Hunt], who were going from the Udall Reservoir works, home to attend the celebration of my fathers 72 birthday, March 9th 1906 [1905]. It was a grand affair, given by the ward to their bishop, who had served them faithfully for 26 years. Held in the Stake house, with refreshments served to every one present. The ward presented him with a large arm-chair for each home, also a beautiful satin banner. Mottoe "John Hunt—Bishop of Snowflake. The right man in the right place." There were original songs, essays & speeches, and everything went lovely and made our father feel well.[1] Daughter Pauline still taught our Dist. school. The preceeding year had been a very hard one on our nerves. We were obliged to keep our boys out of school to drive mail. Tho only 14 and 16 years of age the three older boys drove from Holbrook to St. Johns (70 miles) for many months. In August our reservoir was washed out by heavy storms and we lost all our work & our beautiful lake of water stored for another years crop. We got our grain off the land before the flood covered it, but our garden just ready to use, was all washed away, except cane from which we made molasses after the water had run over it for one month. Our boys had the high waters to contend with in their mail driving and had to risk their lives nearly every day in crossing rivers or flume at Woodruff. The heavy rains and floods continued all through the winter of 1904 and 1905.

PART 3

From Youth to Marriage, March 1874 to May 1882

IDA'S BIRTHDAY BOOK ended in 1905, probably because she had her first stroke just after her forty-eighth birthday in 1906. Ida's memoirs, however, end mid-sentence, and we do not know why she stopped or even when she wrote what she did. She had clearly intended to complete her memoirs, for she left pages blank before beginning her daily journal on page twenty-two of the record book. Her experiences from 1874, when she was sixteen, until her marriage trip in May 1882 can be filled in by drawing from the writings of her sisters May and Annie, her Grandma Pratt, Great-aunt Caroline Crosby, and various church records.

Life at Beaver

For Ida and her sisters, growing up in Beaver held many opportunities to learn social skills, develop their talents, and make lasting friends. Ever after, they looked back on those years as an "oasis" in their lives. Surely it provided a good background for the experiences they were to have pioneering in the Sevier Valley of Utah, in Savoia, New Mexico, and in eastern Arizona. In turn these experiences prepared Ida for the life she chose when she became a plural wife and accepted the hardships of living in polygamy.

Ida loved the town of Beaver, with its many friends, cultural and social advantages, talented musicians, teachers, and writers. Her Grandmother Pratt took delight in providing the best educational advantages of the time.

Ida was considered a fine scholar, a most agreeable child to have around, quite content when away from her mother, self-possessed and amiable, neither bashful nor rude, always obliging. If invited to sing, she readily agreed, "pleased to contribute something to the enjoyment of the company she was in."[1] Ida's Grandma Pratt and Aunt Ellen taught school, and Ida readily did all the work they gave her. Under this additional influence, Ida became a young woman in mind and manners and a lover of books.

While in Beaver, Ida's father gave her a guitar, and Great-aunt Caroline noted in April 1875 that she was playing accompaniments for herself and her sisters when they sang. Ida and her guitar became a center of family and neighborhood entertainment wherever she went.

That same April Ida had her own school, held in the Second Ward schoolhouse. Her account book of her teaching lists the names of her students, their parents' names, and how the schooling was paid for. Some was in cash, but most was in credit at the local store, in produce or such services as making a table, or in woolen yardage from the Beaver Woolen Mills. Ida also listed her expenses. Her account book clearly shows Ida's financial help to her father's family, help that continued until her marriage.

The same year Ida began teaching she was invited to join the Beaver Literary Association, organized by her teacher Richard S. Horne. Besides reading and discussing literature, the members learned how to conduct meetings using parliamentary procedures.[2]

Although Ida's life was fulfilling, her father's life was unenviable. As sheriff of Beaver County since coming there in 1863, he was responsible for keeping the peace between the Mormon settlers and the "Gentile" population, which was coming in for mining, or in connection with the 250 soldiers at Fort Cameron or the first trial of John D. Lee. He also faced problems with his brother Joseph, who had moved his wife and three daughters to Beaver and had a drinking problem. Moreover, his family was growing, and he needed a better income. Since John Hunt's name was repeatedly placed on the ballot by church authorities, he could shed the office only by moving. The possibility of moving from Beaver was not welcome news to Ida, even though she was well aware of all of the problems the family faced if they remained.

The Sevier River Valley, 1875–77

Ida's parents searched the country for a place to locate and decided on a farm in the Sevier Valley, Utah, two miles above the small town of Joseph City (today's Joseph). Ida and her sisters did not want to leave Beaver. When Ida suggested to her father that she be allowed to remain with her grandmother and continue teaching, he told her that he expected her to forget her own desires and do what was best for the family. Ida and the youngest children did, however, remain for a time in Beaver with their mother (who was expecting), while their father and the others went to establish a home on the farm that October. Lois gave birth to her eighth child on 8 November 1875, a girl named for herself. Shortly after this Ida went to the Sevier Valley, and Lois and the baby joined the family as soon as they were able to travel.

Of their experiences Annie remembered, "We attended Sunday School and Meeting every Sunday at Joseph . . . very often walking the distance. Ida taught one or two terms of school there, and boarded with the Bishop's family, Alfonso Farnsworth and three wives, but no children." May remembered that Ida also took a trip to visit their Aunt Lydia, the widow of their Uncle Gilbert Hunt who lived in Utah's Dixie, and that Ida taught one term of school in Monroe.[3]

Shortly after John Hunt left Beaver, his brother Joseph got into a drunken brawl and killed a man. The trial showed there were extenuating circumstances, and he was acquitted on 20 May 1876. Later, Joseph moved his wife and three daughters to Joseph City, not far from the Hunt farm.

The first Christmas the family lived in the Sevier Valley, Ida's cousin Celia Hunt and two of the Murdock boys came from Beaver and took her by horseback to Beaver for the Christmas season, where she attended holiday dances and parties. The following Christmas her Beaver friends went to Joseph City, as Ida's sister May described in her journal in December 1876:

> At Christmas six of our associates came over from Beaver. They were Henry Tanner and Eliza Parkinson, Lyman Shepherd and Sara Ann Stoney, Will Farnsworth and Harriet Shepherd. Two of the Bean boys, Tank and Will, from Richfield also came, and such an amount of fun and merriment as we had. Uncle Joe's folks took the bed from their largest room and we danced, played games, recited, sang, had step dancing, etc. every evening, and Christmas Eve, we spent nearly the whole night in Jollity. Our parents took part with us, and did all they could to make the time pass pleasantly for our visitors. Uncle Joe and Hy were good singers and step dancers, and added much to our entertainment. Our friends went home feeling well paid for their trouble in coming to see us.[4]

The Hunt family was at Joseph City only a year and four months (from October 1875 to February 1877) when John decided to move again. He obtained permission to settle in Arizona or New Mexico.

A Visit to Beaver

Before going off to New Mexico, Ida went to Beaver in January to spend a month with her Grandma Pratt. Louisa Pratt wrote, "Considering my advanced age, I could scarcely expect ever to see them again. . . . I had indulged a hope that she [Ida] would be persuaded to remain with me until the family found a location suited to their minds. She had partially consented; but when the final test came, she could not part from her mother and younger children."[5] The move to New Mexico was also fraught with anxiety for Ida's mother, Lois, who was leaving her mother and two sisters. While in Beaver on 27 August 1876, Ida had received a patriarchal blessing from her great-uncle, Jonathan Crosby: "Blessed art thou for thy purity and gentleness, and the many graces you possess. Thou art the pride of thy father, and the joy of thy mother, a multiplicity of blessings are in store for thee."[6] Ida was now ready to join her family on John Hunt's fourth pioneer venture.

Pioneering New Mexico

The family left Beaver on 21 February 1877, visited old friends as they passed through settlements, and on 26 February reached Washington, where they stayed four days. While there, part of the company visited the St. George Temple, where Ida and May received their endowments.[7]

On the journey to New Mexico, Ida drove a team hitched to one of the family's three wagons.[8] She and May traveled together and slept in their wagon. Each morning they had their wagon loaded and the team fed, hitched, and ready to join the party of travelers. In the group were two newly married couples, Henry Tanner and Eliza Parkinson of Beaver, old friends, and John Bushman with his plural wife Mary, who were en route to a new home in Joseph City, Arizona. Of this trip, George Tanner wrote, "In the party were two young women, Ida and May Hunt, ages 19 & 17, who entertained at evening firesides with their guitar and singing. This was fortunate as most of the party members were homesick and needed cheering up! This would be continued all the way to their destination."[9]

Their route took them from St. George directly south to the Colorado River and Pearce's Ferry. Though the crossing was much dreaded, they found it "far the most pleasant thing" of their journey. Since the water was smooth, the young women, including Ida with her guitar, took a "sail by moonlight." Their trail continued south and eastward

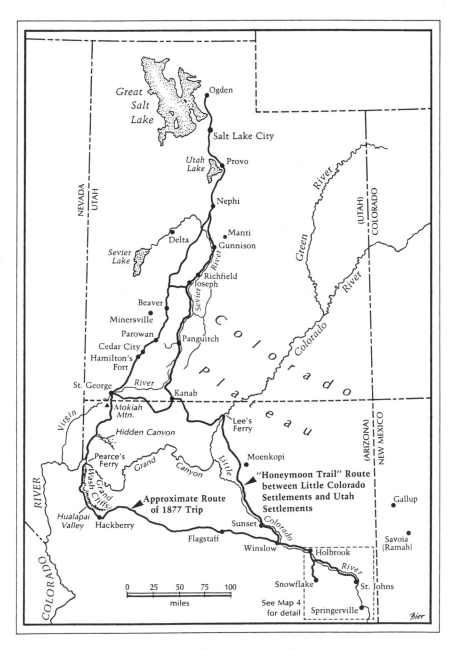

The Utah-Arizona corridor.

to the old Beal and Butterfield route, eastward past San Francisco Mountain to Lot Smith's settlement at Sunset on the Little Colorado, and on past the Zuni village to San Lorenzo, Valencia County, New Mexico. They stayed there three weeks with Lorenzo Hatch and his family. Then on 1 June they decided to go on over to the Savoia Valley, where they met the church's special missionaries to the Navajo.[10]

Pioneering another start, the Hunt family would spend less than sixteen months in Savoia. John was called to be presiding elder over the small congregation, essentially a missionary camp. The family lived in a stockade room while a new double log house was being built. Despite the lonely circumstances, the children were kept busy and derived benefits from their experiences there. Ida earned cash by sewing on the family sewing machine for the Indian women. She and Annie taught the younger brothers and sisters in school. Ida also taught Annie to play the guitar, and she studied the Spanish language. She had taken a Spanish book with her and was helped by her father, who had picked up some Spanish while living in California, and by a Mexican boy, Leopold Mason, who had been taken into the home to learn English. Ida also enjoyed a friendship with a Peterson couple. The husband was about her age. As a child, he had been lost from a Danish immigrant company and taken into the home of a Mexican. After maturing, he had married a Mexican.

On the first of September 1878 a company of Mormons migrating from Arkansas reached Savoia and passed on to the Little Colorado settlements. One of those immigrants brought smallpox into Savoia, and during the winter the colony suffered terribly from the disease, which ultimately took some thirteen lives. Ida, her parents, and her sisters May and Annie, who had been vaccinated in California, escaped the disease and were able to nurse the younger children and others, some of whom were housed a mile away. Ida and May worked the early night shift. As they walked home at midnight, a lantern in the window guided them through the deep snow. "It was a very sad, dreary holiday time for us," Annie wrote.[11]

The Call to Snowflake

The family had been in Savoia a little over a year when they heard a new settlement was to be founded on the Little Colorado, and John Hunt was to be bishop. Annie remembered the event:

> In July we heard that Bro. William J. Flake (a friend from Beaver) had bought the Stinson Ranch, on Silver Creek, Arizona, and in September

Apostle Erastus Snow came out to visit the settlements in Arizona and gave the new place the name Snow-Flake, in honor of himself and Bro. Flake. Our father was called, with a unanimous vote of the people, to be the bishop. He obeyed the call with as much cheerfulness as possible, and we all hailed the change with delight, for our life in New Mexico had been rather lonely.[12]

The townsite was surveyed, and on 24 September 1878 the Snowflake Ward was organized, with John Hunt as bishop. For a short time, his jurisdiction extended over much of eastern Arizona. He was to serve thirty-one years.

Ida went with her father to the site to help pick out a building lot in the new town. Her father returned to Savoia for his family, while Ida seized the opportunity to ride to Beaver with longtime family friends, the Minerlees. The Minerlee party reached Beaver toward the end of November 1878. Ida had fulfilled her promise to return.

A Promised Return to Beaver

Ida was welcomed by Grandma Pratt with rejoicing. Her grandmother recorded in her journal that "as the shades of evening were closing in upon me she came walking in as homelike as though she had only been to a neighbor's house to visit, and returned in due time."[13] Her great-aunt, Caroline Barnes Crosby, observed, "She seemed very natural, the same good kind girl."[14]

Ida was happy to be with her grandmother, aunts, and other relatives again, though she found changes had occurred while she was gone. Hattie Shepherd had married Will Farnsworth, and her cousin Nellie McGary had married Will Jones. Other friends, however, were still there, among them Johnny Murdock, whom she had dated over the years.

Ida was to remain in Beaver with Grandma Pratt for nearly a year and a half, during which time she grew even closer to her grandmother and other family members, renewed friendships, taught school, and became a leader in young women's affairs. Visiting friends and holding dinners were favorite pastimes.

On Christmas 1878 a pattern of having dinners for special occasions began for Ida. She and her grandmother joined the Crosbys for dinner at the home of cousin Nellie Jones. After Christmas she went to the Sevier Valley and visited relatives.[15]

Ida's leadership and influence with her peers was recognized at once, and when the Young Ladies' Mutual Improvement Association

(Y.L.M.I.A.) was organized in the Beaver Stake, she was chosen as a counselor in the presidency. Mary E. Ashworth was president, Flora Shipp Hill the other counselor, and Sarah C. Shepherd the secretary and treasurer. The presidency made regular visits to the ward associations in Beaver, Greenville, Minersville, and Adamsville. Semiannual conferences were held.[16] Caroline Barnes Crosby, her great-aunt, described a midwinter visit to Minersville for the conference there. The Crosbys, Ida, her grandmother, and her Aunt Ellen made the wagon trip "in dense fog with a cold north wind blowing." It was miserable going but well worth it as they enjoyed being with friends and attending the conference.[17]

When there was no teaching job available, Ida earned money copying court records and doing sewing. Grandma Pratt wrote, "My granddaughter was steadily with me, engaged in teaching school; I had the pleasure of seeing her passing out and in every day, and when she was gone for a half day, I did not feel lonely, as I expected her to return, at the set time."[18] Ida was a comfortable companion, engaging in good conversation, reading, preparing a nice dinner, sewing, receiving friends, enjoying an evening of sociability, usually "full of business," but taking time out for a sleigh ride or a visit to the Crosbys.[19] As Caroline recorded, "Evening came Ida Hunt, and Nellie Jones. Ida brought her musical instrument, sang and played for us"; "Last evening called Ida Hunt, and Sarah C. Shepherd with their musical instruments, and played, and sung several nice pieces."[20]

Ida's birthdays were special occasions. Her twenty-first was described by Caroline: "I went, carried a pie, and piece of cheese. Sister Shepherd came, brought milk for the tea, also pickled beets. We had a nice dinner, and a social chat. Ann L. Willis [Ida's Aunt Louisa] was present. Young John Murdock came in, and sat a while with us. Ida took a ride with him to Wm. Jones's. He choped a little wood for Sis. Pratt."[21] By then, Johnny Murdock was seriously courting Ida.

When sickness came to her family, Ida was prepared to assist. She helped Caroline's rheumatic granddaughter by giving her warm baths.[22] When her grandmother injured her shoulder, Ida obtained hops to make a poultice to ease the pain.[23] Her help was really appreciated when her Aunt Ellen came down with inflammatory rheumatism and became "helpless as a baby." Her grandmother wrote, "How fortunate it was that she was here, a help and comfort in time of need."[24]

Of her social life in Beaver, Ida wrote in an 8 September 1879 letter to her parents:

I have been so busy with conference, concerts, etc. lately that I have not had time to answer sooner. It is all over now, though, and the monotony of everyday life is unbroken, for a few days I hope. There are so many calls to go to practices, meetings, sociables, parties, that I get quite tired of preparing for and attending them, and often feel as though the "haven of rest and peace" would be attained if ever I got home again. . . . Saturday night of Conference the Harmonic Association gave a concert to get music. I will send you a program. It was quite a success. The house was crowded, and the singing went off very well.[25]

In the same letter she enclosed a long message to her sisters, telling of mutual friends and of making herself a new white basque (a blouse with a tight-fitting waist) to wear in the concert and enclosing a sample of the material. She also told of going with two friends, guitars in hand, to serenade the neighborhood before the friends left Beaver. Family stories recount Ida's singing "The Star Spangled Banner" at a Fourth of July celebration for the town of Beaver and the soldiers at Fort Cameron.

During October 1879 Ida left Beaver with William Farnsworth and his wife and went to St. George on a short visit, returning by the twenty-first. The winter of 1879–80 was particularly severe, with unusually deep snow and low temperatures. On 1 January 1880 Caroline noted, "Evening there were parties, and sleighriding, bells were jingling in various directions." Two days later Caroline called on her sister Louisa: "The weather had been so very cold, and snow so deep, we neither of us felt like going out. . . . Mr. C. came in and we both took supper there. Ida was full of business, but still took a little sleighride."[26] Louisa had, as she put it, "struggled through one of the coldest winters I ever experienced in my life," and she particularly appreciated Ida's presence, reliability, and companionship.[27]

During that cold February Jonathan Crosby, Ida's great-uncle, made a wooden chest for her, which was to be with her through all her subsequent moves.[28] As February temperatures warmed, women got out more to visit. "Sat 14th quite warm and pleasant. Pm I went into sis P's [Louisa Pratt's]. Ida was washing. Emma Lee [a younger sister of Lucinda Lee] came in. The conversation turned on the womens bill, considerable excitment was manifested. I had very little to say," wrote Caroline.[29] Louisa would have given her opinion, since she was outspoken on women's rights. Emma Lee also had strong feelings on the subject.

On 8 March Ida's birthday was again celebrated by the family. Caroline was there: "I am invited to a dinner in memory of her 22nd birthday, to be given by her aunt A. L. Willis. We were all to contribute a little something, and we had a splendid good dinner."[30]

Besides family relations, Ida had a host of friends in Beaver who enjoyed each other very much, but friends and relatives at home missed her and wanted her to return home. When a chance arose for a ride to Snowflake in the spring of 1880, she finally left Beaver. Grandma Pratt had a little time to be reconciled:

> Her friends in Arizona continued their importunities for her to "come home"; and she was constrained to yield to their entreaties; although we were equally as solicitous to have her remain. But a father and mother have the first claim; a house full of sisters, and brothers, all filled with anticipation to witness her return, to hear her sweet strains of music on the guitar, and be cheered by hearing rehearsed the events of her protracted visit, and a thousand little incidents peculiar to long absence from home.[31]

Of Ida's departure, Grandma Pratt wrote:

> Ida Frances passed two birthdays in Beaver, her 21st and 22d. She took her departure on the 6th of April. . . . It was my youngest daughter's birthday, and we were assembled at her house to dine; when the carriage drove to the door.
>
> With tears and incoherent goodbyes we wished her a pleasant and safe journey home. Nothing could exceed the loneliness in the house the first day where she had so long been an inmate. . . . Her Aunt Ellen was hopeful; she believed the dear girl would come again in due time of the Lord. Since then we hear intimations that events may transpire to bring her back sooner than we had dared to expect.[32]

From her previous residence in Beaver and these months in the home of Louisa Barnes Pratt, Ida received a unique inheritance. She basked in the great love showered on her by Grandma Pratt, her aunts, and others. Her social skills were well cultivated, and she knew good books. Her penmanship and composition alone testify to the quality of that education. Her grandmother taught her to sew, and by teaching school, sewing, and copying court records, Ida was able to take care of her financial needs.

During her years in Beaver she became steeped in the family stories of personal sacrifices for the Kingdom of God, which nourished her through her own life's experiences. There were stories about Grandma Pratt's youth in Canada, where she taught school, and about her move to New England, where she learned tailoring and became acquainted with the Henry Pratt family—Henry, who constructed organs for churches in New England and the South; Rebecca, the daughter who became Louisa's friend; and Addison, her brother, the seaman with whom Louisa fell in love.[33] There were Louisa's and Caroline's stories of the Pratts' and Crosby's conversion to the church, their visits to Kirtland, and their lives at Nauvoo, where they knew the Prophet Joseph Smith and other church leaders personally, because Louisa tailored suits for the prophet and his brother Hyrum. There were the stories of the personal trials and tribulations in Nauvoo, the exodus, the sojourn at Winter Quarters, the trek across the Plains, the mission of her grandfather, Addison Pratt, to the Society Islands, and the experiences of Louisa and her four daughters (including Ida's mother) in going to and residing on the island of Tubuaï in the South Pacific.

All of these stories attested to the sacrifices for the cause, the missionary service, the loyalty, and the obedience of these people Ida had come to know so well.[34] The history they shared those months Ida was in Beaver bound grandmother and granddaughter more firmly than ever. It was a bond that influenced Ida for the rest of her life.

Return to Snowflake, Arizona

Ida's trip to Snowflake was to have another profound impact on her life. When the territorial legislature adjourned, John R. Murdock returned to Beaver, accompanied by Jesse N. Smith, who had recently been appointed president of the Eastern Arizona Stake, headquartered in Snowflake. President Smith had taken his wife Janet Johnson and children to Snowflake earlier and was now moving the rest of his family there. Murdock, Johnny's father, helped arrange for Ida to go with them.

The first week in April 1880 President Smith and his wives Emma and Augusta, "with nine children, left our long time home in Parowan for Snowflake, Arizona. We had 3 wagons, 6 horses, 2 mules, and 2 cows. . . . Louis W. Harris and Sister Ida F. Hunt joined us for the journey."[35]

Word of the progress of the little company reached Beaver, where Grandma Pratt recorded in her journal:

> Long and tedious has been her journey! Instead of performing it as she had hoped in two weeks the company were detained by high water and sandy roads, scarcity of feed for their animals, till eight weeks labor would scarcely suffice to take them through. Returning travelers bring us news of their difficulties.
>
> An explorer brought us word that the company when they reached the Colorado found the river ten feet deep, the wagons had to be un-

loaded, taken to pieces, and by littles carried across the river in a canoe instead of a flat boat. Then the animals were made to swim the stream. What a labor to make repairs, and load up again![36]

Near Flagstaff the Smith party met Charles Flake and others searching for strayed cattle. Ida and Louis Harris joined the men and rode horseback to Snowflake, arriving a few days before the others.[37]

The experience of traveling with President Smith, his wives, and their children changed Ida's life. This was an intimate view of a polygamous family, and she was most favorably impressed. She became aware of "a distinct spiritual quality" in the relationship of the wives and an "unselfish devotion between these wives and a loyal respect for their noble husband."[38]

Ida also made an impression on the stake president. Aware of her experience in the Y.L.M.I.A. in the Beaver Stake, Smith chose her to serve as president of the first Y.L.M.I.A. in his stake. On 26 July she chose her counselors, Nellie M. Smith and Emma Larson, with Nannie Freeman as secretary and treasurer.[39] At the same time, Ida was chosen to be stake secretary of the Relief Society.[40]

In Snowflake, Ida was welcomed with open arms by her family as well. Annie, her sister, was especially pleased: "She [Ida] had owned a guitar every since November 1874, and I spent a great deal of my time while we lived in New Mexico playing it, and had greatly missed it while she was gone. She brought the old one and a new one home with her, and my delight knew no bounds. I played almost constantly, and soon became quite expert. I played the tunes on the new one, and Ida accompanied on the old one, which gave ourselves much pleasure, as well as our neighbors."[41] Her sister May wrote that Ida "soon fixed us up for clothes, as she was so much handier at sewing than the rest of us. She brought many little presents from Grandma Pratt, and made baby Loie many cute dresses, which were the envy of the town women and children."[42]

On 8 September 1880, just five months after Ida left Beaver, Grandma Pratt died. Ida was always convinced that had she remained to care for her, her grandmother would have lived much longer. Filled with sorrow, she nonetheless wrote a comforting note to her Aunt Ellen and cousin Nellie Jones. Nellie commented, "What a sweet comforter she is; I would give anything if I could write such a good sympathetic letter as she can. Oh I do wish she could have been there; We would [have] all felt so much better."[43]

The classroom beckoned Ida, and soon she was teaching school in Snowflake while her sister Annie taught in Taylor. Of a spring festivity, Annie wrote, "On the first day of June [1881], we had a *May Ride.* Ida was queen. [There were six maids of honor, with her sisters May and Annie among them.] . . . The Cottonwood Grove up the Wash was the gathering place. The wind was howling. Ida's speech was a fine one, and it seemed as if the wind ceased while she delivered it. . . . We went on horseback. . . . There was a grand Ball in the evening."[44] Ida was as popular in Snowflake as she had been in Beaver.

Ida's idea of marriage, however, had changed. Her conversion to celestial plural marriage "worked within her to such an extent that when her Beaver sweetheart, Johnny Murdock, wrote that he was coming to Arizona to marry her, she broke the engagement." She hoped that she could marry a man who wanted to practice polygamy so she could share her husband with other wives.[45]

Enter David K. Udall

Soon after Ida's return to Arizona she met David K. Udall, bishop of St. Johns Ward, who had come from Kanab, Utah, the year before, under appointment from President John Taylor to preside over church affairs in that area. As bishop he stood among the top church leadership in eastern Arizona. To answer the call, he had left a promising financial future in Kanab, where he and his partners, Tommy Stewart and L. C. Mariger, were successfully engaged in farming, stock raising, and operating a general mercantile business. (Tommy Stewart was his wife Ella's brother and was married to David's sister Mary, and L. C. Mariger was Ella's sister Sarah's husband.)

David, born 7 September 1851, was the son of English convert immigrants. He had originally come from Nephi, Utah, where his parents had settled in 1852. Motherless at eleven, David from an early age shouldered many responsibilities at home on the farm and away from home, grading road for the railroad or freighting. He handled responsibilities well and was energetic, resourceful, and dependable.

During the summer of 1873, when he was twenty-one, he met Eliza Luella ("Ella") Stewart, an eighteen-year-old woman from Kanab who was traveling through Nephi. They fell in love at first sight and were married in the Endowment House in Salt Lake City on 1 February 1875. Six weeks after the wedding, David was called on a mission to England. During his absence, Ella kept books for the co-op store and assisted in teaching at the village school. As a young woman of fifteen, she had learned telegraphy, and she had operated the De-

David K. Udall, missionary, London, 1877.

seret Telegraph Line out of Kanab and had worked for a time at Pipe Springs, Arizona, earning the honor of being Arizona's first telegraph operator.

The lives of David and Ella were bound together through similar and mutual experiences. Her father, called in 1870 to be first bishop of Kanab, had left prospering businesses in Salt Lake Valley to pioneer in southern Utah. Tragedy struck the Stewart household when a fire broke out in their house in the Kanab fort on the night of 14 December 1870, entrapping and killing Ella's mother and five brothers. Ella was seriously affected by this tremendous loss.[46]

In St. Johns, David turned to farming and was superintendent of the Co-op Store, and in that capacity he hired Ida as clerk. She had the necessary bookkeeping skills and could speak Spanish, which was helpful to the Mexican customers. Just when and for how long Ida was in St. Johns living in the Udall home is uncertain. She was there September 7 for his thirtieth birthday, but the stay could not have been long, for she taught school in Taylor that winter. Annie wrote, "We boarded with Bro. Philip Cordon and wife, and son Lewis. They had a comfortable home, with an organ, and plenty of everything. They enjoyed our music and singing very much [Ida had taken organ lessons in Beaver], and we had a very pleasant time all winter. Our brother Lewis took us up every Monday morning, and brought us home every Friday night. Our sister May had left home on the 4th of October to be married. . . ."[47]

In his memoirs, David placed his hiring Ida to clerk in the autumn of 1881. No doubt the story that Ida had left a sweetheart in Utah had circulated, which might have encouraged Ella to welcome Ida into her home to live. When David learned of Ida's broken engagement, however, he became interested in her. "Before the winter had passed and with Ella's knowledge and consent," David wrote in his memoirs, "I talked with Ida about becoming my plural wife."[48]

David's interest in taking another wife was prompted by word from church president John Taylor that all church leaders should take additional wives. Though Ella came from a polygamous family and said she wanted her husband to take more wives, whenever David had suggested someone as a possibility in the past, Ella had found something to ridicule about her, and David had then lost interest. Ida, however, was not someone to ridicule; she was attractive and talented, as David noted in his memoirs: "My acquaintance with her proved her to be a womanly woman with an abiding faith in the Gospel. She was a charming girl with a wealth of auburn hair and the gift of song."[49] Ida was also poised and self-assured, combining a practical bent with an artistic nature. Ella may have consented to David's proposal, but she clearly was not happy about it, perhaps feeling that Ida had betrayed her.

As soon as David let Ida know of his interest, Ida left for Snowflake and began teaching in Taylor. Until she could be assured of Ella's willingness to accept the marriage, Ida would not discuss it any further with David, as her letter to Ella indicates:

Snowflake, Arizona   January 29, 1882

Mrs. E. L. Udall
St. Johns, A.T.

Dear Sister:

I feel that I cannot allow another day to pass by without writing you to ascertain if possible your true feelings upon a subject which is, no doubt, one painful to us both, but one which, I realize must be disposed of sooner or later, viz: the possibility or probability of my becoming at some future day a member of your family. I trust you will not consider it presuming in me addressing you without permission. In that I cannot allow the matter to go farther, without first having received some assurance of your willingness to such a step being taken, at least that you have no more serious objections to me than you would to any other under like circumstances.

During my stay in St. Johns I learned to love you as a sister, and the very thought that I may have been the cause of bringing unhappiness to you has troubled me day and night. Nothing but pride kept me from writing this letter long ago. But I have finally become convinced that such humiliation is nothing compared to that of receiving the attentions of any man contrary to the wishes of his wife.

I trust, dear sister, that you will appreciate my true motive in writing and favor me with an answer if only a few words. I believe in this matter, it is not only your right, but your imperative duty to state plainly any objections you may have in your feelings and I beg you will not hesitate to do so. I promise you I shall not be offended, but on the contrary, shall thank you for it all my life, and I believe you will not have written in vain, for, unless it meets with your approval, I shall never listen to another word on the subject.

May the Lord bless you and help you to decide in this matter is the earnest prayer of Your true friend,

Ida Hunt[50]

Ella waited a long time before answering Ida's letter:

St. Johns, Arizona, March 12, 1882

Miss I. F. Hunt
Snowflake, A.T.

Dear Friend:

I received your letter bearing date of January 29th some weeks ago. My health has been so very poor that I have felt unable to reply sooner and am scarcely equal to the task now.

The subject in question has caused me a great amount of pain and sorrow, more perhaps than you could imagine, yet I feel as I have from the beginning, that if it is the Lord's will I am perfectly willing to try to endure it and trust it will be overruled for the best good of all. My feelings are such that I can write but briefly on this subject.

With kind regards to all, I remain your friend.

E. L. Udall[51]

David was attracted to Ida, and Ella could only agree with his choice. Despite difficulties, an understanding was reached, and Ida commenced making her wedding dress before school closed that spring.[52]

David K. Udall and his wife Ella Stewart were intelligent, industrious, and attractive people, who were anxious to obey all church principles. Both David's and Ella's fathers were bishops and polygamists, though their family experiences were quite different. Ella's family had a happy relationship, possibly because the two youngest wives were sisters. David's family did not. When David's mother died, David and his siblings lived with the second wife, Elizabeth, until their father married Rebecca. Thereafter they lived with her. Elizabeth and Rebecca did not get along, and their bickering turned David against polygamy. After Ella's mother's tragic death by fire, Ella, fifteen, made her home with her mother's sister, Macy Stewart, who showed her great love. Although the loss of her mother scarred Ella emotionally, it increased her belief in the practice of polygamy. Only after David married Ella and was serving a mission did he become converted to polygamy.[53]

Living polygamy under the most ideal circumstances was difficult for the man as well as for the women. Those who practiced it most successfully were individuals with strong religious convictions that it was a commandment from God. They also needed financial security, a residence for each wife, and an equal share in the husband's time. Even under the most favorable arrangements, living polygamy caused emotional trauma, especially in cases like David and Ella's, where there was deep love between a man and his first wife. Sharing that love with another must have been a terrible ordeal for those involved.[54]

Contrary to popular opinion, polygamy was not especially popular among the Mormons. Most men had to be called, cajoled, and almost threatened into practicing it.[55] Bishop David K. Udall received his call in a letter from church president John Taylor, stating all church leaders were expected to set the example. Despite outward appearances, it was a trial to all parties, and, as Jane Snyder Richards so insightfully observed, "they consider it wholly as a religious duty and schooled themselves to bear its discomforts as a sort of religious penance; and that it was a matter of pride to make everybody believe they lived happily and to persuade themselves and others that it was not a trial; and that a long life of such discipline makes the trial lighter."[56]

Like all polygamous families, the Udalls were to have their problems. Besides individual differences and personality characteristics, there was the closeness of the ages of the trio. Even more basic, however, were the twin problems of finances (the Udalls seemed always to be in the wrong place at the wrong time) and the anti-Mormon crusade that sent men and women into hiding on the "underground" and convicted polygamists to prison.

At the time Ida was converted to polygamy, she expected to marry and then share her husband with another wife, not to be taking something away from the first wife. Ida was by nature sharing, having given up her own desires often to help support her father's large family. In time, Ida's unselfishness became a significant asset for the Udall family.

The plural relationship was difficult for David, and much depended on his management of the two households. He later wrote, "I was sorely tried myself. It hurt me in an inexplainable way to cause Ella any heartache."[57] Ella's feelings were his first consideration, and it fell to Ida to make the greater sacrifices and to be the peacemaker.

One of the most difficult places to live polygamy in 1882 was St. Johns, Arizona Territory. Unlike towns in Utah and Arizona that were settled by Mormons and remained essentially Mormon towns, St. Johns was a Mexican town that had recently been taken over by five American cattlemen (The Ring), who welcomed new settlers but insisted on retaining complete control of the town. Anti-Mormon sentiments that were so widespread in the United States reached into St. Johns, and the federal, anti-Mormon judicial crusade soon took hold in St. Johns. The stage was set for conflict between the cattlemen and Mexicans on the one hand and Mormon settlers on the other. The conflict was to have particularly dire consequences for the Udalls, but that spring they were optimistic.[58]

On 6 May 1882 Ida left her home in Snowflake, Arizona, and went with David K. Udall, his wife Ella, and their two-year-old daughter, Pearl, to St. George, Utah, where in a temple ceremony she would become his plural wife. Her journal opens with the beginning of that long journey.

Of the wedding trip, David K. wrote:

Ella showed her good sportsmanship by complying with my urgent request that she go with us to the St. George Temple in southern Utah where Ida and I were to be married. It was an unusual trip. The girls read several books aloud as we jogged slowly over the desert. Baby Pearl was talking and proved to be our safety valve in conversation. At night in my roll of camp bedding I slept on the ground guarding the wagon in which my precious ones were sleeping. In contemplating the future, as I lay there under the stars, I realized I was placing myself in the crucible to be tested for better or for worse. With all my faith I prayed constantly that I might measure up to the standard that Ella and Ida had a right to expect of me. . . .[59]

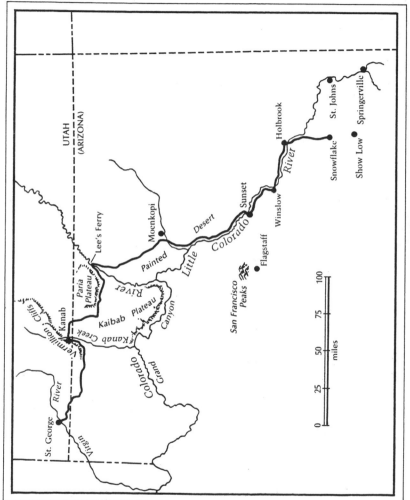

Route of the wedding trip in 1882.

PART 4

Ida's Journal: Marriage and Life on the Underground, 6 May 1882 to 8 November 1886

[The Wedding Trip]

MAY 6TH 1882 On the evening of Sat. May 6th 1882 I left
dearly loved home in Snowflake, Apache Co. Arizona, in comp
with Bro and Sister D. K. Udall, and their baby Pearl to make a sh
visit to Utah. We started about 4 p.m. traveled about seven miles,
made a dry camp for the night, which proved to be a wet one bef
morning, it having rained incessantly all night.

May 7th Reached Woodruff for noon. Took dinner with Bro
Sister Chas. Jarvis. Did some trading at the Central Coop. Were
tained there several hours on account of the rain which continued
pour down. Camped 2 miles below Woodruff.

" 8th Arrived at St Joseph about 3 p.m. Had a pleasant chat w
acquaintances there, and camped for the night 9 miles below on
Little Colorado. We were also on the line of the A. & P. Railrc
During our stay several trains thundered by reminding us that civ
zation was really forcing its way into this new land.

" 9th Beautiful weather, but traveled through deep mud all
morning. Nooned within half a mile of Sunset. From there we
cided to take the road down the right bank of the Little Color
River on account of its being more retired from horsetheives, hi
waymen, etc. with which the Country was thronged. The road pro
to be very heavy. Camped 7 miles below Sunset on a deep gu
which had some water in it.[1]

May 10th 1882 Traveled 25 miles over the worst of roads.

11th Came to the crossing, and good roads about noon. We w
thankful to reach it, for the road we had come, was much farther
heavier than that on the left of the River. Refreshed ourselves in

cool shade and water, till about 3 p.m. when we came down 6 miles below Grand Falls.

" 12th   Reached the Dug-way for noon. That afternoon met Prest [President] Lot Smith[2] and Charles Flake. They were just from Utah. Reported roads good. Big Col. [Colorado River] very high, but perfectly safe to be crossed with the little boat. Bro Watkins whom we had been endeavoring to overtake for company, about one and a half days ahead of us. Camped that night about 2 miles above Tanners Ranche.

13th   Came to the Ranche for Breakfast. Enjoyed the fresh milk and butter which we could purchase there very much. Nooned at Moancoppy Wash. The wind blew a perfect hurricane. Camped that night at Willow Springs.

Sunday 14th   Pleasant Weather. Spent the day in reading from the Bible, and a variety of good books as we journeyed along. Nooned at the Cedar Ridge. Here was the first moments private conversation I had with David after leaving home, so my spirits were considerably lightened. Camped that night at McLellans Tank.

15th   Nooned in the Wash 3 miles from Bitter Springs in the Refreshing Shade of the high Cliffs. Reached Navajoe Springs that night by traveling until quite late.

May 16th   Reached Lee's Ferry on the Big Colorado about noon. Our team, a large span of American horses, (faithful old Dock and Suse,) managed to take the load over the "Back Bone" without help or unloading. Here we found Bro & Sister Watkins, Bro Browning and Frank Crookston whom we had counted on having for traveling companions. Also met Frank & David Farnsworth some of my old Beaver friends. The River was high but by taking the wagons apart we crossed with perfect safety. Put the loads in proper shape and came down to the houses of the ferryman to camp for the night. Here we could buy lucerne and grain for the horses, which helped us nicely.

17th   Weather excessively warm. Nooned at Badger Creek. Our company now consisted of four wagons instead of one. But Bro Watkins team would not permit of their traveling long with us. Camped that night five miles west of Soap Creek on good grass.

18th   Nooned at Jacob's Pools. Weather slightly moderated. Reached House Rock that night. Bought fresh milk and butter from Jed Adair, whose family were living there. The day before our arrival there, they had buried a young lady 20 years of age, Miss May Whiting from Brigham City, Arizona. She had for some years been troubled with dropsy, and had got this far on the road to Utah in company with her mother & brothers when she died. Poor girl! My heart ached to think of her being buried in that lonely place. Here we left the company who did not get into the Spring till next morning.

May 19th   Windy weather again. Came on top of Buckskin Mountain for noon, and that night camped within four miles from Navajoe Wells. The new road over the mountain cuts off several miles, but is much rougher.

20th   Reached Kanab, Ella's old home, about 5 p.m. Just 2 weeks from the day we left Snowflake, and two years from the day I arrived in that place, with Louis Harris, after my long stay in Utah with Grandma Pratt. We put up at Sister Udalls brother Tommy Stewarts, whose second wife Mary, is also a sister of Bro Udall. Unfortunately he was not at home, but his two pretty young wives gave us a hearty welcome. Took supper the first evening with Aunt Macy [Stewart], Ella's Aunt, and also stepmother, and Sister Luna [Stewart], who was the only one of E's family, I had ever met before. I felt much refreshed after a bath and good nights rest, with Sister Mary in her cool chamber.[3]

21st Sunday,   was a beautiful day. The bright fields of lucern, green orchards, and singing birds made Kanab seem almost like a paradise, after leaving such a country as the Colorado traverses. I spent the morning in writing short letter home, and in the afternoon attended meeting with Luna. The Speakers were D. K. Udall, and Wm G. Young. Singing led by Sister [Harriet D.] Bunting, I enjoyed very much. After meeting repaired to Ella's sister Sarah's, wife of L. C. Marriger, where we partook of a bounteous repast, in company with all the Stewart family, also Sister Lulu Johnson. Spent a pleasant evening, in conversation, songs and music. But with all the merriment, I felt lonely and depressed. Like a stranger in a strange land. The sorrow another was passing through seemingly on my account, though I was powerless to help it; the constant strain my mind had been on during the whole journey, lest by word or look I should cause her unnecessary unhappiness, had weighed upon my spirits greatly, and I retired from the scene that evening with a feeling of dread and fear at my heart impossible to describe. Afterwards was greatly reassured by a moonlight walk and conversation with the one dearest on earth to me, who brought light and hope to my heart once more, with his loving encouraging words. So that I finally went to bed, feeling that in striving to obey the commandments of God, with a pure motive I had everything to live for. No matter how severe the trial, what a privilege to pass through it, in such a glorious cause.

22nd   In the forenoon made some necessary arrangements for resuming our journey to St George. All took dinner at Aunt Macy's and started out about 3 p.m. Ella's sister Luna joining our company. Traveled about 14 miles and made a dry camp.

23rd   Reached Pipe Spring about 10 oclock a.m. bought butter etc. of the ranchmen, filled kegs with water, made dry camp.

May 24th   Weather very warm. Reached St George by traveling till after dark. Stopped at Bro Frank Farnsworth's whose first wife is also Ella's sister. They have a beautiful home and treated us very kindly.

Thursday, May 25th 1882   This afternoon at half past 5 oclock in the Holy Temple of the Lord, I was sealed for Time and all Eternity to David King Udall, the only man on Earth to whose care I could freely and gladly entrust my future, for better, for worse. Ella and Bro and Sister Farnsworth walked down to the Temple with us, and after a talk with Prest. J. D. T. McAllister, (by whom the ceremony was performed,) she, Ella seemed to feel much cheered. Oh! if she could only feel happy and reconciled, I should feel that my life was indeed a happy one. Why is it, that in carrying out the commandments of God, his children need be so sorely tried? Today I have made the most solemn vows and obligations of my life. Marriage, under ordinary circumstances is a grave and important step, but entering into Plural marriage, in these perilous times is doubly so. May Heaven help me to keep the vows I have made sacred and pure, and may the deep unchangeable love which I feel for my husband today increase with every coming year helping me to prove worthy of the love and confidence which he imposes in me, and to always be just and considerate to those the Lord has, and may give unto him in a similar way. When he bade me goodnight, the sacred name of *wife* was whispered for the first time in my ear, causing my heart to flutter with a strange new happiness. During the night, Ella, being unable to sleep, and thinking likely I was the same, came into my room, and mentioned for the first time to me our relationship to each other, and we talked long and earnestly of our hopes and desires for the future, both feeling much happier for the same.

26th   We all spent the morning at Booth's Art Gallery where we all had our Photo's taken, after which we visited the Coop and Whiteheads Store doing quite an amount of shopping for ourselves and others. At one oclock I took dinner with Bro Jno E. Pace and wife Phebe. Had a very enjoyable visit with them. During the day met many friends and acquaintances whom I had forgotten I had in St George. In the p.m. Ella & I went shopping again, making some purchases at Woolly, Lund, & Judds and when we got home, I found my old Beaver and Minersville friends Grandma Boothe, Bro & Sister

Ida's wedding picture, St. George, Utah, 26 May 1882.

Rollins, and Phillip Baker and wife awaiting my arrival. Heard much news from my old home. Same evening called on Bro [Thomas] and Sister [Caroline Jane] Cottom in company with Villa Liston and Ida Rollins.

27th   Started from St George at three p.m. arriving in Kanab Monday May 29th feeling much happier than I did when I left it, which I believe was the case with all the party. After our visit to the Temple there seemed to be a feeling of peace and union between us which had not existed before. On the road home Ella and I had several long confidential talks. Told over our mutual trials and sorrows, and got to understand each other better. O, if we could always be frank and open with each other, how many heart-aches would be saved.

30th   Spent the day, visiting making lace handkerchiefs, etc.

June 1st   Sister Mary and I did the family washing. Ella and Fanny [Stewart] getting dinner, in which we were joined by the Marriger family.

3rd   Enjoyed a family gathering at Aunt Macy's. Sort of a carpet-rag bee. Had dinner and supper together.

4th   We made dress, hat and collar for little Pearl.

5th [4th] Sunday.   Called on Grandma [Martha] Crosby & others in company with Fanny. Attended meeting. That evening Bro Tommy, our host, came home for the first time since our arrival. Had a pleasant evening.

6th   The members of the Stewart family, three wagon loads in all, started out for a pleasure excursion to the Cave Lakes.[4] We were supplied with the best of Picnic, and a borrowed guitar which we used to good advantage during the day. These Lakes are the grandest natural curiosity I have ever seen situated about 6 miles north of Kanab. We arrived there about noon, and spread our dinner under the tall Box Elder trees which shade the mouth of what is called the Dripping Cave. Here the water which is cold and clear as crystal drips continually from the roof of the cave into the placid lake below, running out in a small stream. During the afternoon we enjoyed ourselves swinging, talking, reading, singing & eating until near sundown when we started homeward, well pleased with our days amusement.

7th   Spent the day in washing.

8th   All went visiting down to Lon Stewarts.

9th   Visited at Aunt Eliza's, John Stewarts wife.

10th   In the afternoon visited Young Ladies Meeting with Sister Mary who is the Prest. of that Ward.

11th Sunday.   Went to meeting with the Sisters Marriger, Prest. Erastus Snow delivered one of the best discourses I ever listened to.

Preached just 2 hours. After the close of the services, he came and spoke to me, introducing me to his wife Minerva (who was with him) as the grand-daughter of her old friend Sister Addison Pratt. Was also introduced to Bro & Sister Horrace Spencer. That evening went to Sister Marrigers to enjoy some music.

12th   Spent the day preparing for our journey home, but were detained until Thursday.

15th   Left Kanab enroute for A.T. [Arizona Territory] about 12 m. During our two weeks stay there, I had made many dear friends whom it was a trial to part with. It was also a great cross to Ella, who was leaving her old home and all her relatives except one sister who was in St Johns. But we all felt that she was far happier to go, even though we suffered on the road with heat than to remain for awhile with her friends as she had talked some of doing. The load was considerably heavier but the team was in better fix than when we left home. Brother Tommy camped with us the first night out at Navajoe Wells. He was out on Stock business.

16th   Parted with him when we started for House Rock. Brigham and Levi Stewart overtook us during the afternoon driving some wild horses. I immediately offered my services as "Bacaro" and Levi took my place in the wagon so we both enjoyed the change. Reached the House Rock about dark.

17th   Parted with the boys. Reached Jacobs Pools 3 p.m. Filled water kegs and drove several miles farther to camp for the night. There was a nice cool breeze instead of the scorching heat we had expected. During the day read from Mrs S. J. Holmes Novel entitled "West Lawn."

18th Sunday.   Was cool and cloudy all day. Read the "Rector of St Marks." Same author. Nooned between Soap and Badger Creek. Here two men with pack mules overtook us. Their outfit of tools would indicate them to be prospectors. If they were only good men, how glad we should be of their company for it was running a risk to travel alone. Reached the ferry about dusk that evening. Everything looked lovely after the fine shower we had been blessed with during the afternoon.

19th   Weather still cool and cloudy. We crossed the River in the morning, and I never enjoyed a boat ride more, although the water was very high. We were safely over and the wagon put together and loaded up by noon. Reached Navajoe Spring that night. Our friends of the "pick and shovel" remaining at the Ferry a few days.

20th   Watered the horses at Bitter Springs about 3 p.m. & camped for the night at Lime Stone Tanks. During the day were rather unfortunate. Lost the small water keg and David was obliged to go back two miles for it. I also lost small pocket-book containing [a] few dimes. This was the anniversary of little Pearls second birthday, and she chattered about it all day.

21st   Met 4 men with 12 head of mules and horses. Some of them packed. They were a hard looking crowd, but only asked a few questions about the road and let us pass in peace. We nooned at Cottonwood Tanks. Had a pleasant camp and cooked a good warm dinner, which we did justice to. Camped that night at Willow Springs.

22nd   While at breakfast another crowd of Packers came to us. Talked very importantly. Said they wanted to buy some grain, and their manner indicated that if we refused, they would take it any way. So David thinking "valors best part was discretion" under the circumstances sold them a few pounds and they departed. Nooned at Moan-coppy Wash, and that night reached Tanner's Ranche. Here David was quite sick with neuralgia & cold, but by morning felt much better. We bought fresh butter and milk and went on our way rejoicing.

23rd   Was very warm in the forenoon. The first time we had felt the heat to any extent. Camped for noon on the Little Colorado, and made some Molasses Candy, for a change. That night reached Black Falls. A great many Navajoes there with sheep. The grass and water both exceeded our expectations, being rains all over the country.

June 24th   Also enjoyed the benefit of a nice breeze which prevented our feeling the scorching rays of the sun. Nooned at Grand Falls and that night reached San Francisco Wash, or a short distance of there.

25th   Found our friend and brother-in-law Ammon M. Tenney[5] and his little son Nathan camped just above where we were. Much pleased to see them being the first decent people we had met on the road. He was going home so we would have traveling companions. We nooned at the Bend. Ammon fixing up a nice shade for us between his wagons, but the wind and the sand were any thing but agreeable. That night we had a pleasant camp just below Brigham City with nice water, grass, wood, and good company. Thus passed the first month of my married life. It had been clouds and sunshine intermingled, with more happiness, in the mane, than I had anticipated. I can say truthfully that I beleive we are all three far happier, than we were one month ago today, which is indeed encouraging.

26th   Started early. Came through Brigham City, but not Sunset. Crossed the Little Colorado at Sunset crossing. Nooned on the River in nice shade. Here Johney Redd became a member of our company.

He was on his way to St Johns. Passed St Joseph 4 p.m. Called at Sister [Melvina E.] Richards' a few moments, who told us of the murder of Bro Nathan Robinson of Reidhead, by the indians a few days before. I was much shocked to hear it. Camped near Baradoe's.

27th   Met some men from St Johns near Holbrook who told us of a sad affair which had just happened at that place on St Johns Day which the Mexicans were celebrating with a big Bull Fight. In a shooting scrape between the Greer boys and the Mexicans, Father Tenney and Jim Vaughn had been killed by the latter, & the Greers arrested and put in jail.[6] Ammon was thrown into grief at the news and started immediately for home on horseback, leaving his teams in care of the boys. We stopped a few moments at Woodruff. Bro [Charles] Jarvis pulled a tooth for David, and Bro [Joseph] Fish engaged a passage to Snowflake with us, where we arrived about dusk the same evening. Found the dear ones at home all well and anxiously looking for us. Pa was on the eve of starting to California to visit his sisters there, in company with Bro Issac Turley. Oh! it seemed so pleasant to get back home again, to father, mother, brothers & sisters.

28th   At 1 oclock pa started for Cal. and at 2.30 David, Ella and little Pearl left for their home in St Johns   I [am] to remain in Snowflake till we see which way the wind blows, and some arrangements can be made for my safe keeping.

July 18th   David passed Snowflake on his way to Albuquerque to make purchases for the St Johns Store of which he was Supt. Said Ella and Pearl seemed much better in health, for the long trip they had enjoyed.

July 24th   By riding nearly all night of the 23rd David reached Snowflake, on his return from Albuquerque in time to spend that Holiday with us. We had a nice Celebration, and a family dinner. I enjoyed the day very much being the first of Davids society I could freely appreciate, since our marriage. George and Nellie Elsworth from Showlow took supper with us and we all attended the party in the evening.

25th   David remained with us; after dinner he and I called on Sister [Mary A.] West, and Bro Smiths family. Had a pleasant visit with each.

The morning of the 26th he started early for St Johns going clear home that day.

The following month I was busily employed in making quilts, and bedding of different kinds.[7] Sister Anna and I visited Taylor. Spent the night at Bro & Sister [Philip] Cardons, & also visited the young ladies Association. Pa arrived from Cal. the first part of August, having had a very rough trip, suffering with the heat, etc, but much pleased with his visit with his sisters in San Bernardino, also with Ma's sister Frances in Anaheim, Los Angeles Co.[8]

[To St. Johns]

Aug 23rd   Dade arrived in Snowflake, this time coming with the intention of taking me to St Johns to live. He felt that the sooner he got his family together, under each others influence, the better it would be for all parties.

24th   We left S. about 3 p.m. I felt very sorrowful at parting with my parents, brothers and sisters, and in leaving the old home, never to return on exactly the same footing. But I was happy in the thought that I left home with their approval and blessing, and also perfectly happy in the love of my good kind husband. We came that night to the Cedar Ridge. Talked long and earnestly of our past lives and our hopes for the future. Camped by the light of a beautiful moon.

25th   Came by Sister [Thomas L.] Greers Ranche. She insisted on our stopping for dinner. Had a pleasant visit with her, and her daughter Dessie. Reached St Johns about 8 p.m. Little Pearl was at the door to give me a welcome, but no one else. That was a night never to be forgotten. In nearing the town, it seemed that all the powers of darkness were arrayed against me, whispering me "it was no use, I could not stand the test" of going to share another womans home and husband, even though it was her earnest desire that we should live together. Our neighbors on three sides were Mexicans, and I felt that the wicked influence and spirit surrounding the place had something to do with the forebodings I had, but on reaching the house, and finding Ella in the depths of despair, with no welcome for me, my feelings can better be imagined than described: I cried earnestly unto the Lord for help and strength, and He is the friend that never forsakes us in the hour of sorest need. I felt greatly comforted in seeing a great change in Ella's feelings the next day, which we spent in arranging things for my comfort, and also called on Ella's sister Anna Riggs.

Aug 27th Sunday.   David visited the Meadow Ward[9] to hold meeting. Ella went with him and took Pearl for a ride. This was my first Sunday in my new home. I visited my dear old-time friend Sister Jensen, and attended meeting in the afternoon, then called on the Sisters Romney.[10] The following Sunday we both went to Walnut Grove, 20 miles above St Johns, with David, to hold meeting. Had a pleasant ride, and visit.

Sep. 14th   Davids Sister, Eliza Tenney started to Utah to visit their old home in Nephi, taking her two little girls with her.

" 16th   While David was away from home, surveying land at the Meadows, Ella gave birth to another little daughter. We were occupying the same bed when she was taken sick, and were not expecting to be thus disturbed for three weeks at least. Pearl, and Jake, (a swiss boy living with us) were the only other occupants of the house. The night was dark & rainy, but on Ella awaking me at 11 oclock, I immediately ran for Bro Ammon Tenney, our only neighbor, besides Mexicans, who soon brought Sister Rizpah Gibbons, the only midwife in the place. Sister Olive McFate was also called in, and at 2 oclock a.m. a little wee daughter was born. It was the first time I had ever been present on such an occasion, and being the child of my husband, it seemed this little stranger had a claim on my heart no other child had ever had. David returned that morning, on account of the heavy rainfall, and was greatly surprised to learn of the new-found treasure. She was blessed and named "Erma" in due time.

When she was two weeks old, Ella's sister Anna Riggs being there to keep house for us, I attended the Stake Quarterly Conference held at Snowflake, Sep. 25th in company with David. We reached there in time for the afternoon session of the Ladies Conference on Friday, in which the business for the Y.L.M.I.A. was attended to. There being a large attendance from every part of the Stake, another meeting was held at 5 oclock for the officers of the three organizations, in which much good instruction was given by Sister [Wilmirth] East & others. The Stake Conference was continued Sat. Sunday & Monday, largely attended & very spirited. We reached home again Wednesday Eve.

Oct. 12th   I had quite a sick spell, which impoverished my health greatly, and baby Erma was afflicted with colic every night till three or four months old. Her mother lost so much sleep with her, that she was not well any of the time. Pearl & her papa were the only lively ones in the family.

[A Room of Her Own]

November   We cleaned house, and persuaded the folks to let me have the little Mexican room we had been using for [a] kitchen, for my bedroom. Previous to this, I had been sleeping in the Dining room, which made it very unpleasant, especially when not feeling well. (And we did not wish to make any more improvements till it could be done on the city lot in the "Mormon town" Bro Tenneys had just moved onto their lot, leaving us with no near neighbors, excepting Mexicans.) Accordingly we had the little room fitted up. Whitewashed, lined over head with cloth, new door and window put in and painted, and my new carpet down, and I felt proud as could be of my first little room in St Johns. It was cosy & cheerful inside, if it did resemble a mud-daubers nest from without. But before I had ever spent one night in it, Pearl had gone to bed in there, delighted to sleep in "Aunt Ida's new room the first night," while Grandma [James] Ramsay, Ella & I were finishing E's room, we were startled to hear Pearly crying, and I rushed in to find the room one dense fog of smoke, and Pearl nearly suffocated. Coals from the little corner fire-place were thrown all over the room, carpet burned, and cloth-ceiling burned to the wall on all sides without blazing. The mystery was solved when I found the hull of a cartridge laying on the outside of the bed. Jacob, in cleaning up rubbish, had chanced to put a bullet in the fire-place, and when it became sufficiently heated by the pine fire we had left on the hearth, exploded, throwing fire all over the room. I felt very badly in gazing upon the wreck made in a few moments, and wondering if that misfortune was typical of the life I should spend in that little room. The prospect was certainly not very inviting, however we were so thankful that Pearl was uninjured, I could not mourn over any loss I had sustained, and I soon got the damages repaired and spent many happy hours in it afterward.

December, 1882   In the early part of this month I went home on a visit to Snowflake. Saw for the first time, the only grandchild of the family, and my first nephew. The fine son of my Sister May Larson, born Nov 7th 1882 in Snowflake. I spent the Holidays with my dear ones at home, also attended the Quarterly Conference held at Taylor, after which I returned to St Johns with David, Bros [Miles P.] Romney, [Andrew] Gibbons, and [Willard] Farr who came to Conference.

January 1st 1883   We met pa on the road home. He had been attending Court, in St Johns and had spent News Years day with Ella. We reached home the afternoon of Jan 3rd and that evening heard the sad news of the death of Sister Fanny Stewart, Tommys wife. She died with child-bed fever leaving a babe three days old. Sister Mary [Stewart] had a babe two days younger, and was also lying very low with the same fever. Poor Tommy! this was the second wife he had buried, and Mary was left with five little children to care for, only two of them her own.

January and February were extremely cold months. David settled Tithing[11] and Store business for the year. He and Bro [Willard] Farr took a trip to Savoia, which was then a part of the St Johns Ward, to settle tithing. They nearly perished with the cold.

March   In the first part of this month David took a trip to Albuquerque to do purchasing for the Store. He also had the place improved, putting up lumber kitchen, new door & window in Ella's room and the place enclosed with picket fence, thinking these would enhance the value in selling, and be much more comfortable while we remained there.

26th   Stake Conference was held in St Johns. Apostle B Young and H. J. Grant being in attendance.[12] At the Sisters Conference, held Friday, Stake Prest of R.S. [Women's Relief Society] Sister East having moved away, her first counselor Sister [Emma] Smith not arriving in time for the morning Session, I as Stake Supt of Y.L.M.I. Associations was called on to preside, which in the presence of Apostles, and Stake Presidency was no little task, having the Secretary business for the three organizations to look after, into the bargain.[13] To my great relief Sister Smith arrived for the afternoon meeting. My Sister May and husband attended this Conference bringing with them Johney and Loie [Ida's brother and sister]. My father and mother were then on a visit to Utah, from which trip they returned with a new member added to the family. Pa had at last entered the order of Celestial or Plural Marriage, taking the daughter of his old friend Taylor Crosby of Kanab for his second wife. I was much pleased to hear this piece of news, as I beleive were all the family, and my dear good mother, if ever she was tried in that principle, (which she had always been willing and anxious for pa to obey,) she never let her children know it, and she treated Aunt Sadie from the first as she would have wished one of her daughters treated under the same circumstances. If her daughters can only follow her noble example.

April 1883   We had the same as three working men to cook for. David hired a man for a month or so, and with Jacobs help, they cleared land, made ditches and prepared to raise [a] large crop. David worked very hard, but was greatly blessed in his labors. My health, at this time was very poor indeed. I was afflicted with pain around my heart, and shortness of breath which prevented my sleeping at night and soon brought me down weak and thin.

May 20th   My dear mother came to make her first visit to me in my new home. She staid one week, and then Bell and Lewis came after her taking me home with them, thinking a change might improve my health. I remained in Snowflake all through the month of June, riding horseback, going with my brothers to the field and after the cows, which seemed to benefit me greatly.

June 30th   Conference was held at Round Valley.[14] I attended in company with pa, Aunt Sadie, and Sister Anna. She and I took our guitars and we had concerts every night. At Round Valley I met David, also Ella, who was on her way to Riggs Ranche with her sister Anna, taking the children for their health. Little Erma was commencing with teething & summer complaint, and she feared the hot weather in town would be too hard on her. I returned home with David, pa also coming by that way to attend District Court which was then in session.

July 4th   Pa, Sadie and Anna spent with us. We had a Celebration, which reflected great credit on the town. M. P. Romney Orator. Sister [Mary E.] Freeman sang the Star Spangled Banner. Violin Solo by A. [August] Mineer. Duets by Sisters Freeman & [Mary] Farr, and Sister Anna & I with guitar accompaniament. Song by Maud Crosby etc. His Honor, Chief Justice French was present and made a very flattering speech at the close.[15] We all attended the party in the evening.

5th   We were invited to spend the evening at the home of Bro Willard Farr, a social gathering in honor of his birthday. Had a very enjoyable time.

6th   Pa and Aunt Sadie started for home, but I persuaded my Sister Anna to stay awhile with me. This was the first time I had been left to keep house alone, and it seemed strange, and Anna was much company for me. David was in the field from early morning till 8 oclock at night.

24th   Anna returned home a few days before this. We had a nice Celebration. I was called upon to teach twelve little boys and girls to sing "I'll be a little Mormon," which was quite a success. David came from the field long enough to attend the celebration, after which we took dinner at Bro Romneys in company with Bp [Joseph H.] Richards of St Joseph. David then returned to the field where he had been for nearly a week night and day attending to the irrigation of his crop. I went to the party at night with Sister Eliza Tenney & Sister Jensen. We heard from Ella frequently. The baby was still very poorly. There was also much sickness in town. Grandma Ramsey made her home with me when she was not attending the sick.

August 17th   We received a letter from Ella, saying that she also was confined to her bed, worn out with waiting on the baby. David started immediately after them reaching home Sunday noon Aug 19th   Erma was nothing but a little skeleton and she and her mother were both very feeble for several weeks. Pearl was fat & well.

Sep 7th   Davids 32nd birthday. We gave him a complete surprise. Sisters [Mary] Freeman & [Mary] Farr were the instigators only they spoke to us thinking it would be more agreeable all round. We set two long tables in the dining room. Cooked chickens, potatoes etc. while they invited a nice company, and attended to other matters. The guests were all assembled, and supper waiting, when David arrived from the field weary and dirty with his arms full of green corn. The evening was spent in music, speeches, the reading of original poems by Sisters Freeman and Farr, appropriate to the occasion, and would have been a success in every way had not Ella been so poorly she had to take the bed before the evening was half over.

25th   Ella and Sister Ramsay attended the Quarterly Conference held at Taylor, in company with David. They took little Erma, but Pearl stayed with me, and was a very good girl. When we were lonely at night, Aunt Eliza [Udall Tenney], with Olive and Phebe, bore us company.

Oct   Grandma Hunt, with Bell and Johney, who had just recovered from Mountain fever visited us.

November   David had the threshers three days in the field. He was blessed with a splendid crop. Made two trips to Camp Apache with grain; to cancel his indebtedness on Mail Contract. During this month Pearl and Erma had the measels. Got along first rate.

21st   Apostles B. Young and H. J. Grant visited us. My father was with the party. Bro Youngs wife Lizzie was with him. They held meeting at St Johns one day.

December 8th   Quarterly Conference was held in St Johns, but on account of so much sickness, among the children with measels, the attendance was much smaller than usual. During conference Bro Ammon Tenneys lost their sweet little baby Lula, with pneumonia which set in after the measels, and two weeks later their little Abby died in the same way. This was a very severe trial for poor Aunt Anna, the mother. My Mother and Sister Bell attended the Conference and I enjoyed the visit with them very much. The Choir gave a concert on Sat evening, in which I had several parts, and it made a great deal of extra labor.

15th   I commenced to assist Bro [Willard] Farr, in teaching the large District School. My health was not what it should have been for the task, but the trustees could find no one else who would or could accept the situation. We hired a girl, as Ella's health was also very poor. I enjoyed my labors very much.[16]

25th   I attended the party Christmas Eve, with Charley, (our hired boy) as David nor Ella cared to go. On arriving home, I found that Santa Claus, in the form of my dear husband had called and left a much-wished for little sewing-chair by my bed-side. Christmas day passed pleasantly. Bro Ammon Tenney and family, who were feeling so sorrowful over the loss of little children, spent the day with us. After a bounteous Christmas dinner was partaken of, David and Ammon discussed religion, politics, etc. by the fireside, while Anna and Ella called on Sister [Ada] Babbitt, and Sister Eliza and I took a walk to Sister [Mary] Farr's, who had been quite sick. We returned, had supper, and spent a quiet social evening together, feeling greatly blessed in the possession of peaceful homes, and the association of our friends and dear ones.

Jan. 1st 1884.   On New Years Day, I was happily surprised by the arrival of my father and Sister Anna in time to take dinner with us. Pa came on business, and Anna, who had lately returned from her wedding trip to Utah came specially to see me, leaving her husband to the care of one of his sisters. She had been married the latter part of September, 1883, in St George Temple to Orrin Kartchner, a young man from Snowflake. I rejoice to say, one in good standing in the church, and whom our parents could approve of. While in Utah they had visited our relatives in Beaver and Richfield, and she had much to tell me of all the dear friends she had seen. We all attended the New Years Ball that evening, and the next day at noon they started for home, leaving me only half satisfied with the visit I had enjoyed. I continued my labors in the school-room until the latter part of February, when the term expired. Pa happened to be in St Johns again on Court business, and in company with David and Ella attended our exercises on the last day of school.

February 23"   I returned with pa for a short visit to the dear ones at home. While there, (in riding out with my brothers and sisters, to look at "Silver Creek" which was a raging torrent, caused from rains in the mountains,) I contracted a heavy cold, and commenced having toothe-ache, and neuralgia incessantly. My dear mother and sisters did everything they could think of, but only temporary relief was given.

March 7th   Conference commenced in Taylor. I attended the Sisters Conference, that afternoon, which through lack of time was curtailed to one half day. David came to Conference, bringing with him Bro A. S. Gibbons and Sister Olive Moffatt,[17] but on account of high water had to go directly to Taylor without coming to Snowflake, and we that were on the opposite side of the River from the meeting house, had to be ferryed over to meetings on a flat-boat. This was something quite novel, for as dry a country as Arizona so early in the season.

10th   About noon started for St Johns. We managed to ford the River, by my brotherinlaw, Alof [Larson], piloting the way on horseback. That night we camped out. It snowed and blowed, and I suffered everything with neuralgia. Sisters [Mary A.] Freeman and Moffatt applied hot salt, etc. and finally the brethren administered to me, after which I became easy and slept all night. Reached home about five oclock p.m. Found Ella and the children moderately well, and for eight long weeks, I was confined to the house, suffering with neuralgia and rheumatism in every part of my body. Oh! those weary days of suffering! Had Ella not been a natural doctor, I don't know what I should have done. She was always ready and willing to try every remedy mentioned or thought of, and relieved the pain first with hot applications, then cold, and dear little Erma must always have a hand in the rubbing. Sister [Rizpah] Gibbons and [Sister James] Richey, too were very kind to come and help care for me, and my dear patient Dade. What can I say of him. Working hard as he did every day in the field, and coming home to find us all sick and low-spirited, it was certainly discouraging, but he always had a kind word of sympathy, and great hope for the future. His great faith and cheerfulness, were of untold value to me at this time, for I sometimes lost all hope of ever being well again. I had a number of old teeth, which by filling had only been made worse, and I imagined that no one but a scientific dentist could extract them, as I had tried on several occasions only to have them broken off. I had suffered from the time I was sixteen years old, with toothache every little while, and made up my mind it was to be my everlasting doom.

[The Anti-Mormon Crusade in St. Johns]

March 1884   During this month the persecutions of our enemies also became, seemingly unbearable. A newspaper was published in St Johns, by one [George] McCarter, whose sole mission was to misrepresent and vilify our people. The "Secrets of the Endowments" were claimed to be exposed, and every issue contained low vulgar articles about some of our leading men's private affairs. My name frequently come out in glowing colors, calling me a prostitute, mistress etc. This was very hard for our brethren to bear, but they treated it with silent contempt, and quit reading the paper altogether.[18]

In the latter part of March one of the nicest city lots in the place was jumped by three outlaws by the name of Nicolson, Lewis, and Compton, who were discovered fencing the same early one morning.[19] David and others remonstrated with them kindly, but in vain. The lot belonged to Bro Don C. Babbitt and he immediately engaged carpenters who began taking down the land-jumpers fence and putting up one of his own. This kind of work was kept up nearly the entire day, until the Sheriff, a Mexican came and ordered both parties to stop work, and then went and hid while the outlaws continued their labor. I mention this as one of the most exciting days of my life. All day Ella and I stood watching the proceedings from the window, listening and dreading to hear the first sound of a pistol. Our brethren were knocked down and mistreated with no chance of redress. These outlaws were backed by the whole, jew, gentile, and Mexican town, who were waiting anxiously for our people to give them the least cause for an outbreak. The spirit of bloodshed seemed in the very air.

But thanks to an overruling Providence our brethren kept perfectly cool, the whole day through and when night came, they all looked as though they had had a spell of sickness. David and others were on the ground all day, simply as peacemakers, and on the following day, he with six of his brethren were arrested on a trumped-up charge of "unlawful assembly." They were tried before a Mexican Justice and acquitted, by paying a lawyer fee of $10.00 each.

The following week, a part of two other lots were jumped, each of these having houses on them, and the brethren were arrested again on a charge for the same offence, got up in a different shape. This time they waived examination to appear before the Grand Jury.

It became evident that St Johns must have help, in the shape of more permanent substantial citizens of our people, or the place would have to be abandoned. The persecutions of the County officials, in depriving the people of School money, water rights, and the extortionate taxes were more than they could stand. It being just before the April Conference, held in Salt Lake City, Prest J. N. Smith and others had already started for that point. So it was thought advisable to send some one from the Ward to explain the true situation of affairs, to the First Presidency of the Church, and Quorum of the twelve Apostles, and leave it for them to decide. Bro Miles P. Romney was the one decided on for this mission, and he was ably assisted by Prest Smith, when he reached Salt Lake, who fully realized that if St Johns was abandoned the whole Stake would have to be. Accordingly, about two weeks after his departure, Bro Romney wrote David that he believed the Authorities were fully arroused to our necessities, and there was a private call made on the different Stakes, for one hundred families, or missionaries to go to St Johns. This was joyful news indeed, and served to cheer the people greatly.

May 1st Was a day of rejoicing with us, and was greatly enjoyed by old and young. The Y.L.M.I. and Primary Associations joined together in celebrating the day, each crowning a Queen and braiding a Maypole. I learned the little girls of the Primary, the crowning exercises for their Queen, all in song. The exercises were all in the meeting house, the morning devoted to the crowning of the Queens, appropriate songs, recitations etc. and the reading of the "Young Ladies Advocate" of which Ella was editor, but I did the reading. A bounteous picnic was partaken of at noon. In the afternoon the primaries engaged in the dance, and in the evening a Leap year Ball was given by the Young Ladies.

About 5 oclock a shooting affray between Mexicans and cowboys took place, chasing each other through the "Mormon town" firing their guns incessantly, and many threats were made that our party would be broken up at night, but their courage failed them before putting their threats into execution, and the party was a complete success. Ella and I retired at about 10 oclock, much gratified with our days pleasure, being the first time we had all been able to be out for several weeks. We left David to the care of a young lady partner (Miss Ada Babbitt).

May 8th & 9th   A Special Conference was held in St Johns, which was attended by Apostles B. Young, and F. M. Lyman,[20] and a large concourse of people. The Saints were much encouraged and built up, by the exhortations and promises of the Apostles. On Sunday the large congregation fasted till the sun went down, and prayed the Lord, to release us from the bonds and persecutions of our enemies, and the spirit of God was poured out upon all present.

Bro Lyman carried a set of Dentist instruments with him and made a practice of pulling teeth for the people wherever he went. When he found I had some decayed ones, he gave me not a moments peace about getting them out, and on Sunday evening after Conference he made a commencement on them. Extracted two bad ones, and was trying the third, which broke off, and my jaw was pulled out of place. Bro Lyman, never having had a case like it thought it was merely a contraction of the muscles of the face, or lock-jaw. David and pa were with me & they with Bro L. administered to me immediately, and repeatedly through the night many of the Priesthood laid their hands on my head and pronounced great blessings upon me. Ella and Sister [Rizpah] Gibbons worked faithfully, trying every remedy they had every heard of for lock-jaw, but all to no purpose. My mouth remained wide open, my tongue became badly swolen, and I was unable to swallow a drop of anything, and no surgical assistance to be had in the place, only from our bitter enemies. The following morning found me in a sad fix, and the brethren counseling together, decided that help must be had, and so it was thought best for pa to go and explain the case to Dr Denney, who was very kind, explained in a moment how my jaw was dislocated, and showed him how to set it, and at 10 oclock on Monday 10th Bro Lyman performed the operation. Thankful indeed was I, to feel my teeth close together once more. That night will be one long to be remembered.

11th   The Apostles and party started early for Round Valley to visit the settlements in the upper part of the Stake. After they had gone, Sister Olive Moffatt came up to see me, & before starting home, she asked me if she should do as she felt inspired to do. I eagerly answered "yes," and with no one in the room but we, two, she placed her hands on my head, and gave me one of the greatest blessings I ever received, promising me life and health, and the blessings of sons and daughters that should be mighty in the Kingdom of God. Although a young woman, she is one of great faith, and I felt great joy in listening to her words, knowing there was a power in them.

May 12th   The week following, I suffered greatly with the old tooth that had been broken off. At the expiration of that time Bro Lyman came back, but I did not have the courage to let him make another attempt at pulling them.

[David Arrested, Tried]

The morning they got back from Round Valley David was arrested on a charge of Perjury, a low-down saloon-keeper by name of Darling serving the papers. He gave bail to appear before U.S. Commissioner for trial. This was another trumped-up charge, simply got out through malice on the part of the "ring" and because they had no other way of making a living. Bro [Miles P.] Romney, in preempting a Ranche, had desired David for one of his witnesses & in giving evidence in the case they claimed he had perjured himself. The Apostles went on to Prescott on business, and Prest Smith, pa, and others returned to Snowflake.

About this time the first companies of emigrants arrived by Rail from Utah, and soon after some began to arrive by team. David had been very busy since the first lot Jumping, securing all the land between St Johns and the Meadows, building Section houses etc. and missionaries had been sent from the different settlements to assist in holding it for the new-comers.

June 14th   The Apostles returned from Prescott, and I underwent another ordeal of tooth-pulling. This time by the earnest solicitation of Bro Ammon Tenney, I took brandy to deaden the pain, and

Bro Lyman with Dades help, succeeded in pulling eight more teeth, dislocating my jaw the second time, but was prepared by former experience, to set it instantly.

15th   My health began to improve rapidly from that time on. I acknowledged the hand of the Lord in sending Bro Lyman to that part of his vineyard, just when I so much needed help.

16th   After holding one good meeting, and riding with David all over the field, with which they were delighted, Bros Young and Lyman bade us goodbye, and started for Salt Lake, by way of Navajoe Ward in New Mexico. They left many hopeful hearts, where they had found heavy ones, and their visit will never be forgotten.

20th   The week following, David stood his trial for perjury, before U.S. Commissioner, [George A.] McCarter, and by paying Lawyer [Harris] Baldwin, $150.00 to defend him, (through counsel of the Apostles) was honorably acquitted, for lack of evidence. Unjust and unlawful as this charge was, we felt greatly releived that he was once more *free*. There began to be rumors afloat now, that our leading men were likely to be arrested for polygamy, being blessed (?) with a U.S. Commissioner in our midst, who had power to issue such warrants whenever he chose. *Report* said papers were already made out for David, Ammon [Tenney], and Bro [Miles P.] Romney, but we knew not whether it was true or not.

July 4th   Was celebrated with considerable zest, notwithstanding the political bondage of our people. David was called on for a speech on "Religious liberty" which was rather a *sore* subject for him just then. The two Young Missionaries, just arrived from Beaver, (Gillies, and Yardley,) who had formerly been school-boys of mine, took dinner with us. That evening, the baby of Bro John Plumb's family got a piece of paper in its windpipe and choke to death. David was there until midnight, and Ella and I spent the evening in writing.

5th   At 4 oclock a.m. we were suddenly aroused by Ella being taken sick, and at 7 a.m. she gave birth to a fine 9 lb. daughter, Sister [Rizpah] Gibbons officiating as M.D. It was a beautiful healthy child, and Ella was getting along much better than ever before. With the help of little Lena Jensen, I was getting along splendidly with the housework, and it really looked as though there was a prospect of our all being well once more, and able to go out and do something as other people did. But alas! for our hopes!

[The Raid]

10th   When baby was five days old, just as I was clearing away the dinner table, Ammon [Tenney] and Joe Crosby, suddenly came to the door, to say that he, (Ammon) had been arrested, in town on a charge of Polygamy, and before Sister Eliza [Udall Tenney] had heard anything about it, she had been subpoenaed as witness against him. She had told the officer she would not be there and immediately left the house. They thought the next call would be for me, and it might come any moment. So David said I had better disguise myself and leave the house immediately. Oh! how my heart sank at the thought of leaving home, with Ella helpless in bed, and no one we could depend on to take my place. There sat little Erma, just woke from her knap, eating bread & milk. She could not talk a word, and would not make friends with strangers. After her ma was taken sick, she had adopted me without a murmur, and seemed perfectly happy in my care. I shall never forget the feeling I had in leaving her.

I threw a shawl over my head, and without waiting for a word further, walked down through the Mexican Town to Mother Gibbons' [widow of Andrew Gibbons] who lived in the edge of the field. Explained the situation to her, and she immediately consented to go and look after Ella's wants, and spend the night there, while I remained in her stead. I arranged things for an early breakfast for Bro [William H.] Gibbons, and had just retired for the night, when David rapped at the door, and requested me to get ready for a ride into the country. I hastily dressed, and walked with him, across the field to Sister Freemans, where I found poor Sister Eliza, and Sisters Catherine and Anna Romney already in waiting to bear me company. Bro [Miles P.] Romney was getting a team in readiness, and at half past eleven oclock he and David started with us, for the farmhouse of Bro Joel White, which was about three miles out of town, and entirely out of the way. After traveling the worst of roads, getting stawled in the mud, several times we reached Bro Whites about 2 oclock a.m. They welcomed us very kindly, although they were not a little surprised to be visited by so many ladies, at that time of night. After David and Bro Romney had assisted us in arranging our beds on the shady side of the house, under the blue canopy of heaven, they returned to town.

[Ida's Exile Begins]

July 11th 1884.   Thus passed our first night as exiles from home. Eliza had left her two little girls, to the care of neighbors, Aunt Anna [Tenney] being on the farm. Sister Catherine had left five children at home, and Sister Anna two, and had with her, her baby boy three months old. So they all felt they had more to worry over than I, and I was quite willing they should think so. Eliza stood guard for the party; with a pair of field glasses, she descried every object for miles around that came towards the house, and when anyone really came, we got behind curtains or under the beds.

16th   We remained with the family of Bro White, until the evening of Tuesday July 16th when it was decided we [should] be shipped in the direction of Snowflake. Bro Romney took his wives and myself in a wagon, while Eliza, being the only criminal of the lot, dressed in masculine attire, rode horseback across the trail to Concho, accompanied by Ammon and Will Berry for guide. Oh! that night! Shall I ever forget it? Before starting I had ventured home after dusk, and hastily packing such things as I would need, kissed Ella and the children goodbye, for the last time in many, many, long days, I felt impressed at the time I left them. We got started from the bench, back of town at about 11 oclock p.m. David driving the team to the top of the hill, when he bade us goodbye, and walked back. We traveled all night. Took breakfast at the Tanks, and reached Snowflake at 2 p.m. Found Sister Bell afflicted with kind of a fever sore which made her a cripple for several weeks. The rest of my dear folks were all well, and so glad to see us.

July 18th   Aunt Sadie [Hunt] had a cute little sister, three months old to show me. She was named Martha, for her Grandma Crosby. Bro Romney rented a room near by in which he got his wives quite comfortably located, before returning, while Ammon made arrangements for Eliza to board with my Sister May, thinking it would be more retired than staying at pa's. However, living so near, we were like one family, most of the time. Eliza kept very close, being like a prisoner but I went out whenever pa thought it prudent to do so.

23rd   Sister Catherine gave birth to a fine daughter, and got along splendidly. She was blessed and named Emma.

24th   I attended the Celebration, and assisted some of the girls in singing. Poor Bell, was too lame to go. In the afternoon pa took Eliza, Bell and all of us out in the carriage to see the races. We had only just got home, when a deputy marshal from St Johns came into town with subpoenaes for Prest Jesse N. Smith and wife, Ma, Bell and I, claiming they wanted us as witnesses in pa's case, which had been pending in the District Court for nearly two years, adjourned from one term to another. Now they wanted to prove that he was a polygamist at the time of his election and not entitled to the office. Of course I was not to be found in Snowflake. Pa expressed surprise that the Marshall had not found me in St Johns, as I had been there all the Spring. David and Ella had been subpoenaed on the same pretence, and it was evident they wanted witnesses in some other case than pa's.

August 1st   The officers went to the house to inquire for me on two occasions, even questioning little Pearl, in the yard, as to my whereabouts. But she adroitly answered "I don't know." Between August 1st and 12th Pa & Ma accompanied by Bro and sister [Jesse N.] Smith made two trips to St Johns and back, hoping to get the case disposed of, but it was never called up. This was Chief Justice Sumner Howards first term of Court and from his deportment, and the experience our people had previously had with him in Utah, we dared not hope for the justice that even Judge French had shown us.[21] While the folks were in St. Johns Ella's baby was blessed and christened Mary. They also had the pleasure of meeting, Joseph Udall (David's youngest brother) and his wife Emma.[22] They had been called from Nephi, as missionaries to St Johns, and arrived there August 2nd after a journey of nearly three months. They were detained on account of high water in the Big Colorado. Eliza and I felt very much grieved that we were not permitted to see them. We had looked for them so long. David's mother, died when he was ten years old, leaving the four children, two boys and two girls. Aunt Rebecca, their fathers third wife, having no children of her own, had been able to do for them as their mother would have done. As they grew up, they had each in turn married and moved far from their old home, and now Joe, the baby whom she hoped to keep near her, was called to go too. We received heart broken letters from poor Aunty after she was left without a child in the old home. Much as David sympathized with her, he rejoiced to have his brother near him, and every note I received from him, spoke of the comfort they would take together, working as they could, to each others interests.

11th   Aunt Sadie started to Utah, with little sister, to visit her parents in Kanab. Bro Johney and I accompanied her as far as Woodruff, where she joined the company she was to go with, (pa being in St Johns at the time.) We soon heard of her safe arrival, having had a prosperous, pleasant journey.

16th   Sat evening, about sundown, I was very much surprised to see David riding up to the door on horseback. Not very happily so either, because I knew it was no pleasant errand that would cause him to leave his work at that busy season of the year. He soon informed us that he had been hastily summoned to appear as a witness before the Grand Jury in Prescott, a distance of 275 miles. He could have lawfully refused to go, on account of the short notice given him, but being a *Mormon*, he thought best not to give them any cause for complaint against us. Bros [Miles P.] Romney and [John T.] Lesueur were also subpoenaed and would go via Woodruff. David remained over Sunday. Attended meeting, after which we all took a ride in the field.

At 3 oclock next morning he started for Holbrook where he would join the other brethren, and take [the] train for Prescott. I felt very badly at seeing him start for I was strongly impressed that this was only the beginning, of a long train of annoyances and persecutions for our people, in Apache County.

All the leading members of the St Johns *Ring*, our bitterest enemies, were also summoned as witnesses before this Jury, and it was apparent that "indictments for Mormons," was the chief object.

David and party, were detained in Prescott over a week, under heavy expenses, their witness fees only serving to cover a small portion of the same. The Jury seemed bent on finding indictments for perjury against David, Bro Romney, and Joe Crosby, but could not find evidence sufficient. Before leaving Prescott however, he, David, was arrested on a charge of Polygamy, an indictment having been found against him, and six other brethren before this U.S. Grand Jury. The witnesses names signed to the indictment were, [J. Lorenzo] Hubble, [E. S.] Stover, Bunch, [George A.] McCarter, [Alfred] Ruis, and [Louie] Trawer, all of the "St John Ring" men who never came to our house, and who knew nothing whatever of our family affairs, except from hearsay. Had never, in public or private, heard me called by any but my fathers name. He gave bonds in the sum of $2,000.00 two of the leading men of Prescott proffering to sign them, assuring him at the same time that the evidence before the Jury was of such a flimsy nature there was no chance for conviction. The other brethren indicted, were Bros. [Ammon] Tenney and [Christopher J.] Kempe of St John Bro W. J. Flake of Snowflake, and Bros J. N. Skouson and P. J. Christofferson of Round Valley, who were each arrested and taken to Prescott to give bonds. They offered no resistance, thinking they had nothing to fear under the Edmunds law, and it was thought wisdom by the Authorities to stand their trial. David did not return via Snowflake, so I did not see him again till Conference.

About this time Aug 24th my poor mother had a very sick spell, which worked on my mind and feelings greatly.[23] For two or three years she had been subject to these attacks which effected her for days, sometimes, and she would have no recollection of them after they had passed. They were caused from the critical "time of life" she was passing through.

27th Sister Bells birthday, she had so far recovered from her lameness, as to be able to walk over to Annie's which caused great rejoicing. We all had supper at Mays, after which a feast of water-melons from Bro Alof's garden. The days passed pleasantly with my dear ones at home. My sisters and I improved the chance of getting some quilts made. When evening came we generally took a ride to the field with my brothers; these rides poor sister Eliza enjoyed very much, being so closely confined to the house through the day. I felt very grateful that inasmuch as I could not remain at the home of my husband, I was permitted to be associated with my dear parents, brothers and sisters. I also had great reason to rejoice over the improvement in my health, and felt to acknowledge the overruling Hand of God, in hearing and answering my earnest prayers at this particular time.[24]

September 12th   Quarterly Conference convened in the new brick Meeting House which was termed the Stake House, in Snowflake. There was a large attendance. Many people from St Johns whom I was pleased to see, Sisters Freeman and Farr, among others. On Friday afternoon, Sep 12th the Ladies Conference convened, at which time my resignation as Stake Secretary for Relief Societies was accepted with a vote of thanks for past services tendered, and by my suggestion Miss Della Fish was unanimously sustained in my stead. My many other offices and duties prevented me from doing justice to that calling, and with minutes, reports, etc. complete up to date in the Record, I gladly gave it up to my predecessor [successor], having filled the duties of that office for four years. Immediately after the close of the conference, a meeting of the officers and Secretaries of the different organizations was called, in which I explained, to the best of my ability, the making out properly, of reports, on the printed blank forms.

David arrived on Friday noon, in company with Bro Romney. This was the first hint I had had that it would not be safe for me to remain longer in Snowflake, and the thought of having to make another move, arroused a very serious train of reflections. It was counseled by all means to keep witnesses in these polygamy cases out of the way, and when David related to me all his experiences in Prescott, and the many falsehoods the Evil One, had put it into the hearts of those wicked men to testify to before the Grand Jury, I was greatly exercised.

September 15th   It opened my eyes to the great power of the Adversary and I realized that I would not be safe to stay with my friends or relatives in any part of that country, and I tried to reconcile myself to do cheerfully whatever David thought was for the best. He prayed about the matter, that he might be directed aright, and before starting for home on Monday morning, he had almost decided to send me back to Nephi, Utah, his old home, to stay with his father and Aunty until after his trial in November. The thought of going so far from home, among people I had never met, almost broke my heart, but my dear boy talked to me long and earnestly of the many dear friends he had there who would give me a hearty welcome, and make my stay a pleasant one, in the home of his childhood. Of his Mothers grave, where, when a boy, he had always gone to pour out his soul in prayer, when in trouble or sorrow, and which he wished me to visit. All this served to strengthen and encourage me, and then too, he thought that Ammon would also send Eliza, so that I should not have to go alone. Prest Jos. F. Smith, Apostle Erastus Snow, and Bro Jno Morgan with their wives, were expected at St Johns the following week. He would counsel with them, and if they thought advisable to send me, he would return with their party to Snowflake to make arrangements for my journey; in the meantime I made what preparations I could, in case I decided to go, Grandma Hunt also preparing to visit her daughters in Cal. hoping the Apostles party would return via San Francisco so that she would have company.

September 24th   Wed. evening at 4 oclock the Apostles and Co. reached Snowflake. Bro and Sister [Erastus] Snow were our portion of guests; David and Ammon drove through in one day and did not reach town till about 8 p.m. David was still strongly of the impression to send me to Utah while Ammon thought Eliza could be just as safe to stay nearer home, by going up in the mountains to an out of the way place called Willford,²⁵ and the Apostles thought it perfectly right for each to follow their impressions. Here was another trial in the thought of giving up Eliza's company. We had shared our exile, thus far together, and it was a sorrow to both to part. My poor mother, also felt very badly to have me go, but said "Davids will be done."

25th   Meeting was held all day in the Stake house. Some of the best preaching and instruction I ever listened to. That evening meeting was held in Taylor, many of the S. F. [Snowflake] people attending; The boys D. & A. did not go however, and we all spent the evening at Mays, eating grapes (a treat from Ammon) and counseling on what course to take, for the best.

26th   The Apostles party started, Friday morning for St Joseph, pa going with them, and taking with him dear old Grandma Hunt, who had decided to attempt the journey to San Bernardino alone, as she could now go through in two days and a half, by rail. It was quite an undertaking for one 79 years old, but she was real spry, and enjoined it upon all to pray that she might make her visit, and return to Zion to be buried. She did not wish to die away from the Church. As the company would not leave Holbrook for Salt Lake until Sunday noon, I had a little longer to remain at home, which time was busily occupied in making necessary preparations for the journey.

27th   Saturday at 2 p.m. I bade goodbye to my dear mother, brothers, and sisters, and to poor Sister Eliza, and started in company with David and Ammon for Woodruff arriving there at dusk where we spent the night. Here David purchased trunk & valise, giving me at the same time many instructions and warnings as I had never traveled any distance by rail before.

[Into Exile in Utah]

28th   Sunday Morning, I parted with my dearest boy, with a heavy heart, and started for Holbrook in company with Bro Hatch. We took train at 1 oclock. In reaching the passenger coach, I had to pass through a large crowd of staring men, but being thickly veiled, I think no one recognized me. I merely had the chance of shaking hands with pa, just as the train started. This was a sorrowful hour for me. I was leaving home and dear ones for an indefinite length of time, expecting to travel hundreds of miles, to tarry among relatives, whose acquaintance I had yet to make, until the persecutions of our enemies should cease sufficiently to allow me to remain at home.

I was fortunate in having so nice a company to travel with.[26] Prests Smith, Snow, and Morgan with their wives of the Salt Lake party, and from our own Stake Bro Lorenzo H. Hatch, Bro Jos. James, and Sister Mary Bushman from St. Joseph, with two children. Bro Morgan was my cavalier from the first hour of my journey. He looked after my trunk, and arranged my satchel and shawl-strap, where they would be handy, talking cheerfully to me the while, but I dare not trust my voice in answer. I kept my veil pulled closely down to hide the great tears that chased each other down my cheeks for two or three hours after leaving Holbrook.

All this ground I had traveled over by team several times before a R.R. was thought of, and it brought up so many reflections of the days I had spent in New Mexico, when we had gone as pioneers to the country. Sister Bushman had been one of our Company in making our first move from Utah. As we passed "Isleta" about 10 oclock p.m. the Indians came on board the train by dozzens, selling the passengers delicious grapes and peaches very cheap. Reached Albuquerque at 11 oclock to where we had half rate tickets, but through some misunderstanding had to pay full fare from there to Pueblo, (which however was arranged satisfactory afterward).

29th   Took breakfast at Las Vegas, New Mexico. Dinner at Raton. About 2 p.m. passing through Wooton Pass or Tunnel. Darkness reigned supreme for about 5 minutes. 7 p.m. reached La Junta where

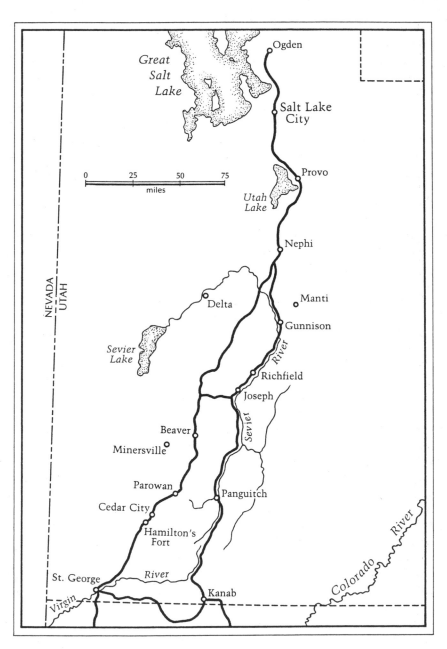

Ida Hunt Udall's sojourn on the underground in Utah, 1884–87.

we stayed two hours and changed cars, for Pueblo, arriving there at midnight. Here with much regret we parted with our friends of the Salt Lake party whose passes took them via Denver. Before leaving us Bro Morgan assisted in securing a pleasant room with two beds, and everything nice in Strane's Hotel for Sister Bushman & I, which we were fully prepared to enjoy. Bros Hatch and James occupied an adjoining room, and acted as our escorts from there on.

September 30th   We rested here until 11 a.m. when we took train on the Denver and Rio Grande R.R. for Salt Lake. Being fortunate, through Bro Hatch's influence in securing half fare tickets. This line is a narrow gauge R.R. and being crowded with passengers, we were rather uncomfortable as to seats, but the scenery on this route is grand past all description. Soon after leaving the dirty, noisy town of Pueblo, we come in sight of the Arkansas River, and the track winds up its banks for many, many miles. In passing through the "Grand Canon," we took an observation car, and I enjoyed the magnificent scenery to the fullest extent. Was sadly disappointed in finding that the greater portion of Marshall's Pass, was crossed after dark. Two engines were attached, and we began the ascent just at sunset. There chanced to be a pale moon, and with the aid of that, I lost no opportunity of getting a glimpse of the apparently topless heights we were scaling, filled with awe in contemplating the works of man, on this one Rail Way. Passed Gunnison at 10 p.m. Here many of the passengers got off, which made it more comfortable for those remaining.

October 1st   Wed. Morning found us passing through a most barren desolate country; in great contrast to that we had last beheld in the evening. The wind was blowing a perfect hurricane, and the dust sifted in at every crevice. Passed Green River Crossing at 8.15 a.m. Took breakfast there. Noon found us at Sunny Side Station on Price River. Wind still blowing and country desolate. The force of the gale and showers of sand was sufficient to almost stop the train, which at 1 p.m. Price Station, was three hours behind time. Here another engine was attached, and we made a little better time. 2.20 halted at Castle Gate on Price River, one of the Natural Curiosities on the Route. During the afternoon passed Springville, Provo and Lehi. At the latter place, Bro Hatch and Sister Bushman got off. I reached Salt Lake 8 oclock, instead of 4 p.m. when the train was due.

[Salt Lake City]

I felt truly like one alone in a strange land. I knew I had friends if I could only find them, but that was the trouble. Before leaving

Bro Morgan, at Pueblo, he had given me a card with his address, and instructed me just how [to] reach his residence, by hiring a certain hack, thinking I would reach the city before they did; but it was so dark and strange, I had to accept the services of the first cabman that offered, and instead of taking me to the residence, as I charged him, he deposited me in front of the Morgan College and drove off and left me, standing with my luggage in the street.[27] This building was formerly occupied by Bro Morgan's family, and as a schoolroom, but is now rented to every class of people. I inquired for John Morgan of a lady (boarder) who stood in the door, and she stared at me as though she had never heard the name. I was ushered into a room where a crowd of rough looking men were playing cards, & they served me as the woman at the door had done, while I stood there, the beating of my heart almost smothering me, and thinking "why oh why did I ever leave my home in Arizona!" Finally one man more gentlemanly than the others, went in search of the landlady, who soon explained that Jno Morgan had not lived there for several years, and told me how many blocks and in what direction he did live, but being an entire stranger in the City, that did me no good. I timidly asked if she would not go with me, but she called to a young fellow by the name of Sam and asked him to take me.

I felt very reluctant about accepting the assistance of a strange man, but I thought it could not be worse than staying there, so we departed. On the road down there I learned that he was a Southern boy, who had formerly lived at Bro Morgan's, & I felt much relieved. I was delighted to find Bro and Sister Morgan had reached home ahead of me and were just at supper. They gave me a hearty welcome, and treated me with the utmost kindness, so that I soon felt perfectly at home. Made the acquaintance of Sister Jenny Whipple, who had been the housekeeper during their absence, & Bro Morgans daughters, Melly, Eliza, Ruth & baby Flora.

October 2nd   Was a dark rainy day. I did not go out of the house. Met several of the Groosbecks[28] who called to see Sister Morgan. Helped with the housework, and wrote short notes home to Snowflake & St Johns.

3rd   Called on Bro and Sister Richard Horne, my old schoolteacher. Had a pleasant visit. Sister H. went shopping with me. I bought Hat at Mrs Dye's (Miliner) and Dolman & gloves at the Coop.[29]

4th Sat.   Conference convened in the Large Tabernacle, & I attended meeting in that grand building for the first time. But strange to say, every thing seemed as familiar to me as though I had always

been used to it. Met many old and dear friends from Beaver and elsewhere, all apparently glad to see me. That evening Father Udall[30]
called to see me; and I saw for the first time the father whom I had
so often heard my husband talk of. I was rejoiced to meet him, and
he gave me a very kindly greeting. Said on receipt of Davids letter
telling of my arrival in Utah, he had come to Conference with the
full expectation of taking me home to Nephi with him. I also met
my old Uncle [Jonathan] Crosby from Beaver, Uncle Wm McGary,
Sisters White and family, and my dear friend Wm Ashworth, accompanied by a Young lady Miss Emma Westerman, (whom I judged to
be something nearer to him than a friend). He was the same brotherly attentive fellow as of yore. Insisted on my going to Beaver with
them, and he would pay my fare, but I had come to make my home
in Nephi and so I declined.

6th Monday.   I not only attended the Conference meetings, but
likewise a review of Bro Evan Stephens singing class, of 200 children.
It was held in the Assembly Hall, and was really splendid. I had the
pleasure at this meeting of hearing the famed Salt Lake Vocalist, Mrs
Olsen, Thomas, [sic] render a solo. In the evening, in company with
Bro Morgan's family I attended the Sunday School Union, held in the
Large Tabernacle. The building looked grand, when lighted.

7th Tues.   Conference still continued half day but this was the
only meeting I did not attend. Father Udall started home that morning, reluctantly consenting for me to remain a few days in Salt Lake,
to see more of the City, before going to Nephi. He left me a ticket,
with the promise that I come down on the Sat. Morning train. Bro
Geo. W. Bean from Richfield called on me. Aunt Jenny [Morgan], and I,
who were already fast friends, went out shopping together.[31]

8th   Sister [Jenny] Whipple obtained the use of the Groosbeck
buggy, and took me out sight-seeing. Rode by the "Gardo House,"
Brigham Street, Walker Block, etc. Enjoyed the ride very much. Afterward went with Sister Morgan to call on her brother and sister. That
night I spent at the house of Sister Lizzie Horne.

9th Thurs.   Visited the Salt Lake Temple, now in course of erec-
tion. The Supt. a Bro Jones, took me to the top of the walls, where
I had a beautiful view of the whole City. After leaving the Temple
Grounds, I called at the Woman's Exponent Office. Met Sister [Emme-
line B.] Wells, her daughter Louie and also Bro Jno Q. Cannon.[32] Sister
Wells appeared much pleased to see me. Presented me with the Book
"Representative Women of Deseret" and two pamphlets on Plural
Marriage by H. M. Whitney.[33] She was pleased to hear I was going to
Nephi. Said I would find many nice people there who would sympa-

thize with one leaving home under the circumstances I did. I canceled my indebtedness for the Exponent, and she insisted on my calling again next day. The same evening I attended the "Carlton Opera" held in the Salt Lake Theater. The play was "Fra Deivolo," and the characters were well sustained. Being the first *real opera* I had ever had the pleasure of seeing I enjoyed it immensely. Sister Whipple & Melly Morgan were my companions.

10th Friday.   Spent the morning in packing my trunk and valise preparatory to an early start Sat Morn. Sisters Thatcher and Calder, visited at Sister Morgans. That night Sister Whipple occupied the same bed, and talked most of the night. She was a widow lady formerly of Chicago, one of Bro Morgan's converts, and had only been in the Church a little over a year; she confided all her trials and sorrows during that short time to me. Wished me to pray for her and if I saw any opening for her to get a situation as teacher or governess in the place where I was going to let her know.

11th   Bro Morgan and Jenny accompanied me to the Depot. Sister M. said she felt as though she was losing one of her family. Invited me to stay with them as long as I could feel contented. I was very grateful indeed for the kindness they had shown me, and felt that the Lord had surely answered my prayers in raising up friends unto me in my hour of need. I met Prest J. R. Murdock of Beaver at the Depot and had the pleasure of his company as far as Lehi, where he was to wait the 4 oclock train.[34] From there I visited with Sister [Louisa] Lyman, Mother of Apostle F. M. whom I had not seen since I was a child. She was on her way to Filmore. Arrived at Nephi 12 oclock.

[Nephi]

Father Udall was awaiting me at the Depot, and I accompanied him to the house of Aunt Rebecca who had a nice dinner waiting, and gave me a hearty welcome. I had strange sad feelings on entering for the first time the old home that had given shelter to my dear husband, from almost infancy to manhood. The very yards, and walks, seemed hallowed to me. In the afternoon visited the family of Aunt Elizabeth. Saw the room where Davids Mother died, and sat in her old rocking chair. Took supper there.

12th Sunday.   Attended meeting in the p.m. after which many of the old friends and neighbors called in to see me. Spent a pleasant evening in company with Sisters Pitchforth and daughters.[35] Following week visited at Sister Brian's.[36] Louise Udall assisted me in making [a] black dress.

18 & 19th   Quarterly Conference was held in Nephi. Aunty had

been notified that Apostle F. M. Lyman and wife would be her guests. They came Sat. morning. I had not seen Bro L. since the severe ordeal of tooth-extracting I passed through under his hands. He seemed gratified to note the improvement in my health and appearance.

Oct. 20th   Aunt Rhoda and their little daughter Lois came also, and stayed till Monday 3 p.m. We had a splendid visit, and attended some of the best of meetings. Sat. Evening Apostles [Wilford] Woodruff and [George] Teasdale called in to see us.[37] Asked me many questions in regard to St Johns etc. On Sunday we were all invited to a nice dinner at Prest [William] Paxmans.[38] He was a dear friend to David when on his mission in England, being Prest. of the London Conference where he labored and seemingly took the same interest in me. They have a beautiful home and a nice family.

24th   Thursday, was Bro Paxman's 48th birthday. His wife gave him a surprise in the evening. Tables all set and guests assembled when he returned from business. I was among the honored ones. Met some of the leading people of the town. Sister Sarah A. Andrews the famous singer was there and favored us with many nice songs. The Supper was splendid, and the evening devoted to music, speeches etc. until 11.30 when all retired wishing the host many such happy returns of the day.

26th   Bros [John] Morgan, Marks and Parry were missionaries to the S.S. [Sunday School] Conference in Nephi. I attended meeting all day. Had a good visit with Bro Morgan.

28th   In company with Aunty attended wedding party of Messrs Norton and Broadhead, in Social Hall.

30th   Sent letters to David and Sisters at home. Friend Jenny Whipple arrived from Salt Lake to visit me for a week or so. In the afternoon we attended Relief Society meeting. Several Sisters blessed with the gift of tongues.

October 31st   Aunty, Jenny and I visited at Sister [Emma and Julia] Bryans, and the following day at Sister Paxmans, on Sunday at Wm Bryans, and in this manner passed the week.

November 4th   I had a narrow escape from being seriously hurt. Started down cellar for potatoes, leaving the trap door open above my head. When I had nearly reached the bottom, the door fell, knocking me senseless for a moment. Aunty was much frightened; called father to administer to me, and I was soon all right.

Friday 7th   My Dear Aunt Kit, arrived just after dark from Richfield.[39] She had come purposely to take me down there on a visit. She had a light carriage, and team furnished by her two Sons-in-law, and one of their little brothers for driver.[40]

8th   Bros Morgan, Marks and Parry took dinner with us, on their

[way] to San Pete as missionaries. Sister Whipple would return with them on Monday to Springville.

[To Richfield on a Visit]

2 p.m. we started for Richfield. Left poor Aunty Udall with a severe headache. She and father reluctantly consented for me to go, with the promise that I would return in a few weeks. Reached Little Salt Creek that night, distance 15 miles. Stayed at Sister Emma Whitbecks, who treated us very kindly. Sunday 9th reached Gunnison. Put up at Bro Mitcalf's, just returned from a New Zealand mission.

10th My Dear Grandma Pratts birthday. We reached Richfield. Saw for the first time in four years my cousins Celia, Ina and Ida. Celia was now the mother of two large boys while Ina had three children. Aunt Kit and Ida had a cozy little home.

16th Attended meeting and had a pleasant evening at Sister [Elizabeth] Beans. Monday reced. good letter from Sister Eliza, who was up in the timber above Snowflake keeping out of the way of the officers. Said she had been lonely and broken up since I left. Was looking for David and Ammon to pass there on their way to Prescott to stand their trial.

20th Received letter from David written from Snowflake from which I quote.

Snowflake Nov 10th—We arrived here 1.30 p.m. today. Will leave here at 5 in the morn. Five of us are going, Tenney, Kempe, Christofferson, Flake, myself and one of our lawyers, Jno B. Milner, (formerly of Provo.) [41] *We are going by team. Will take Ammons team and he will be driver. Please write me two or three times at Prescott, as we will likely be there several weeks. The place here seems so lonely to me without you. Prest Smith has put me in charge of the company while we are gone. I feel the responsibility very much. He feels very hopeful over our cases and so do I, but no doubt we will have a strong fight. Ella and all the folks felt very badly yesterday, when we left home. Some of the brethren were reminded of the days of Missouri. xxx [Ida's ellipsis mark] I am so thankful you are treated so kindly and are so happy. God bless you is my constant prayer. You must make Nephi your home while in that country. Of course go and visit your kindred in Richfield. I do not think I would visit Beaver at present.*

Oh! how thankful and happy I shall be to hear they are that far on the return trip.

22 & 23rd   Attended Stake Conference of Sevier. Apostles Lyman & Teasdale and Prest. S. B. Young preached powerful sermons on the laws of life, Word of Wisdom, etc. I never enjoyed a Conference more.[42]

25th   Reced the first letter from D. K. after reaching Prescott where they arrived Sunday Nov 16th. On Monday they were arraigned before the Court. Chief Justice Sumner Howard presiding. The poor boy feels that only the power of faith and an overruling Providence can keep them from the Penetentiary. My heart sinks when I read the list of witnesses. Some 30 of our peoples worst enemies from Apache Co. (Barth, Hubble, Stover, Traner, etc.)[43] Surely the Lord will not permit His servants to suffer long through the persecutions of such men. David says they have hired Rush and Herndon of Prescott, for the sum of $18,000.00 and John B. Milner (Mormon) for $600.00 [$6,000.00] making in all $24,000.00 for lawyers. In conclusion he says

If I go to prison I will endeavor to do so cheerfully. Who would not go for the sake of God's law, and the blessing of as good a family as the Lord has given me. Dear, what we have to endure for conscience sake, and for the love we have for each other in the Gospel Covenant, and the other holy ties we have formed with each other, let us do it in a Godly manner, which will bring happiness in its-self. Though we are seperated yet we are near each other. God bless you in your wandering! I know that you are among kind friends, yet I cannot express my feelings in having you away from home, through force of circumstances brought upon us by our enemies.

I was very much exercised on receipt of this letter. The outlook was so dark. That night we were all praying earnestly for their deliverance, when in answer to my cousin Celia's petition she received a strong testimony that David would not be convicted. The good spirit prompted her to open the Bible, when the first words her eyes fell upon were "I cried unto the Lord, in my distress and He answered me. From lying lips and a deceitful tongue the Lord has delivered me." [Psalm 120:1–2.] This comforted me not a little.

Wed. 26th Today visited with Celia & Ina at Mrs Etta Wrights had a pleasant time but my mind is so filled with anxiety and suspense, that I feel most of the time as one in a dream. The deliverance of my poor boy from the hands of his enemies is my first & last thought.

27   Received letter from Sister May saying that my dear mother had been sick but was mending slowly. Pa had gone to Kanab after Aunt Sarah [Hunt, his wife]. They were expecting him home soon. Friday night, in company with all my relatives, I attended Y.L.M.I.A. party. Enjoyed myself as well as I could under the circumstances.

Dec 1st   Sent for one of Moodys Systems of Dress Cutting, Aunt Kit proffering to learn me. Attended Joint Session, p.m.

Dec 2nd 1884.   Received letter from David written Nov 25th. Things look very dark for them in Prescott. Ammon's case is the first to be tried. He is standing it manfully but evidence very strong against him. His own admissions to Hubble, Stover, etc. several years ago. These men are now sworn witnesses against him. Also same evening received kind affectionate letters from Father and Aunty at Nephi, containing a scrap of News-paper telling of Ammon's conviction on the 27th of Nov. This had come by telegraph without any particulars. Poor Ammon, Anna and Sister Eliza! How my heart aches for them! and I know not how soon the same sorrow will be mine. Still my faith and hope is exercised in behalf of my husband, feeling certain there is less evidence for conviction against him than his brethren. Next day was a sad one for me.

Thurs. 4th   Fast morning, I spent in prayer and in writing to David. Took dinner at Ina's. Friday & Saturday Celia and I washed and ironed. Both sad days filled with foreboding and suspense.

Sun. 7th   Wrote letters to Snowflake, attended meeting, after which Aunt Kit and I visited and took supper with Bro and Sister [Ed] Thurber. Family spent the evening at Pam's and Ina's.

8th   Reced following word from David.

                                        Prescott   Nov 30th

My Dear Girl:

Since last writing you Bros. Tenney and Christofferson have been tried and convicted of Polygamy! It looks dark for the rest of us too. Nearly all the rulings of the Court are against our cause. The law of limitation or the fact of being married in Utah out of this District cuts no figure in this court. Nearly all kinds of testimony is taken. Several witnesses in both cases swore falsely. There seems to be no law or justice for Mormons in Arizona. The public feeling is very strong against us. If we have any friends here they are afraid to manifest it. The Judge & all the members of the bar, (except our lawyers,) Officers of the Court and citizens in general are the Prosecuting Attorneys, and every ruling of the Judge or speech of the prosecution seems to intensify the feelings of the people. It is generally understood that they are going to send us all to the Pen. Such talk as "the Tennessee way is the best treatment for Mormons" is indulged in on the street, as we overhear at the Post Office & elsewhere. I don't beleive the situation of the Saints in northern Arizona is understood. We have two of the best lawyers in the Territory but rulings of the Court have almost demoralized them. Jno B. Milner has but little influence at this Bar, or with the Court. I feel that the Atts. are doing all they can for us. We have tried, and still exercise great faith in God that deliverance may come but how and when we cannot see. I beleive that He is permitting this imprisonment for some wise purpose in himself. To see our brethren cast into prison in the dead hours of the night as they were, and our little party going one by one, with but little hope for the remaining ones, makes us feel terribly lonesome. I hope you are sufficiently acquainted with me to know that I will make the best of it, therefore I ask you to not worry over me. The Lord will look after us, and I pray that He may cheer and comfort you. I thank God for my lot and calling! If we are faithful victory is sure! So be of good cheer, and prepare your mind for the worst! If I am convicted the Lord will certainly provide in some way for my family. I worry over that more than anything else, and then there is so much unsettled business at home, pertaining to the St John Purchase, Tithing Office, Store and other things that the brethren do not fully understand. But some disposal can be made of it, so I shall not take trouble about that.

I received a letter the other day from Ella. Poor girl; she is having a hard time of it. The children have been sick and she is worrying over our circumstances. Bro Kempe joins me in kind remembrance to Celia and her family relations. I promised to be at the Hotel to see Bro Milner before this hour. Peace and Heaven's blessings be with you.

David.

I was filled with grief inexpressable on receipt of the above letter, but I thanked God for the love of the true loyal heart that dictated it, and come what may, pray that I may ever be worthy of it.

Dec 9th 1884   Reced. letter from pa, of Dec 1st. All well at home. Sister Anna Kartchner had just been blessed with a fine baby girl (my

first neice) named Celia. Pa still had great hopes for David to be acquitted. Said there was no evidence to convict him. A few days later
the following letter came from David.

Prescott, Dec 6th 1884

Dearest Ida:

*Bros Tenney, Christofferson, and Kempe have been convicted of
Polygamy, and the day before yesterday Bros. Flake and Skouson
plead guilty to the charge, or Indictment, which was brought about
by the friendship of [C. E.] Cooley, Scotts, and others of Flake's
friends. They made the promise that if they would plead guilty the
sentence would be light; so it was thought best for them to do so, as
we could plainly see from the trial of the other cases, that they would
be convicted. Yesterday at 10 a.m. Bros Tenney, Christofferson and
Kempe were sentenced to 3½ years imprisonment in the Detroit
House of Correction and $500.00 fine each. Bros Flake and Skouson
to six months in the Yuma Prison, and $500.00 each. My case has
gone over to next term of Court, six months from now. We tried hard
to go to trial, but the Prosecution claimed that they could not get
some important witnesses, and until they could get them, they had
no evidence to warrant them in going to trial. This is a hardship on
us, and a great one, but I fully expect that had I been tried this time I
would have been convicted. With such a Judge and such a Jury they
would have no trouble to convict any one. It may be by another term
of court there will be a great change in affairs. Such is my faith. If
not what will the people in Arizona do? I know this news will make
you feel sad, but dear, you must not give to despondency. You are
among kind friends and will be well provided for I hope. It has been
one of the severest trials of my life to see my brethren imprisoned in
the way they have been. Six of us came here together and one only
left to go home and report. Bro [Miles P.] Romney is here and we
are indicted for Purgery again. Bro R's indictment was quashed on
a technicality so my case will probably not be tried for a year. We
start home tomorrow. Goodbye for a short time. Yours truly,*

Dade.

I had prayed so earnestly that his case might not be continued, so
that I should be permitted to return home in safety. But now after
five of his brethren have been sent to prison on the same charge how

thankful to hear he is allowed liberty for six months longer, when perhaps something will intervene in his favor. I feel worried about his being indicted for Perjury. The same charge from which he was cleared last spring, for want of evidence, by the U.S. Commissioner in St Johns.

Dec 11th 1884   Celia, Ina and I visited Sister [Elizabeth] Ramsay and her daughters. Packed my trunk preparatory to my journey to Nephi. Spent the last evening at Ina's.

Before leaving Richfield I wrote the following lines in Celia's Autograph album.

> My more than cousin, dearest friend, in girlhood days
>   we strove,
> To share each others joys and griefs in confidence
>   and love.
> Those long bright days filled up with beaux, books,
>   music light & gay,
> Or talking of our coming life, its future mystery.
> Now when we've older grown, and care its blighting
>   sorrows send,
> I've come to you, and find the same dear cherished
>   faithful friend.
> Been cheered and strengthened by your faith in Gods
>   Almighty power.
> To send deliverance and peace in this my darkest hour.
> O may our friendship ever thus with sweetest links be
>   rife.
> Till in a fairer better world we gain eternal life.

[Return to Nephi]

12th   Friday morning early, bid goodbye to my dear ones in Richfield and started for Nephi where I was to make my home for the winter. Had a fine team & light carriage, and my driver was Jack Gray, an old Beaver acquaintance, who was going to Juab to bring B.Y. [Brigham Young Academy] students home for the Holidays. The morning was pleasant when we started. Sharp air, with about one inch of snow on the ground, but before reaching Salina the wind was so bitterly cold I had to get in the bottom of the carriage, with blankets over me to keep from freezing. Stopped at Salina two hours, and in the afternoon the wind had changed into the south and we continued our journey in comfort. Reached Gunnison about sundown.

Accepted the kind invitation of Bp [Christian August] Madsen & wife
to spend the night with them. They made us very welcome. Attended
theater with them in the evening, Salt Lake troupe Plays "Camilla's
Husband" and "Loan me Five Shillings." After the theater spent two
pleasant hours in singing and converse at home.

Early Sat morn 13th started for Juab, 25 miles, reaching there in
time for the 2 oclock train, which soon landed me in Nephi where I
reced a hearty welcome from Father and Aunty. Many friends called
in to see me on hearing of my return. Prest. Paxman & Sister [Sarah
Ann] Teasdale among the number. The following week was a very
lonely one for me. Aunty was much of the time at Bro Bryans who
was very sick indeed and the poor old ladies [Julia and Emma] felt
that they could not do without her. Miss Mary Linton, who clerked
in the Coop Store through the day, was very kind to spend the night
with me as often as possible, for which I shall ever feel grateful.[44]

18th & 19th   Was at Sister Pitchforths helping her sew, for Christmas.

20th   Old Beaver friend, Bro [Marcus] Shepherd, called on me.
Insisted on my going home with him. Also received a letter from
Cousin Nellie [Jones], Beaver Co., begging of me to come and spend
the winter with them.

21st   Rained and snowcd all day as it had been doing for a week
past. Attended meeting, and afterward went to see Bro Bryan who is
still very low.

24th   Christmas Eve 1884, finds me all alone in my husbands old
home. Aunty has gone to spend the night with Bro B. which leaves
me "Monarch of all I survey." But solitude is what I most enjoy in my
present state of mind. My thoughts are busy with the past. I find myself wondering how many Christmas Eve's my dear Dade has passed
under this roof, a happy lighthearted boy, ere the cares and responsibilities of life had changed him into an earnest, sedate man. It is
certainly the first I ever spent alone. Being reared in a large family,
there was little chance at such times for solitude or quiet. One year
ago I had been with dear ones at home in St Johns. Bro Tenney and
family had spent the day with us. Now how changed were our circumstances. Poor Ammon is spending his Christmas in the Michigan
Prison. I am an exile, while those who remain at home are no doubt
feeling sad over the change in affairs.

Dec. 25th 1884.   Christmas morning, instead of the usual bustle
and din I had been wont to hear, over the mysteries of Santa Claus,
not a person greeted my sight until 9.30 a.m. when Aunty came
home, and presented me with a little painted tin bath tub for Christ-

mas present. 10 a.m. attended Christmas Jubilee of Sunday School in Nephi Tabernacle. Listened to an excelent programme. Rain poured down all day. At 2 oclock Aunty & I joined in a sumptuous family dinner at Sister Bryans. In the evening went to the Theater. Play entitled "The Orphans." Star performers, Mrs. Lizzie Bryan & Clo Pratt. Mary L. spent the night with me.

Jan 1st 1885.   New Years Day passed much the same as Christmas. Attended fast meeting in the morning. Tabernacle crowded. Bros Teasdale, Paxman & dozens of others bore very strong testimonies. I returned home feeling almost in despair of ever hearing from David again, the time had been so long since his last writing. On reaching home was not only happily surprised with a good long letter from him but also by a call from Bros Bushman & Standifird just from A.T. [Arizona Territory].[45] Had left there through fear of indictments being got out against them. Prest J. N. Smith and other leading men of the Stake were with them, but had taken train at Juab for Salt Lake. They took dinner with us, then continued their journey. Bro S. Linton and family also took dinner and spent the evening with us. From Davids letter of Dec 20th written from St Johns I extract

On Saturday following the date of my last letter to you I made contract with Rush & Herndon to appeal Bros Tenney, Kempe, and Christoffersons cases to the Supreme Court of the Territory for the sum of $800.00. I paid down $500.00 of this amount. The cases will come up the first Monday in Jan. xxx On Sunday morning 6.30 they started for their respective Prisons. The brethren stood it like men. Much better I think than I did. Bro R. [Romney] and I left Prescott at 9 a.m. same day. It was a very cold windy day in keeping with our circumstances as a people and as Prisoners. I left with two indictments hanging over my head, as though I were the worst criminal in the land, but my conscience is void of offence therefore come what may I will try and make the best of it. I hope to be able to wait the time of the Lord in these things. Vengeance is His and He will repay.

It rained and snowed on us every day from there till we reached Snowflake Sat night at 10 oclock. The snow was so deep we would only find our way through the mountains by following the marks on the trees, and by having one of the best teams in the country. Had we not arrived the night we did they were going to send a party out in search of us. To our great satisfaction Prest. Seymore B. Young arrived from Salt Lake in time for a portion of our Conference. I was much pleased to see him as it relieved me of a heavy weight on my

mind. He was sent by the first Presidency of the Church to ascer-
tain the facts in these late trials. He intended to go on to the Salt
River Country but he got such a buget [?] he returned immediately
to the city.

This whole affair is of such vital importance to the Saints in this
country that it needs the best legal ability to look after it. We were
partly sacrificed for want of the same. We went like a lot of Lambs to
be slaughtered, and were shoo'ed into the gulf not realizing where
we were going. We had no friends to take our part, or work for us in
Prescott, went one at a time, with no one to say "why do you so"?
until but one was left to report. Oh, Ida, no one knows how my feel-
ings have been wrought upon during these trials. I did not think I
could love man as I do, but the love of my brethren I find to be the
most devout of all. All these things and many more, I gave vent to,
to Bro Young & the Conference until many shed tears. I was scarcely
able to sleep until I met with the saints after which I felt like a new
man. xxx Father and the folks treated me very kindly at Snowflake.
They are all well and getting along nicely with the new house. xxx

Left there on Monday, arriving home Tues. afternoon. Found Ella
and Mary and the sweet babes all well and so glad to see me home
again. Ella weighs 120 lbs and seems much happier since my re-
turn than she has for several years. I start next Monday visiting the
Settlements above, to raise money to assist in these lawsuits. This is
the first mission I ever asked for, but I want to see something done
for the brethren in prison. They can't help themselves and we must
try and help them. Eliza came home two weeks ago. Poor girls feel
very badly.

Mary, spoken of above is Davids sister, Thomy Stewarts wife who
with her five little children went to live with them last October. Her
husband is on a mission to New Zealand. She is occupying my room,
while I am in the one that was used by her when a girl at home.

14th   Bro Bryan passed peacefully and quietly to the other side,
and the two dear old ladies were left in their big house alone. Aunty
& I spent several nights with them after his burial on the 16th.

17th & 18th   Stake Quarterly Conference was held. Sat a.m.
Apostle Teasdale preached a powerful sermon. His last one in Nephi
for some time. He took train that day for the South. Prest Seymore B.
Young was in attendance in the afternoon; having just returned from
Arizona, he gave a detailed account of his visit there, his spending
two nights with David at my fathers house in Snowflake, and the

sorrowful account he gave him of the trial imprisonment and unjust treatment of our brethren in Prescott. Bro Young seemed very much in earnest over reciting the persecutions and situation of the people there and was listened to with marked attention. After meeting he and Bro Campbell visited us, took supper, and Bro Y. [Young] read a letter from David written on the 3rd in relation to the money raised for lawsuits, etc.

20th   Reced. a letter from pa, saying that Ma and Sadie were sick also telling of the nice visit they had had from Prest [John] Taylor and party at Snowflake. That evening, with father and Aunty I attended a party at Bro Goldsbrough.[46]

21st   Old Folks party was given in the Nephi Social Hall. A bounteous dinner was served at 12 oclock [with] about 140 persons participating, after which a nice programme was carried out for the amusement of the old people. Aunty was chairman of the committee. Every thing went off satisfactory. By urgent request of Bro Paxman and Sister [Mary] Pitchforth I sang "The Dearest Spot on Earth to Me," assisted in the chorus by Sister Andrews. That day reced letter from David containing following items.

Jan 14th

It is a great comfort to know that Saints in my old home remember me in my hour of trial, and show such kindness to you. I am glad you returned from Richfield when you did, as I know you will be comfortable at home during the winter. I appreciate our Richfield relatives' kindness, and hope some day to be able to repay it. We will pray that Celia's testimony may be true in regard to my acquittal. If I would give way I could worry the life out of me but I know that will not do. I think dear, I am as happy and serene over these things as man can be under my circumstances. The future I rejoice in. I know that God's Kingdom will prevail, and that we will yet meet and have much happiness in this life as well as through Eternity. If we work unselfishly for the cause of truth our lot will be a pleasant one, through our conscience being void of offence.

The children are well and growing nicely. They are such a comfort to me. Bro [William] Gibbons and I made a trip through Round Valley & Luna Valley. I never was treated better in my life. The people showed a very sympathetic feeling. We raised $500.00 with a promise of $300.00 more in a short time. It was sad to see the sorrow of Bro Kempe's Christofferson's & Skousons families, whom I visited. Have not heard from the brethren in Detroit yet. We learn *they cannot write but one letter a month, which will be a great cross to them. Their cases before the Supreme Court, are postponed till the 3rd Monday in Feb.*

The Y.L.M.I. Associations are doing well. Their Joint sessions are a success. I must admit the girls are ahead of the boys. There are 125 families in the Ward now. Many of them poor and destitute. Looks like we will have a hard time to get through the winter or the next year. On Friday last at 3 p.m. I received a telegram to come to Snowflake and meet the Presidents party. I started at 6 p.m. same day, rode all night, arriving there at 7 the next morning, when I had the great pleasure of meeting Prest Taylor and the brethren who were with him. Bro Taylor gave me great encouragement that my cases would not amount to any thing. He says many of these crooked things will be straightened out shortly. I went with the party to Holbrook where they took train. I left Woodruff Monday morning, reaching home same night at 12.30 being away from home three days. We commence settling tithing tomorrow. It is a very busy time with me as you know. Will try to be a better boy in the future, to write.

The following week I visited at Sister Paxman's also at Sister House's.

Feb 1st   Wrote long letter to David. Thos Wright called on me.

3rd   Father took Aunty, Nora Pitchforth and I down to Wm R. Mays farm for a visit. Distance about four miles. Went one mile out of the way to show me the grounds where David and he had built a large dam for a reservoir, put in a large crop and lost it all through the dam being broken one night by some low, jealous persons. David & Ella first went to house-keeping there. Staid three months, and after the dam was broken, they moved up to town. Tore down the house and moved the logs back. They laid here on Aunty's lot all those years, and since I came, father got a chance to sell them to Ed Kendall for $30.00 cash, of which I had the disposal. I considered it quite providential. After losing all his winters work, D moved to Kanab, got a good start in business, and was called from there to St Johns, A.T. [Arizona Territory] where undoubtedly his mission lay.

We had a pleasant visit at the farm and a nice ride home.

4th   Reced the first letter from poor Ammon written from the Michigan Prison. They were only permitted to write one letter a month. That, Ella copied and sent to us enclosed in one written by herself to father, Aunty and I. He said that in view of a prison his fare could not be better, but they were not allowed to speak to their brethren, nor even pass any mail back & forth which was a very great trial to them. He worked at a table, running a circular Saw. That same day I was visited by Bro David H. Cannon of St George, who was sent by Apostle Erastus Snow to tell me that he felt strongly impressed that it was not safe for me to remain at Father Udall's any longer. It was evident that officials from A.T. had been making inquiries from this part of the country about me and he felt very desirous that every precaution should be taken, as he was certain no stone would be left unturned to obtain the desired witness in "Bro Davids Case." Bro Snow thought that I must be immediately taken over to San Pete or some other place where I was unknown, also change my name, so that no clue could be found. I was in despair at the thought. I had just got comfortably located in the little room where I thought I could be safely taken care of through my *trouble*, and I felt so helpless now to either travel or go among strangers. Dear Aunty comforted me by telling me that I should not go alone. If it was really necessary for me to leave the place she would go with me; but when she and father suggested the idea of my taking a room at Sister Bryan's where there were only the two faithful old sisters and no children he thought that would do nicely, providing our nearest neighbors and friends were kept ignorant of my whereabouts. This releived me greatly.

5th Thursday.   I spent a lonely, homesick day, making preparations for my change of location. I felt as though I would give anything in the world to talk with David if only for one hour. Oh! what a sacrifice to be so widely seperated from those nearest & dearest when we feel that a little of their company would be such a comfort and solace. When the shades of night came down, in company with father and Aunty I took flight to my new quarters. I found a comfortable little room on the second floor, with a bright fire burning in the open fire place awaiting me. I soon felt quite at home. Had been there about one hour when I was joined by Miss Kate Love,[47] who was also seeking refuge, feeling impressed that it was unsafe for her to longer remain at home.

6th   Deputy Marshalls came into town and subpoenaed 8 important witnesses to appear before the Grand Jury in Salt Lake. Sister M. E. Teasdale, her father Bro [James] Picton and Sister M. E. Neff practicing midwife among the number. That evening at eleven oclock, poor Etta Picton, (supposed to be the wife of Apostle Teasdale) with baby eight days old, was carried through the deep snow to the room below me, by Prest. Paxman and others, to prevent the marshalls from finding her. Bro P. came up and talked with Kate a few moments when it was decided that she return home for the present.

But Etta and I remained. I wrote letters to Ammon, Eliza, Ella and dear ones in Snowflake.

11th   Reced letter from Richfield saying Celia had been sick in bed four weeks with typhoid fever. Was mending slowly. That day Apostle F. M. Lyman arrived at Aunties to stay two days and in the evening sent for me to come down and visit with him. This was my first "out" for a week. He had much to tell me about his late trip to Ariz. and Mexico. Meeting David at Holbrook, visiting with the Brethren at Yuma etc. He congratulated me on the improvement in my appearance, since the time he took up a labor with me in Arizona. Said he told David when he met him, that whatever the results of his tooth-pulling operations might be, he expected to credit himself with a good share of the honors. Bro Lyman thought that it would be perfectly safe for me to return to Aunties by keeping quiet as I had done, now that everybody was under the impression that I had left the place. This was a great relief, as it was too much for Aunty to care for me, being away from home, and in an upper room.

12th   Reced. good letter from David from which I quote,

                                        St Johns. Feb 6th 1885

My Dear Ida:

It seems a long time since I received a letter from you; I do not remember the date, as I have complied with your request and destroyed all the letters received from you, much as it was against my natural feelings. Before doing so, however, I have read and re-read them, trying to fathom your true feelings, and wondering as I do now, how you are bearing up under all the fears and anxieties woman is prone to, under your circumstances. If I could but see you, and talk to you I know we would be cheered in the glorious prospects before us. I now have a few quiet moments, such as I have not enjoyed for weeks. I am writing in the Store. Clerks and Customers all gone. I wish I could write my true feelings to you but I cannot. My heart is full of joy in you, and the gift of God to us, and I thank Him for the day we met. Our lot has been hard to bear, particularly yours. It seems we have been tried in many ways, until we have learned that God is in our acquaintance and union. You must not forget to write to me often. It is such a happy change. My life is such an active, hurry-blury one, that I am no criterian for you to go by in writing.

Since my last letter to you, we have settled Store business for *the year. Declared a dividend of 25%, added to the reserve fund $6,000.00 and settled Ward Acct. of $202.00 that hàd accrued during our many lawsuits. (This was a donation to the Ward.) We done over $34000.00 worth of business on a Capital of $6000.00 The average per cent on goods was 4½. I am elected Prest. and Supt. for the coming year. I get 6% for doing the business, & as I cannot be here much of the time, I have hired Bros Farr and Lesueur again paying them 5% to do all the manuel labor.[48] We are building brick warehouse 45 × 24. Our Coop Store is a great help to the people here. In fact it is our bank. When there is money to be raised we go to the Store for temporary relief. I have just sent off the Tithing report for 1884. The Tithing for this ward was a few dollars less than $4000.00. There were only eight non-tithe payers in the Ward. We are working on the City ditch. It will probably be completed this spring. Will cost $6000.00 in labor. We have started on the Reservoir below town, and also have one nearly done one mile above town. The two will contain about 200 acres. Joseph [Udall] is taking hold and doing well. He and I will farm together this summer. I am about to sell the place in the Mexican town, to Roman Lopez, for $3.25.00. Cash next Oct. and 10 cows and calves in the spring. Have commenced to make preparations to build on the city lot. We have hauled 50 perch of rock and got the cellar about half dug.*

We are having good times in our meetings and public gatherings. I never saw the people feeling better, though many are very poor.

The District Court is now in Session here. Judge Howard is bitter as possible, but I think he has done his worst. I think this St Johns Ring is weakening too. Your pa, Bro [Oscar] Mann and others were over several days ago. Since he has gone home I hear his case is decided without ever coming into Court, in consequence, they claim of his being a Polygamist and not entitled to the office.

I will have to close. Have been plowing sod all day and am tired. We are all well. Yours as of yore,

David.

21st   Reced. a letter from Sister May with the startling intelligence that Prests Jesse N. and Lot Smith accompanied by every polygamist in the country, my father among the number, had taken a portion of their families and gone to the land of refuge in Mexico.[49] There was also a little farewell note from pa written the morning he started. I felt very sorrowful on learning that so many good people had found it necessary to leave their homes, and was especially grieved over pa going when my dear mothers health was so uncertain. Aunt Sadie and little sister accompanied pa, leaving the rest of the family very lonely.

Feb 23rd 1885   With a grateful heart I returned to my little room at Aunties. The dear old Sisters Bryan had been like Mothers to me, and I regretted to leave their company but it is always pleasanter to be as near home as possible. March was ushered in like a lamb indeed. Warm, sunshiny days in which it was the greatest trial for me to stay indoors. I took all the exercise I could in the house, and when night came down, would venture forth for a walk in the streets.

March 8th   Sunday, My 27th birthday, dawned beautiful & bright. I arose, made my toilet, and looked forth on the glorious sun, wondering what there would be to remember this birthday by. Aunty and Sister Bryan gave me small keepsakes. After Sunday School Prest. Paxman called in to see me, and finding it was my birthday, gave me a good hug and kiss for David he said. Aunty suggested that as he was so seldom at home now-days, it would be a fit time for he and father to give me a blessing, preparatory to coming events. They gladly consented and oh! such a blessing as I reced. Bro Paxman promised me every thing that I most desired to hear at the time, and I felt greatly comforted, and felt to praise God, that I was associated with His servants, who had power to promise such great things. The infant child of John & Ida Wright, near neighbors, was buried on my birthday. It died of croup very suddenly. Aunty made the clothes & laid it out. My Dear friends, Kate Love and Mary Linton took supper with me, and in the evening we went to Sister M. E. Teasdales and spent a few hours very pleasantly. Etta [Teasdale] and baby were in San Pete.

March 15th Sunday.   Another beautiful day. I rose at daylight, and took a walk before any one was stirring. That day noon, I reced a good letter from David written on my birthday, while attending Conference at Snowflake. I make a few extracts.

Snowflake, March 8th 1885. Arrived here Friday. That day had the extreme satisfaction of meeting Apostle [George] Teasdale. He is on his way to Mex. and was only seen by a few people here. He gave me words of encouragement. Said my enemies would not have power over me and all would be right in my trials in Prescott, and told me to tell you that you would get through your sickness all right. xxx The camp grounds on the road, the Conference, the old home, the kind greeting of mother, brothers and sisters, the gates and streets and every where I go in this quiet, sainted town, reminds me of my poor girl, who is in exile, and oh, how lonely the feeling. Today you are 27 years old! We have been talking of you, and all wish you many happy returns. What changes during the last six months! You are away from me, Father and Sadie are gone to Mexico, Prest. Smith and some fifteen others from this place, as well as many others from the adjoining settlements are gone too. Mother and the family are usually well. Annie & Orrin [Kartchner] are here. They have a sweet little babe. They all treat me so kindly I feel proud of my kindred.

24th   Reced a good letter from Sister Eliza [Udall Tenney] who seemed much more hopeful. The Hon Thos. Fitch had given an able argument, before the Supreme Court, in behalf of the imprisoned brethren, and they were anxiously awaiting the decision of the Court. I also received another letter from David written from St Johns on the 13th. He had returned from Snowflake, on Wed. the 11th. I knew by the tone of his letter that something was troubling him of which he did not wish to tell me. This worried me greatly.

[Death of Ida's Mother and Birth of Her Baby]

25th   Bro [Samuel] Linton kindly brought his wagon, and took Aunty and I up there for a visit. We had a pleasant time until about three oclock, when Julia [Linton] brought the mail from the office. There being no letters, I eagerly opened the "Orion Era" our St Johns news-paper thinking to glean some items from that. The first words my eyes rested upon were *"Death of Sister Lois Hunt of Snowflake."* My feelings can only be imagined, never described. O the utter sense of lonliness that took possession of me! They took the paper from me, and for three long weeks that was all I knew. Not a particular in regard to her death. Not a word of sympathy or condolence from any direction. I only knew that the dear kindly eyes that had always smiled so tenderly on me were closed forever, and I was left motherless. Dear Aunty and Sister Linton said and did all they could to comfort me. Though feeling very unwell I walked home just at dusk accompanied by Mary L. [Linton] who would spend the night with me. At 10 oclock that evening I was taken in labor. At 1 oclock Aunty went for Sister M. E. Neff the M.D. At 8 oclock the next morning Father and Bro [Charles] Sperry administered to me after which I seemed to take a change, and at 10 oclock a.m., Thursday, March 26th, through the mercy of God, I was blessed with a dear little daughter of my very own. She seemed so bright and healthy, weighed 8 lbs. Had blue eyes and long, dark hair. Oh! how proud and thankful I felt. Father wrote that day to David apprising him of the fact.

April 2nd   When baby was eight days old, it chanced to be fast day, and as Grandpa Udall had been to meeting and got "his hand in" blessing babies, we thought it a fit time to have ours blessed. I had always fancied the name of "Pauline" and as there seemed no objections to it, we called her that and Brother Linton came in and united with father in pronouncing upon her a great blessing. In listening to the same, I shed tears of joy and sorrow. My heart ached that the kind loving papa so far away, was privileged to take no part in the blessing of his child, but felt very thankful that we had a Grandpa to officiate. During my confinement I had every care and attention that love could bestow. Words cannot express the gratitude I feel toward father, Aunty, and all the kind friends who supplied me with little dainties etc. and by their cheerful faces and words tried to comfort me in the great sorrow I felt for my precious mother. Sisters Pichforth, Bryans, Lintons, Neff, Sparks, Paxman, Teasdale, Millard, and others are names that will always recall pleasant memories while life lasts.[50] When baby was two weeks old I was able to sit up & felt quite well; was visited by my dear old friends Wm Ashworth, his wife Emma and Sade Maeser of Beaver.[51]

April 10th   They spent the night with us and I enjoyed their visit very much. Received good letter from David, rejoicing over the news he had received of my safe delivery and containing many words of sympathy for me. Said he had requested Aunty to keep the news of my mothers death from me until I was strong enough to bear it, and that accounted for the sad feelings he had in the former letter of which he could not write me. He sent kisses and blessings to his dear babe, and wished Grandpa to give it a fathers blessing, for him.

Sat. April 11th   Letters from my dear Sister May, from David and from Sister [Mary Jane] West of Snowflake were put into my hands by Aunty, containing the dreadful particulars in regard to Ma's death. Shall I ever forget the anguish which filled my soul on that fatal morn. The grief of having to give up the love and companionship of our dearest friend on earth, seemed nothing compared to the sorrow I felt in hearing the dreadful way in which her death was brought about. I copy the letter received from Sister M. J. West, Prest. of R.S. [the Relief Society] in Snowflake.[52]

Snowflake   March 12th 1885

Sister Ida:

My very dear friend: I have thought for a long time that I would like to write to you, but felt that perhaps it would be as well that you did not have many correspondents: but at this time I feel to write to you, not to add to the bitter which has already been in your cup, yet it will add to it for a very little season but after it your cup will be filled with sweet, and I pray that you dear Ida, may have strength given you to bear every trial that may be given you, and acknowledge the hand of the Lord in everything. Our Quarterly Conference ended last Sunday evening. We all felt happy.

Our company had started home Monday morning, (March 9th) when soon after your brother Lewis came up and asked me if I could come down. He said "Ma has had a bad spell, and fallen into the fire and almost burned to death!" I thought he was excited and that it was not so bad as he thought for. When I got there Sisters Emma Smith, [Lucy] Flake, Fish, [Mary Jane] Minnerly and others were already there and were taking off her clothes, while she was trying to tell them what she could remember of how it all happened. She said she was sweeping the floor, when a very bad feeling come over her. She said to herself now I will lie down just as soon as I get through sweeping. That was the last she remembered. May, Annie and Bell had gone out for a few minutes to see a sick friend. They asked her if she would be all right. She said "oh yes!" and they left Annies babe with her, asleep in the rocking-chair. Alof and Lewis were working at the back of the house. Alof heard her talking and went to the back window, listened—but thought it was not her voice, but that some sister was talking with her. Presently Nettie came from school, passed the door, and knew something must have happened. She hastened to call Alof & Lewis and together they ran in.—The room was full of smoke—she was sitting near the center of the floor, trying to put the fire out of her clothing, and talking in tongues. They soon called Bro [Willis] Copeland and [Albert] Minnerly who administered to her, after which she talked in her own language, and was perfectly rational, but was burned very badly. The Sisters did everything in their power to releive her suffering. At the same time the brethren, (almost every man in Snowflake was there) left their plows and labor of every kind, met at Bro Minnerly's and formed prayer-circles, and Bro [Oscar] Mann said they would continue to pray until she got ease. The sisters formed around her bed, while your sisters and others formed in the other room. In the meantime a messenger was sent to overtake Bro Udall who had started home, but returned, I think, near 3 p.m. This seemed to comfort the girls and children very much, to have him there. Your precious mother kept saying Oh! my dear Heavenly Father, if it would only be thy will to let me die but "Thy will be done, thy will be done, thy will be done." She was so patient! Oh Ida, you are not alone! We are all mourners! At near 4 p.m. she rested easy and continued so until about 5 when she went to sleep, to awake in the arms of her dear mother and all the friends and saints, who would, I feel if they had permission hasten to be among the first to welcome her over.

Ida, dear, she will not have to suffer any more. Our mother,—our sister—who was so good—so pure, so noble. Our leader,—leading us to meeting, leading us to be charitable, leading us to be noble— teaching us to live above the little ills of life, showing us that the things of this life are fleeting—showing us by her example that knowledge is better than riches. Our loss is great, but it will be her gain—her good deeds and noble examples cannot be taken from us.

You can imagine the feelings of the children far better than I could write them. Yet I firmly beleive that as time goes by, they will feel to acknowledge a Providence in it.

The finest of linen, and every thing in the clothing line was the best that could be got. Bro Mann and J. H. Willis arranged the pro- gramme for the funeral which was very nice indeed. Sister Eliza Rogers deserves praise for the nice piece of work she did consisting of a Gate, an angel pointing up to it, and just over the gate were these words "Well done—Enter into the rest of thy Lord!" which was placed just under the stand. I will tell you what Eliza told me. One of the speakers mentioned these words and pointed to them. When she said your mother said to her "Thank you, they are nice!" Eliza said, "you are welcome, and I would have saved your life if I could." Your mother replied "O I am so happy! Comfort my children!" then she seemed to move up. Eliza said "Why I could not have shed another tear; I know she is happy and it is right for her to go." Dear sister, I have been particular to give you nearly all the details feeling you would like to know the truth. Many prayers have been and still are offered up in your behalf, and also for your dear father who is absent. In my personal experience, when the comfort was taken from me, the comforter was sent and I feel assured it will be your experience also. May you be blessed and comforted, and may all be blessed who in any way add to your comfort, is the prayer of your Sister in the Covenant.

Mary J. West.

At the same time I received long comforting letters from David and Sister May, giving every detail in relation to her sickness and death. David had been mouth in administering to her [he had spoken the words of the blessing], a few moments before her death, and stood by her side when the pure spirit took its flight. This was a very great comfort to me. My poor father, in that far-off land! How my heart ached for him, and also for the sorrowing brothers and sisters at home. It seemed cruel indeed, that one so good and pure, should die in that dreadful way, but it seemed that "it was to be." In reviewing all the circumstances, I could only acknowledge the Hand of Providence in it, hard as it was to do so. I shall never forget the kindness of dear friends in Nephi during this sorrowful time. I visited quietly as soon as my strength would permit, at Etta Pictons, Sister Pitchforths, Bryan's, Bessie Sparks and others.

May 1st Went riding for the first time with baby. Father took Aunty and I down to Wm R. May's farm where I visited four days, enjoying the fresh air and sunshine very much after my long confinement. Soon after my return I reced. letter from David saying that he expected to start in a few days for a short visit to the home of his childhood, before going to trial again, also that the place in the Mexican town was finally sold, and he had rented a house from Jno Leseuer, for one year, situated on the opposite corner from Ammon's, and the family were comfortably located in it. Ella and Sister Mary [Stewart] had sent east for $100.00 worth of millinery goods and were going into the business together.

All this news was very gratifying, especially the part that bade me hope I might see my dear one again. How should I pass the time, until his coming which would probably not be until the 20th of May. The days dragged slowly. Almost every day little Lula Bryan came to take a music lesson on the guitar. With the assistance I had given her she was becoming quite proficient.

[David's Visit to Nephi]

David left St Johns on Monday the 11th. Stopped off at Albuquerque one day and in Salt Lake two days doing business. Reached Nephi on Tuesday May 19th 12 m. As he wished to keep his visit quiet, to avoid getting in the news papers, he had requested us to meet him below town, and he would ask the conductor to let him off, but the letter was delayed, and Aunty returned from the office with it, several minutes after the dear boy himself had come in at the back door, having walked from Tulleys farm two miles below town.

He was looking well and natural, and oh! how thankful I was to see him again. I had passed through so many changing and trying scenes, since I parted with him, that I could scarcely believe my eyes were not deceiving me.

He told us he had only five days to remain, in order to reach Prescott by the 5th of June at which time his trials were appointed. I tried to enjoy his visit to the fullest extent but womanlike, the thought of the sad parting so near at hand, almost banished the joy of the present. The first afternoon Sister Pitchforth's, and family and Wm R. May were all in to see him. Sister Lintons in the evening.

Wed 20th　Aunt Mary Pitchforth, Nora [Pitchforth], Sister Sophia Taylor, Sister [Margaret] Paxman & others were in to supper. In the evening David and I visited Bro [George] Teasdale's wives Etta and Tillie.

Thursday 21st　Thos. Wright, Wm R. May & others spent the entire day visiting with David. In the evening we visited Aunt Elizabeth for a short time.

Friday. 22"　We all visited and took dinner at Aunt Elizabeth's. After dinner called on Sister Bryans when David expressed his gratitude to them for all the kindness they had shown me through the past months. Went from there to Sister Pitchforths where we had supper, and the evening D. and I spent at Bessie Sparks. Had a pleasant visit with her, also Sister Neff and Lizzie Bryan.

23" Sat.　D. Cazair, and Bro Sperry[53] spent the forenoon with him, and I never felt more sadly depressed than on that day. The thought of David going back without me after being absent from home so long, and the uncertainty as to when and under what circumstances I should see him again, seemed more than I could bear. I wept and prayed unto the Lord, who has never forsaken me in times like this, and He sent me relief. Bro Sperry staid and took dinner with us, and he gave me words of encouragement. The heavy load at my heart seemed lightened a little.

24th Sunday.　The morning was spent in packing, getting lunch and some little presents for Ella & the children prepared, and by David in saying goodbye to the many old friends who called in to see him. Poor boy! I never saw him feel so badly. He could not keep the tears back every time he looked at the dear little babe. He gave us both a blessing and dedicated us to the Lord & His service. After dinner Bro [Henry] Goldsbrough came around with his close carriage, and by promising that I would not shed a tear he consented for Aunty, baby, and I to accompany him down to Tulley's farm where the Conductor understood, and would take him on the train. When oh when should baby and I be so privileged again. Shall I ever forget the feelings I had on seeing the cruel old train bear him off. There seemed not a friend left me in all the world   only my little helpless one to love and cling to. What a blessing she was to me, in those days. Her little evenly cut features and bright dark hair constantly reminding me of the dear papa who was so proud and pleased with her and yet was denied the privilege of caring for her. It must be my pleasure and duty to do that for him, or fill the place of both parents. Bro G. took us for a ride in the suberbs of town, then deposited us at Sister Lintons where we spent the afternoon.

25 Monday   Was the 3rd aniversary of my wedding day, and a sad one it was. I spent the morning in writing to Mrs. Lizzie Peterson in San Pete & in the p.m. visited with Tillie & Etta Teasdale. Everyone thought it advisable for me to leave Nephi for a short time preceding the trial. I should have gone to my relatives in Richfield or Beaver, both having written me very urgently to come, but I could find no way of going, so I wrote to Mrs Lizzie Bean Peterson, in Ephraim, telling her if it was aggreeable I would come and spend a short time with her.

26th   Following day reced. an answer from her giving me a hearty welcome, and stating that Parley, her husband would be at the depot, at Moroni, to meet me on the following day. That evening, I got every thing in readiness to start; Mrs W. A. C. Bryan called and took me for a two-hours drive in her buggy, while Mary Linton took care of baby. What dear kind friends I found in Nephi. So thoughtful of my happiness and comfort. Baby Pauline, just two months old, and weighs 13½ lbs.

[A Visit to San Pete Valley]

May 27th   Wed. 12 m. I bade goodbye to dear father and Aunty and started out on my first pilgrimage with a baby in my arms. How much company she seemed, although such a little helpless creature. I thanked God that I now had something to live and labor for. I took train on the San Pete Valley Railroad, reaching Moroni, at 2 p.m. Was met by Bro Peterson, and had a very dusty ride of 12 miles to Ephraim. Had the pleasure of meeting for the first time, Sister Lizzie, eldest daughter of Bro Geo. W. Bean, of whom I had heard all the family talk so much about. I felt like an old friend, and she and husband certainly treated me as such. They have a nice little family of five children, and I had a pleasant home with them.

June 1st   I expected every day to get a chance to go on to Richfield.

Celia & Ina were trying to get a team and come after me but were disappointed two or three times. I remained there four weeks. Made many nice friends. Visited at Prest. Petersons, Mrs. Carrie Olsen's, Miss Helen Armstrong's and others, all of whom were very nice people. I must not forget to mention the young German Drugist, who played the Zither, a stringed instrument, which lies on the table, and is the most heavenly music I ever listened to. In company with Lizzie and others ladies, I went to hear him twice, and enjoyed it very much.

Reced letter from David saying that on reaching St John on his return, he found notice from his Attorneys that there would be no U.S. Court held in Prescott in June so his cases would not come up before the middle of July if then.

17th   D. Harrington, Editor of the Home Sentinel in Manti, with his sister Mrs Jennie Tanner of the B.Y. Academy, visited at Sister Peterson's. We had a nice time; I had heard so often of Sister Tanner that I was pleased to meet her. They told me they were boarding in Manti with an old Beaver acquaintance of mine, Mrs Jakeman, formerly Ellen Lee.

18th   Following day, Thursday, Mrs Jakeman came to Ephraim in a buggy, to take me to Manti a distance of six miles to visit them a few days. I gladly accepted her invitation, and hastily getting myself and baby ready were soon on our way. I visited the beautiful Temple fast being completed there, situated on an eminence a little north west of the city. It was the grandest sight I ever beheld. In going through the rooms where hundreds of men were at work, I found Bp [John Henry] Standifird of Taylor, Arizona. While keeping out of the way of officers in A.T. [Arizona Territory] he was employed in working on the Temple. He seemed delighted to see me: carried the baby for me while taking in all the points of interest. I visited his boarding house, a large commodious dwelling, where he had a pleasant room and was so comfortable. He showed me photo's of his family just reced. from home. Thursday Eve. I attended in company with Sisters Tanner, Jakeman and Co. a musical and ice-cream soiree at Miss Vorhees. Had a very enjoyable time. Music, singing & charades, occupied the time. Met several of Prest Taylors family there, who reside in Manti.

19th   We visited at Miss Luella Snow's. Sister Tanner was being feted by the elite of the city, and being her company I fared likewise. Saturday 20th we went on an excursion to Funks Lake six miles from Manti. This is the loveliest summer resort I ever saw, but the fatal accident seven years ago, when 11 people were drowned there at one time has been a great detriment to the place. Our party consisted of

Mr. B. W. Driggs, D. Harrington, J. Jakeman, Sister Tanner Jakeman, Miss Kenner, myself and the two babes. We had a nice lunch spread on the rustic tables under the shade of the Grove, after which we enjoyed a two hours boat-ride in the real steamer, they run on the Lake. Taking a guitar along we had "music on the water." Returned to town at 4 p.m.

21st   Sunday we took dinner at Sister Christoffersons, and supper at Dr [Scipio A.] Kenner's where we spent the evening.

22nd   Monday, I returned to Ephraim, delighted with the visit I had in Manti which will never be forgotton. While there I called on Amasa Mariam an old friend of my father, in the California days.

[Visit to Richfield]

25th   Thursday, I found a good chance to go to Richfield with Mr George Baker and wife of that place. At five p.m. I bade goodbye to Parley and Lizzie with many regrets, for I had come to look upon them as among my dearest friends. We came to Manti that night. I put up with Mrs Jakeman again. She and her husband treated me with the greatest kindness.

26th   Friday, when baby was three months old, I traveled 50 miles, from Manti to Richfield, reaching the home of dear Cousin Celia, at 12 oclock midnight. We camped twice on the road. During the sunset camp baby screamed with the colic and I walked up and down the road with her, until we were both fairly exhausted. Sister Baker made some brandy sling; and we fed her till she got quiet. But it was several days before she got over the effects of the trip. I was warmly welcomed by Celia and Ida who were together, Aunt Kit and the boys, not coming down from the sawmill till the following day. When I enjoyed a good visit with them all. But the thought of the great loss I had sustained, since seeing them last, brought many sad feelings.

July   I found long letter from David waiting my perusal. He had attended Conference held in Snowflake June 13th & 14th. A Board of trade[54] was established and much business attended to of which he wrote me. Had a good visit with sisters May and Anna. Said Ella's health was quite poor.

July 4th   We all took dinner at Sister [Elizabeth] Bean's. There was no celebration. After dinner we adjourned to Ina's and made ice-cream for the company. In the evening the boys hitched up two carriages and took the family out for a ride. The night I passed with dear Aunt Kit. Thus passed the Glorious Fourth 1885.

14th   Reced another letter from Dade, which cheered me very much. There was a prospect that he would have a hearing of his cases. He and Bro Jos Crosby indicted for perjury, were notified to be in Prescott with their witnesses July 15th. Some of their witnesses had started by team over the mountain while they were to follow by Rail. They had had a pleasant time on the 4th. Emma [Udall], Mary [Stewart] and families had gone to the mountain for a week. Many of the new missionaries were poor and discouraged. Some were returning to Utah. He is cheered in the thought that he has "the faith and confidence of his brethren."

Celia and Ina presented me with a nice autograph Album, which I hope to get filled, by my friends.[55]

15th   Reced letters from May, Bell, and Mary Linton from Nephi. Mays boys who had both been sick were recovering. Pratt the eldest, was kicked by a colt making an ugly wound in the face. Would probably leave a scar for life.

Dear friend Lizzie Peterson came down to her mother's on a visit and we, the family, had pleasant times together at Celia's, Ina's, and elsewhere. Bro Richard Horne and wife Mary, old friends from Beaver, formerly, visited Richfield at the same time. They were traveling on the "Under Ground," the same as myself, the greater part of the time.

23rd   Reced. the first letter from David after reaching Prescott. I will make extracts for the same.

Prescott, A.T.   July 16th 1885

We arrived here on the evening of the 14th tired and heart-sick, having had no sleep to amount to much for three nights previous, and coming to this city in the way I have so many times, is enough to almost discourage one, much better than I am. It looks as though this cannot exist as a business center very long. The place is going down fast, and times are very dull. The following witnesses for the Prosecution have already arrived, E Tee, Mr Porter, Jno. Nicolson, and Trauer. They expect more some time this week. I do not think public feeling is as strong against us as it was last winter. We brought the following named brethren as witnesses for the Defence. Wm Sherwood, Jas. Ramsay, Richard Gibbons, F. Froerer, and Wm Platt, that we will use in the Perjury cases besides Ruis and some others (Gentiles) that we will probably put on the stand to testify as to our good standing in the Community. I will use Bro Doxey, and probably some of the other brethren, as witnesses in the Polygamy case if I feel it advisable at the time. I do not feel that the Prosecution can get a conviction in either of these cases still we do not know what is in store for us. xxx

Pray my dear that I may have fortitude to be a man. *God alone can give us power to withstand temptation   see how Peter failed when, in an evil hour, he denied his Master. I have felt that this would be the snare the Judge and the prosecution would try to lead me into, (pleading guilty) in the absence of the proof they so desire. I have met and had a nice chat with Judges Howard, French, and several of the leading citizens here. Our cases will not be called till the middle of next week. The U.S. Marshall & the money not having arrived to run the court. We have rented the same house we had last fall at the rate of $12.00 per month. We all board there, but J. Crosby and I room at the William's House. Sol Barth is here under two indictments for forgery. They say conviction is sure. A friendly word is appreciated by him, even from a Mormon.*

How I long for the day when the common enemy will be bound, so that we can enjoy the society and love of dear ones. It is now over a year since you had to flee from our home and my protection, to save liberty to me. As long as I have enjoyed it, I have felt almost to censure myself for allowing it. Better, it has been my feelings some times, that I had suffered imprisonment, than to have you going by another name and running here and there for fear of being known. It touches the manly feelings of any man to such a degree that it is almost unbearable. I feel that you understand me. If I thought you looked upon me, as a coward, not having sufficient courage to meet the results of the law, my feelings would be past endurance. But I trust you know me too well to chide me in the least in your feelings. I remember you in my labors, in my journeying, in my dreams and in every avocation of life, and thank God for the day I met you, and for the sweet babe He has blessed us with. Kiss her for me, and may God bless you both, as I do, and more abundantly. Yours devotedly,

David King.

Celia had company. Mrs Peterson and family. Mr & Mrs [Richard S.] Horne and Mr & Mrs Abram Johnson. We had a pleasant time.

24th Friday.   There was a programme to be carried out in honor of Pioneers Day. A nice time was anticipated, but a telegram announcing the death of Gen. [Ulysses S.] Grant put a vetoe on all celebrating.

I spent the day and night at home. In the p.m. the girls and husbands went to the races, and in the evening to the party, but I with my little one tarried at home, and wrote a long letter to poor Bro Ammon in prison. My heart was too full of sorrow and anxiety for my dear one in Prescott, to participate in any merry-making. The following week cousin Ina went to the Saw-Mill and I staid most of the time with Aunt Kit at her house. Reced good letter from pa containing a splendid photo of himself. All well at home and he expressed hope for David. Spent a pleasant evening with Tank and Celia at Sister Bean's also at Bp Horne's.

31st   Reced another sorrowful letter from D. He had been in Prescott over two weeks and neither case called up. He seemed to have very little hope and said his lawyers had less, than he. He would try to be reconciled to the will of God. Could say with Paul, he rejoiced in tribulation. These times made his family, his brethren, and his religion dearer than ever before. The thought of going to prison did not seem to trouble him like leaving his family without a home of their own. Living in a rented house, and nothing but the proceeds of the farm for support, which would leave them dependant, more or less on the charity of others. Poor boy! I hope his fortune will take a turn some day, when he can be permitted to enjoy a little ease and comfort, which is something he has never had since I knew him.

Aug 3rd Monday.   Aunt Kit started on a tour through Grass and Rabbit Valleys with Sister [Elizabeth] Bean in the interest of R.S. [the Relief Society]. Celia and Ina attended a big horse-race six miles from town. I wanted very much to go, but feared it would scarcely be safe, so little Lizzie and I kept all the children.

4th Tues.   My old friend and cavalier in girlhood days, John C. Murdock called to see us. He had come over from Beaver to the horse-race. Was still unmarried, but a wealthy man, of thirty-five. He seemed very glad to see us, as we were to see him, but was ill-at-ease and in a hurry to go, vastly different from the days when we were 17 instead of 27. He could willingly let his horse stand at the gate two-thirds of the day, then. I think, from the impression I had of him, he takes little stock in the *great cause* which we are interested in.

5th Wed.   Reced. the following letter from Dade.

Prescott, A.T.   July 29th

My Dear Girl:

I am still here under bonds. Instead of my trial coming up on the 23rd as I wrote you, they concluded that Joseph's was the best case for them, therefore he went to trial on that day instead of me. On account of Gen. Grant's death his trial was put off until next day. We had a hard fight for four days at the end of which time the Jury brought in a verdict of "not guilty." The first ballot 6 to 6. the next 8 for us, and 4 against, the next 10 for, 2 against, etc.   they were out about four hours. Judge Howard showed his bitterness all the way through. Was very severe in all his rulings, and would not, under any considerations, allow [Alfred] Ruiz, [Joseph] Crosby or myself to make statement in regard to the expla[na]tions Ruiz made to us in his office. (He, Ruiz, was willing to testify.) It seemed like in doing this he cut off every avenue we had to make our intentions known to the Jury. The Judge, and Prosecuting Atty. were fearfully mad, when the verdict was brought in, and immediately set my trial for 10 a.m. today.

This morning, instead of going to trial as he ordered they have postponed till next Monday. We understand they have sent for more witnesses also that they have determined to convict me if possible. My faith is, however, they will not realize their fondest hopes. There are many things connected with these trials which I cannot write but will tell you when I see you, which may God grant will not be long. (If I should be in Utah before long do not be surprised. This, however, do not breathe to any one.)[56] *It is the feeling of my Atty's that if the Judge gets hold of me on this Perjury case he will give me the full benefits of the law, which is five years at hard labor, and $2,000.00 fine. Our Attys are working hard. I am well satisfied with them.*

The brethren here with me are true friends but unable to do much. Messrs Ruiz, Tee, Huning, Barth and others from Apache Co. testify as to my truthfulness and veracity. Being unacquainted, this has weight in the community. From appearances they are all willing to help me all they can, which I greatly appreciate. Bro Crosby telegraphed the Deseret News, which no doubt you have seen, ere this.

My Dear, when will these times come to an end? I know these delays are as hard on you as on me. How do you stand it? Sometimes, no doubt you feel as though the Lord and your husband had forsaken you. Dear, it seems as though fate has been against our enjoying much of each others society, which I have sorrowed over many times, and my constant prayer is that the day is near at hand when we will enjoy that happy boon. I am so thankful Pauline is growing so nicely. I know she must be a great comfort to you. The thought of her is a source of joy to me. Do not be surprised at almost any thing you may hear. Trust me, that I will try and do right. A kiss for you both. Goodnight.

David.

O, my Father in Heaven! What hast thou in store for us in the near future. Deliver my loved one, I implore thee, from the hands of his wicked persecutors; Grant O Lord that he may not be imprisoned, nor yet be a fugitive in the Earth!

From the tone of Davids letter, I know not what course he intends to persue. The days drag wearily by, filled with anxious forbodings. Hoping yet dreading to hear the result of Davids trial. My little Pauline is my one great comfort. Were it not for the love and attention she hourly demands I should be almost distracted with this weary suspense.

10th Mon.   Visited at Albert & Ella Thurber's.

12th Wed.   Spent the day at Ina's in company with Bros & Sisters Horne. Reced. letter from David containing following items.

Prescott, August 4th 1885.

Yesterday 10 am I went to trial on the perjury case. It took all day to empanel the Jury. 48 men were summoned before they could get 12 trial-Jury-men. The Judge, in all his rulings, shows that he is strongly in sympathy with the Prosecution. We have had two long sessions today. The Prosecution has rested their case, and we have got through with most of the witnesses on our side. Our boys did well in giving their testimony. Kept cool and told a straight story. The witnesses on the other side were not very vindictive with the exception of Mr. Porter. He did all he could against me. I am informed by my Atty's that the District Atty. will make a strong effort to have my Polygamy case put off till next term of Court in Nov. We will do all we can to have it come up this term in case I am cleared on the perjury charge. But I have little hopes as we never get any thing we ask for from the Court. These perjury cases will probably cost us, not less than $3000.00.

August 5th 9 p.m.   I am nearly tired out, tonight, been in court all day. Got through with all the testimony and the Atty's made a two-hours argument. Court adjourned till 9 a.m. tomorrow. There is still 4 hours more for the Attys. 2 on each side. The cases will be submitted to the Jury about 4 p.m. tomorrow. All I have talked with think I will be acquitted. I surely pray that I may be. The Prosecution in referring to our people settling in this Territory, compared them to devil-fish, having claws in every direction. The issue of this important case of ours you will no doubt learn by telegraph through the News, several days before this short letter will reach you. Hoping you are bearing up under your severe trials, and praying the Lord to abundantly bless you, I subscribe myself, As of yore—

David.

Aug 14th   And still no word from Prescott through the News. Vainly do I search the papers to find some item. What can be the cause of the delay?

Celia and I have been all ready to visit Beaver, for nearly a month past, but have been waiting to hear something definite in regard to D's trials. Today Celia & all the relatives are at Sister Beans. They insisted on my accompanying them, but my heart was too heavy. I preferred to spend the day in prayer, and in writing to dear ones. This morning reced. good kind letter from father and Aunty Udall. They wish me to come back home to Nephi.

17th   Not until August 17th did I receive the following letter from my poor boy.

Prescott. Aug 9th 1885

My Dear and loving Sister:

*I will try and muster courage this morning to write you a few lines. At about 5 p.m. on the 6th inst. [of this month] I was con-*victed *of* perjury. *I have been in the County Prison since that time. May God have mercy on me and all of you, that we may be able to endure this trial. There is this consolation, I am not guilty. They have convicted an innocent man. You will see from the paper I send you why I was convicted. I will be sentenced tomorrow at 10 a.m. My lawyers do not think it will be to the full extent of the law. The Court would not allow Ruiz, Crosby or myself to testify to the interpretation of the law as given to us by Ruiz the Clerk of the Court, before whom we made the deposition (prior to signing).*[57] *The boys that came over with me, as witnesses, are still here, and will remain till after the sentence. I hope my friends will do all they can to test the rulings of the Court in the higher Courts. I am perfectly powerless to do any thing for myself. My Jailor and other officers are kind to me, and give me every liberty, they can. It will take some time for me to become reconciled to this kind of life, but I hope to be able to endure it without murmuring. You must try and bear up under it, although this is a hard blow on our good name. The thought is almost unbearable to me, to think after we have cherished honor as we have, to be thus disgraced. My God! what will we do, and when will this life of sorrow end? It has been a hard one for many years, but we must be patient and wait the time of the Lord. My companions are four chinamen, one Mexican boy, and three white men. They are all very civil to me. I have a pretty good bed and as comfortable as could be expected.*

What will my poor family do? No home of their own and no means to live on. I have told you of the many reverses I have had since being in Arizona. I have lost a great deal of means through a false friend and in other ways, until I now leave my family in poverty. Write to father, and when you see him talk to him in regard to the condition of my family. If they were comfortable and could be happy, I could bear this trial much easier, but when I know they are not, I am in misery. My little children will not know what it is to have a father for years, maybe, and then when I come home they will not know me. Write to Ella and try to comfort her; she is now in delicate health, and little Mary is sick with summer complaint. How is your health and the health of that little red-headed girl. Kiss her for me. You will remember in my Patriarchal Blessing, that I am told I will be tried as Joseph in Egypt and that the Lord remembered him and so he would remember me, which I pray I may be worthy of. I may not stay here long but until you hear where I am sent to direct to this place. Give my love to our many relatives and friends. They must not forget to pray for me, that my mind may be led to think of those things that are beneficial, and my imprisonment may be of some benefit to me. I hope some one will see that I have the Salt Lake papers all of them. I will try and write you again in a few days when I know the worst. May the angels of light be with you to comfort and cheer.
    From Your Affectionate Brother

                                                           David.

Oh! My dear journal, not even to you can I ever express the feeling of gloom and despair that seemed to settle down upon me, on perusal of the foregoing letter. Why was such an outrage permitted? I cry unto the Lord for strength and resignation, but it is slow to come. My dear Aunt Kit, and cousins Celia, Ina Tank & Pam do and say all they can to comfort me, which I greatly appreciate. My little babe, deprived of the care and protection of her father by the cruel persecutions of our enemies, seems the only, only comfort left me on Earth.

18th.   This morning Sister [James] Ramsay stoped to read me a letter from her son James at Prescott, containing David's sentence, which was "*Three years imprisonment, in the House of Correction, Detroit, Michigan*" Bro Bean & Tank had encouraged me that he could not be sent to Detroit on that charge, so this was an extra blow for me. The weary hopeless days that followed I shall never forget, nor shall I the words of comfort spoken by Bro Richard Horne and my dear relatives.

22 & 23.   Quarterly Conference was held in Richfield. I only attempted to attend one meeting, and the baby cried, so I had to retire. I wrote long letters to David, also to Ella, saying everything cheering I could possibly think of, but that I fear was not much.

[To Beaver with Celia Bean]

Sunday Evening 23rd Celia & I made preparations to start to Beaver. We left Richfield about 5 p.m. in Celia's little buggy, drawn by large trusty horse, which Albert Nagely had kindly loaned us for the journey. We drove and held the baby alternately, and as the road was all perfectly familiar to us, we had no trouble whatever in making our way safely to Beaver. Celia's boys went to the Sawmill with their Grandma Hunt, while Ida kept house for Celia during our absence. We came 12 miles the first night, to *Jerrico*. Reached the home of old friends Frank & Melissa Farnsworth, just at dark, where we were kindly entertained for the night. Found them the possessors of a little family of four girls.

24th.   Mon. we traveled 32 miles, passing through Clear Creek Cañon[58] and past our old home at the mouth of the same. Oh! how familiar everything looked and how many bygone recollections, were brought to mind as we journeyed over the road through that beautiful canon, with its wild and romantic scenery, that we had traveled so many times before when merry light hearted girls of *seventeen*. It was just three years from the day I first went to St Johns, with David, to make my home. What changes had come to us since then!

We reached Pine Creek at 5 p.m. Here resided my old school mate and dearest friend Hattie Shepherd, with her husband and 4 beautiful children. The youngest only three *weeks* of age. Their eldest child a nice little girl five years old, was named for me. We visited there until 2 oclock next day then drove into Beaver 20 miles, and took Sister Shepherds [Harriet and Cederissa] greatly by surprise. Found no one in the big house but Sister S., Edna and Julia. It did seem strange. They thought it wisdom for me not to be seen by every body as the news of Davids conviction and sentence had not reached many. Every thing looked so familiar although there had been so many many changes since I left Beaver. My poor Grandma Pratts old house where she lived for 22 years previous to her death, and beneath whose roof I had spent so many happy hours in childhood and girlhood, now stood empty and alone across the street. I could scarcely bear to look at it. The place seemed so forsaken.

26th Wed.   Baby 5 months old. Everybody pronounces her a fine child for her age. We slipped down to dear friend Mary's [Ashworth]

to spend the day. Found Emma [Ashworth] (the second wife) in one
of the bedrooms with a babe three days old which was a profound
secret from all but their own family. They had to dismiss all hired
help, which left the work very trying on Mary's strength, but she
seemed so happy and cheerful, and the household were in such a
state of peace and union that it did one's very soul good to enter
the house. Oh if the world would only investigate this principle of
marriage, when practiced in purity, before denouncing it, how much
unhappiness might be avoided.

Thursday 27th My dear friend Lu Dalton[59] called to see us. She
is the same good noble woman she always was. Is teaching school
in the Beaver Central, to support her family of four children, being
a widow now. Her salery is exceedingly low considering her ability
as a teacher, but they have the same class of trustees in Beaver as of
yore. They consider the *sex* and not the qualification of the teacher.

[Ida's friend Lu Dalton penned the following poem, taken from
Ida's Autograph Book.]

To Ida, rich in love

Beloved friend, me thinks it true
　Upon your natal day
　　The star of love watched over you
　　And beamed its brightest-ray

Where e'er you go, in gloom or mirth,
　Love blossoms ever new;—
　　The rarest gem that shines on earth
　　Is love, when pure and true.

How sweet it is to love with pride
　Untinged with doubt or fear!
　　Your love, though absent from your side,
　　Your heart holds tenfold dear.

"When for My sake ye are reviled,
　Thrice blessed then are ye."
　　Thus spake the Pure and Undefiled;—
　　This promise he shall see.

The baby-treasure you have won,
　That pearl beyond all price,
　　And troops of friends (Love, I am one)—
　　These might your soul suffice.

So rich in these, can you be poor?
　Thus blessed, how *can* you grieve?

The minor trials you endure
Must not your soul deceive.
Lu S. Dalton
Beaver, August 28", 1885

That eve. Bro [William] Fotheringham our old S.S. [Sunday School] Teacher, called by request to see us, and entertained us with an account of his life in the Salt Lake Pen, from which he had just returned. He seemed filled with the good spirit. He pictured my situation as the most enviable one to be imagined, and even complimented me on being much better looking than I used to be. The neighbors tell me that my Aunt Louisa's husband, Tom Willis, who is an apostate has become very bitter, and does all that he can to injure our people. I felt very sorry to hear this and knew that it would detract greatly from my enjoyment while in B. They say he has threatened that he would report me to the officers instantly if he only knew my whereabouts, and would consider it his duty. What a contemptable coward! This is all the gratitude he shows to my generous noble mother, for making a gift of her entire share of the estate at the time of Grandma's death to *them*, because they were so destitute. Now he is living off of her kindness, and doing his worst against her family and people in payment.

28th   In the morning Sister [Harriet] Shepherd and I called on Sister White and had dinner with her. In the p.m. Sister S. went up after Aunt Louisa in the buggy, to come down and see me. She seemed very much surprised at seeing me, and I could see that she did not feel quite at ease, although she was just as kind as possible. The folks say she fairly *raved* on hearing of Ma's death, attributed it all to polygamy. Poor woman, she will find out her mistake some day. She and I went together down to see dear old white-haired Uncle [Jonathan] Crosby. We found dear Auntie's face missing, & his eldest Grand-daughter married and keeping house for him.

Sat. 29th   We went to Aunt Louisa's to dinner. Although it was distasteful to both Celia and I to visit with such as Tom Willis, for Ma's sake I had to go. He takes the daily Tribune, and can talk of nothing but the low-down trash it contains. Their five handsome boys that I used to love and attend with such pride when they were babies, are now great rough fellows, who smoke and swear. Even baby Pauline seemed to partake of the spirit in the house for she cried till we had to bring her back to Sister Shepherds. We then went and took supper with Uncle and Carrie.

30th Sun.   We went to Sunday School in the morning and in the afternoon Sister S., Aunt Louisa, Celia & I visited & took supper with our dear old friend Sister Lee. How natural it seemed to be there. How many times dear Emma [Lee] & I, in the happy days of yore had paced up and down those cool shaded pathways, or worked, read, talked and sang together in that pleasant sitting room. Since then Emma has realized fondest hopes, and becoming a first class reporter has gone out into the world to make her own *way*. She is getting splendid wages in a R.R. office, but has backed out entirely from the Church. Her mother shed tears in speaking of her, and wished that she were only in my position. An exile & wanderer, but with the love of the gospel in her heart. That evening Johnny Murdock and Kent Farnsworth called to see us and we had a nice time eating water-melons at Mary Ashworths. Jno. seemed so natural and jolly. He made friends with the baby; danced her round the room and remarked that she was much more active than her mother used to be in the days when he took her horse-back-riding so often.

31st   Monday, we visited Sister Lizzie Farnsworth and daughters. That night I spent with my dear friends, the Ashworths. We had such a good visit and Billy presented me with navy-blue flannel for baby and I a dress, and yarn for stockings, while Mary gave baby a traveling coat. How grateful I am to my Heavenly Father for blessing me with such kind, generous friends.

Sept 1st Tues.   Celia was afflicted with sick-headache. I visited Sade Maeser, Louis Harris's, and Mary [Crosby] and I took the buggy and called on Julia Murdock Farnsworth. She is natural, Friendly and sociable, and has every desire of heart, so far as this worlds goods is concerned.[60]

2" Wed.   We started early for Rocky Ford Farm, the home of my dear Cousin Nelly [McGary Jones]. I had sent postal card to Aunt Ellen [Pratt McGary] who lived at Milford, to meet us there. We passed over the old familiar thoroughfare through Greenville and Adamsville, arriving at Nellies about 2 p.m. Found her comfortable, and happy, blessed with four sweet children, and a good home. But she is so much alone that it makes it bad for one of her timid, despondent disposition. Will was away & had been most of the time for the two years working in the Cave Mine. She had a hired boy and girl when we were there.

3rd Thurs.   Wm. Ashworth passed on his way to Philadelphia. Took dinner with us. The same evening cousin Will arrived, Nellie having sent for him to come home and visit with us. He seemed just the same dear old rough boy. He is truly one of the "rough diamonds."

4th Fri.   Dear Aunt Ellen came. O how it brought back all the sad and happy past to look on her face. She was so very fleshy that she scarcely looked natural at first. The Dolson family hearing we were there came up from Minersville to spend the day with us. Bro & Sister D. had been present at my dear mothers funeral, and had visited her several times just previous to her death. Sister Dolson told me many things I was glad to hear, and said she had never met any one whose company she had enjoyed more than she did my mothers. She was possessed of such a happy peaceful spirit that it was a pleasure to talk with her. Aunt Ellen and I slept together, and talked nearly all night.

5th   We had a pleasant visit. My dear relatives all seemed so natural and good. Cousin Will shod our horse which had become lame through getting his foot hurt. We had music, from Nellie on the organ in the evening, which sounded like old times.

6th   Sunday, with many tears we parted with our dear ones. It had been five years since I had met them and I knew not how long the seperation might be this time. We reached Beaver at 2 p.m. Sister Shepherds were looking for us. I visited Sister Ashworth & Uncle Crosby in the afternoon. Celia & Edna called on Julia Farnsworth and took supper. Sade spent the evening with us.

7th Monday.   My dear David's 34th birthday I wrote a letter to him directed to the prison at Prescott. Made several calls, did shopping and called at the Beaver Central School to bid dear friend Lu Dalton goodbye. Then went to Uncle Crosby's and copied patriarchal blessing for Celia, and returned to Sister Shepherds to get ready to start home. In company with Sarah and Edna we went to take a farewell dinner with Sarah Ann, Lyemans [?] wife. While waiting there I took the buggy and went to bid Aunt Louisa goodbye, and together we visited the last resting place of dear old Grandma & Aunty [Caroline Barnes Crosby]. I was much pleased with the beautiful marble slab at the head of Grandma Pratts grave.

[Return Trip from Beaver]

At 3 p.m. we bid the dear folks goodbye. Sister Shepherd had been just as kind as an own mother. Before starting she gave me a nice brown flannel dress-pattern and flannel for the babies underwear. We reached Pine Creek at 8 p.m. Found Hat [Hattie] & Will [Farnsworth] and family well.

Next day Sep 9th reached Jerrico just at dark. One of our satchels had lost out. Frank Farnsworth kindly went back at daylight the next morning and found it half a mile from the house. Reached Richfield at 11:30 a.m. Ida had everything in the best of order, but Celia's boys were still at the Mill which was a disappointment to her. Before leaving Beaver I reced letter from pa saying that dear Sister Bell had started with Charles L. Flake to visit the St George Temple, to consumate their union for time and all eternity. This gave me pleasure, for Charly is a promising young man, and if Bell ever stood in need of the love and companionship of a good kind husband, it is now while she is feeling so keenly the loss of our dear good mother. Pa said he expected to start for Utah on the 14th of Sep. Would attend Conference at Logan and take baby and I home with him. This news seemed almost too good to be true. It gave me a lighter heart than I had carried for many a day. I also reced letters from father and Aunty containing a copy of the letter sent to David by the First Presidency. It was such a comfort to me, that I copy it, verbatum.

P.O. Box B. Salt Lake City   August 20th 1885

Bishop David K. Udall,

Dear Brother:

We have been favored by your father with the perusal of your letter to him written under date of the 11th inst [of this month] from the prison at Prescott. We cannot express to you the regret that we feel, at your position. We might write to you many things that would be of interest, but we do not know whether the letter will reach you, or what the rules of the prison may be, respecting communications such as we would like to write.

We, and all of your friends feel perfectly satisfied respecting your innocence, of the charge made against you, and for which you have been convicted. This should comfort you. You will emerge from the trouble, without a blemish on your honor or character, and your word will be esteemed and relied upon as firmly as if this never had occurred. You express yourself to the effect that your character is gone for life, and that your signature and word will hereafter be doubted by many. This will not be so. The men who have contributed to your conviction believe that you are a man of honor and are satisfied in their secret souls that you are no perjurer but an honest man. You have been selected as a victim, and it will redound to your credit in time to come, to be convicted as you have been as much as if it were for the practice of some principle of our religion. If you could have been seized and punished on the latter account with

greater ease, than for perjury without doubt that would have been
taken advantage of in place of the charge upon which you were tried.

We say to you be of good cheer. Do not let your courage fail, nor
your faith waver. Rely upon the Lord and He will sustain and bless
you. With love and prayers for your preservation and deliverance, we
remain Your Brethren in the Gospel

John Taylor
George Q. Cannon

P.S. We have instructed your 1st Counselor to use $300.00 for the
benefit of your family.

I felt very greatful for the above letter, for I knew how it would
encourage the poor boy to whom it was directed.

When I reached Richfield the following letters from David and Ella
were waiting me, also two Photo's of D. taken with no beard on his
face excepting a mustache.[61] As I had never seen him without a full
beard they did not look natural, and oh so thin and care worn that
they made me feel sad to look at them.

[Letters from David and Ella]

Prescott. Arizona. Aug. 23rd 1885

My Dear Sister:

Enclosed find two of my photographs. What do you think of them?
It has been over ten years since I shaved before. Can you recognize
any of my features of long ago? I expect you will all feel like dis-
owning me for shaving, but I feel like I had been most unmercifully
shaved of late, therefore you must excuse. I have sent three of my
photos to Ella & one to Father. They cost $5.00 per half Dozen. The
other day when I had my hair cut and the shave what do you think
I had to pay? Only $1.50   Every thing is very high here.

H. B. Clawson[62] of Salt Lake is here. He visited me on Friday last.
He will likely call and see me again before he leaves. I do not know
his business. I think however, he is friendly to my cause. I received
a letter from father yesterday. He manifests a strong fatherly feel-
ing for me. The machinery of time produces but little news in this
secluded spot, therefore excuse brevity. My health continues to be
good. I have every opportunity to bathe and keep clean, which I con-

sider to be a great privilege and blessing. The Jailor is a tidy, cleanly man and tries to have prisoners & the jail kept clean. You must keep me posted of your welfare. I hope the day is not far distant when your husband will return from his mission. Then a happy time you may expect. His experiences in the world will be of untold and lasting benefit to you and yours. These seperations from our dear ones are grevious to bear, but many times good is gained. We step out of the old groove of life (for a season) a new field of thought is before us, we see where we have erred, a feeling to forgive & forget touches our heart of hearts, and a new life brighter, purer and more heavenly is wrought for our rejoicing and salvation. May the time of peace soon come, when there will be no seperation of families, relatives and friends, causing the sorrow that many have to pass through in these days of trouble. I remember you dear sister in my prayers by day and in the silent watches of the night, in my lonely cell, when hours and hours pass away and the sleep I used to sleep refuses to come sometimes until about the dawn of day. You must not worry over my condition. I feel that my youthful days of hope and jollity will soon come to my complete rescue when the thought of my family & people, with all their troubles and reverses will be all I think that will trouble me.

God bless the widows and orphans. Yours most truly,

"Dade"

I cannot express the comfort and relief this letter gave me, although I had to be adressed as *sister* by the one dearest in all the world to me. The brave hopeful, yet submissive spirit it breathed, was cheering and refreshing. Ella's letter was reced. with much pleasure, and read as follows.

St John, Arizona   August 31st 1885

Dear Sister Ida:

Your comforting letter reached me last night. I was much pleased to hear from you and that you were well. Many thanks for your kind words. (Kind words always melt me but more especially now, at this trying time.) I am in poor condition for writing, as I have not had a good night's rest for nearly six weeks, and scarcely a moment's rest through the long weary anxious days. Dear little baby has been so sick and low, her life was despaired of for days, by some, in fact nearly every one, but thanks to our Father in Heaven she is alive and gaining slowly.

I can never describe my feelings during the past six weeks. Between receiving word of David's conviction and sentence was when it seemed as though death was upon her. Either trial alone would seemingly be all one could bear up under but the Lord blest me with strength according to my trials. I feel like if our lives can only be spared we had not ought to complain. Of course it is very hard to have one's companion imprisoned and subjected to the strict prison rules, but when we know he is innocent of crime, we can conceive of much greater trials. I have passed through many worse ones. I feel too like this had been permitted for some wise purpose, and that good would result therefrom.

I cannot feel that he will be held many weeks longer for this case, as there will be a petition got up for his pardon. The Judge, Prosecuting Atty. and Governor, with other leading Citizens have agreed to sign the petition & this explains why there had been so little said in our papers, as it was thought best to give them a chance to redeem themselves by liberating him. It would take considerable time to write the particulars, but be comforted by the fair prospect there is for a release. Judge [Sumner] Howard will be here next week and David has sent me word for me and the children to see him. I cannot tell how much I dread the ordeal for even if he is disposed to deal justly in this case, I cannot but think of the three brethren suffering so unjustly in Detroit now, for none of them according to law could have justly been sent for more than six months. I have persuaded Bro [John B.] Milner to write to Pheonix to see what can be done for them. Heretofore they have been afraid to write for fear of more harm than good being done.

David passed Navajoe Sunday (yesterday) on his way to Detroit. Joseph Crosby saw him, and brought me a note from him this evening. I should have liked so much to have been there. He will only be permitted to write one letter a month now. Jos. said he was looking and feeling well. In fact David said he felt better than he could have hoped to and was kindly treated by the officials. Did not think his stay would be long in Detroit.

Your father took me quite by surprise last evening. I was so pleased to see him. He told me he was going to Utah and you would likely return with him. If great care is observed it will probably be as well, & in many respects of course much better. The other case [polygamy] remains as it was, and as soon as he is liberated on this they will try and get him on the other, but without more evidence than they are now in possession of it cannot amount to much. I am often led to exclaim "Oh how long will this condition of affairs last." I do hope the end is near.

Sept 2nd   I have to write just a few minutes at a time when I can get baby down. She is dreadfully cross and requires my whole attention and time. Mary [Stewart] is feeling first rate. She went with Eliza [Udall Tenney] to the farm on Sunday, so the children and I are alone. I have everything outside and in to do, only what little Pearl can help me. We get along with very little being done the most of the time. Pearl said the other night, "I wonder what Aunt Ida thinks of papa being in prison?" Baby hardly misses a day of calling "Oh Papa." While she was very low and would revive for a little while, she was sure to call him. Pearl says "Mamma, if the men who keep papa could hear little sick baby call him, they would let him come straight home." Erma awoke early a few mornings ago and asked if that drawing of W. R. Mays was Aunt Ida. I told her no. She says is Aunt Ida dead? I told her no. she says well where is she then? You see she remembers you. The night I reced. David's photo's I found Erma fast asleep on the floor, with her papa's picture under her face.

Mr [Harris] Baldwin called this morning and told me that the papers would be all ready to send to Washington by the last of next week, and thinks they will be acted upon at once. Ruis will make affidavit before Judge Howard as to the conversation between himself & David, and this with quite a number of explanatory letters will accompany the petition. He thinks it is sure. I asked him in case the pardon was not granted what he thought of an appeal. He said the Supreme Court would be almost sure to sustain the lower Court so about the only hope is the pardon and we will know in three or four weeks the result. He said the Territorial as well as the County Officials would sign, and if they do this it looks like it is sure.

I hope you can make this all out. I have had to hold babe part of the time while I've been writing. Everybody has been so good and kind, especially dear Grandma Gibbons, Sisters Romney, Jensen, Richey and many others. Give my love to Grandma Ramsay. I often think of her and wish for the company of the dear old soul. My poor sister Annie is in deep trouble which will likely result in a seperation between her and Bert. She will be here soon to see me. There are many items of interest I could write if time would permit. We had a fearful fright the night Crosby's & Co's store burned. The explosion was horrible and filled me with feelings that could not be described. I hope and pray that these sad anxious days will leave no bad effect

upon us, for with all the rest, I must be nearly three months gone.—
which likely you already know.

The last mail that left here was robbed. I had a long letter to
David also to the folks at Nephi, and Society Report in the mail. I
do hope they will get them ok. There is much I would like to say if I
but could. Be of good cheer. There must be brighter days ahead for
us, at any rate for you. I do hardly dare hope for myself, as I feel like
my life on earth is blighted. I can scarcely endure the thought yet it
is ever present.

In writing to David I endeavor to treat our home and financial
affairs lightly, yet they worry me greatly, as there must be a thou-
sand dollars raised on that Wilhelm note by the last of October. If
we can collect amts. due, and dispose of the Wilhelm places we will
be all right. Bro Joseph [Udall] is very kind, and feels that while
David owes a cent, he does too, and will assist all he can. He is on
the thresher and only see him once a week. Bro [John] Taylor sent
T.O. [Tithing Office] order for $300.00 which will be a great help in
settling accts. These law-suit expenses run up fearfully.

I must stop for this time. Give my love to your Aunt & Cousins,
and Ida try and make the best of a bad situation, hoping it will not
last long. Kiss the little stranger for me. I hope you will keep all well,
and be blest in every way. Oh if baby was only well what a load
would be lifted from me. I feel so worn out and weary. Goodbye, &
may God bless and comfort you.

Ella

P.S. Jos Crosby tells me he telegraphed the Deseret News, also wrote,
concerning Davids conviction.   E.

10th   I answered this letter immediately, for I was much pleased
to receive it, being the first and only one from Ella, since I left home.
I said all in my power to comfort her, for I realized how sorely tried
she was. But I also told her, I could not see where mine was the enviable position, or where there was hope for me and none for her, as she
expressed. If David was pardoned, as she had faith he would be, she
could look forward to having, a husband, home, and a *name*, which
were blessings I might never enjoy in this life certainly not in the
near future, and I could not even enjoy the companionship of my
father, brothers & sisters. But still I do not feel to murmur. The Lord
can make the heaviest burden light if we lean on Him.

Sep 11th   I also wrote long letters to David addressed to Detroit
and to my dear Sister May who was so faithful to write to her exiled
sister. Spent the week in writing and preparing to return to Nephi,
to visit the dear folks there and tell them goodbye, before the coming
of my dear father. Friday I had baby's picture taken.[63] Sunday following Sister [Cederissa] Shepherd arrived from Beaver, to escape Court
time and subpoenaes there.

15th Tues.   We all visited Hannah Ramsay Baker. Had a pleasant time.

17th Thurs.   In company with Sister Shepherd and as passengers
of Albert Nagely, on his way to Provo, I started for Nephi. I expected
Pa and Bell in Utah in a few days. We had not a very comfortable way
to ride having no cover on the wagon, and the sun was very hot. Poor
little baby got so badly sun-burned that she did not look natural for a
week, but she was so goodnatured, around the camp fires and traveling along that the boys in company pronounced her the "best kid"
they had ever seen. First day came within seven miles of Gunnison.

18th Fri.   Reached Little Salt Creek and spent the night with
Davids sister Jean Schofield.

[Return to Nephi]

19th   Reached Nephi, Sat noon. My dear old Grandma Hunt's
eightyeth birthday. She is spending it away in California. We were
heartily welcomed by Father & Aunty. Sister S. started immediately
after dinner, on the train for Provo. Albert resumed his journey by
team at 3 p.m. leaving baby and I for a short sojourn in the dear old
home where she first saw the light. Many friends called that evening.

Sunday I called on Sister Bryan & Aunt Elizabeth and attended the
Y.L.M.I.A. Conference in the p.m. Aunty keeping the baby. I enjoyed
it very much. M. E. Teasdale presiding. The speaking and singing by
the S.S. [Sunday School] Choir was splendid. The sisters Teasdale and
their sister Mrs. [Hannah] Grover, Sister [Julia] Linton and Mary took
supper with us. We read of the course taken by Bp Jno. Sharp.[64] How
he had cast off his wives and made promises to the Court in order to
escape imprisonment. Shame on such men! Who will fail next?

Following week I visited many old friends. Reced letter from Bell
and Charley dated Sep 23rd from Beaver, saying they were married
on the 16th of Sep. by Bro James G. Bleak in the St George Temple.
They had had a splendid time visiting & attending Conference in St
George, and were now visiting in Beaver. Edna [Shephard] was going

with them to Richfield, where they hoped to meet me soon. Aunty gave the baby a beautiful piece of blue French merino, and I bought some white silk braid and took my first lessons in braiding her a suit, dress and cape. It looked lovely when finished, and I imagined she looked like a royal little princess in it. To complete the suit Mary [Linton] and Alice [Udall] "got up" a beautiful little bonnet just to match it, and presented her. She was certainly born lucky, so far as presents are concerned.

[Oct] 1st   Sister Shepherd returned from Provo. We had a good time visiting and working together.

[Visit from Her Father, Come to Take Her Home]

3rd   Sat morning at 11 oclock I was completely overcome with joy and surprise to see my dear father drive up to the gate. Although I was expecting him I could scarcely beleive my eyes, and words cannot describe my feelings on seeing his dear familiar face once more. It brought back all the sorrow we had passed through since last meeting. The memory of the dear face and voice that would never join him in welcoming their child, on this earth again, & oh! how lonely the thought. He was looking well and in good health and spirits, but had made a long lonely trip, camping every night alone, since he left Snowflake. He had come all this distance, mainly to take me back home, and now come a letter from Apostle [George] Teasdale to Aunty, offering me a home with either of his families in Utah but saying it would not be advisable for me to return to Arizona. If David was likely to be pardoned, they would commence immediately in the other case, and if they could get any evidence, would no doubt send him right back again. He had written the same word to Snowflake and I reced. a mournful letter from poor sister May on account of it. She had so set her heart on my coming home.

Pa wished me to go to Springville with him to visit Aunt Lydia and cousin Mary there,[65] and I gladly accepted his invitation; Father Udall and Aunty were contemplating a visit to St Johns right away and they hoped to be ready to start by the time pa returned from Logan so as to travel in company with him to Arizona. What is to become of poor me when they are all gone?

Oct 4th 1885 Sunday.   Pa attended Sunday School while I prepared for my trip. Several came in to dinner. Albert Nagely and Bro White's folks from St Johns among the number. Bro [Henry] Goldsbrough & wife kindly called and took us to the Depot in his carriage.

Oh how it reminded me of the sad parting from my poor boy, four long months ago. We took train at two p.m. leaving Aunty and dear friend Mary waving their hands at the depot.

To our great joy we found Apostle E Snow, his wife Libbie, their daughter & husband Bro & Sister Tony Ivins & other friends on the train. They were all so friendly and apparently so glad to see me. Bro Snow took my baby in his arms looked at her from head to foot, kissed her and blest her. He was very hopeful about Davids pardon and told me many things concerning the Prison etc that I was pleased to hear. He thought it rather *risky* for me to return home, but said he would give the matter his earnest consideration and let pa have an answer at Logan. We talked just as fast as possible, but were only half through visiting when we reached the Springville Station.

I had not seen Aunt Lydia & Mary for nine years. They nearly shook me to pieces. We were delighted to find Cy and Mary good solid Mormons with a good comfortable home & eight children. Poor Aunt Lydia had burried her two sons since last I saw her and was full of trouble. Pa continued his journey to Logan Tues morning while baby and I visited there till Friday then returned to Nephi, to find Aunty nearly ready to start south. They are going to visit their poor sorrowing children in St Johns. Take them fruits and do and say all they can to comfort them.

10th Sat. Morning.   While Aunty, Mary and I were at breakfast, who should surprise us, but my dear, newly made brother Charley. He had come in on the freight train and left Bell and Edna visiting at Richfield while he took a short trip to Provo to visit his many schoolmates. We had a very pleasant visit till 2 p.m. when he took train for Provo.

11th Sunday.   It is one year today since I landed in this dear old home. How little I dreamed then, that one year would pass before I should return to my loved home in A.T. [Arizona Territory] but it may be for years and it may be forever, for today I have had letter from pa at Logan saying that the Apostles will not consent for me to return with him, and say that I must *lose* myself again if possible.

This a.m. I attended the funeral of Davids sister Lizzie Udall MacFarlane's little blind girl. In the p.m. attended meeting, afterwards visited Sisters Love & Neff.

13th Tues.   Sister Shepherd returned from a trip to Mt. Pleasant & Charley returned from Springville. Tom Wright came in to supper and we had a pleasant visit. Charley was invited to a party, by some of his schoolmates. He was very anxious for me to go with him. Aunty also urged me to go, saying she would keep baby. I objected because

I thought it would not look well. Then I thought if David were here, he would say, "go, by all means, and enjoy yourself all you can," bless his dear heart, so I made up my mind to go providing Mary Linton would join us. We started out at 8 p.m. in high spirits.

There was every thing to make the *ball* an enjoyable one. A nice crowd in attendance and the loveliest music I ever listened to. But the very first strain that reached my ear, sent a chill to my heart. Beautiful music always effects me like an eloquent sermon, either joyfully or the reverse. Tonight it seemed to picture to my mind, as nothing had ever done before the exact position of my poor boy. Banished far from home, and all that is dear, buried, as it were, in the confines of that dreary prison. Oh! how my heart ached. I could no more have danced, than I could laugh at a funeral. I sat shivering on the seat a little while, and begged of Charley to bring me home, which he did. Oh Dade, I never missed you as I do tonight! Will this great unquenchable longing in my soul for your society and companionship never, never be satisfied? The world seems so lonely so loveless without you. How long will the Lord require his poor weak children to be thus tried? The beautiful lines I have lately read, on "Parting" haunt me continually.

> When thou art gone there creeps into my heart
> A cold and bitter consciousness of pain
> The light, the warmth of life with thee depart,
> And I sit dreaming oe'r and oe'r again
> Thy greeting clasp, thy parting look & tone
> And suddenly I wake—and am *alone!*

But I am not alone, for I have my precious babe. My treasure sent from Heaven to comfort me. I clasp her in my arms and she seems to warm my heart through. Thank God for the blessings I do enjoy.

14th   Aunty reced letter from Emma Udall, saying that after suffering ten long weeks with summer complaint and teething, dear little baby Mary had passed to the other side. Poor Ella, she will feel that her cup is full to overflowing, to have to bury one of the dear little ones without their papa's presence and aid. And what sorrow will be that poor father's, who is thus cruelly detained from his sorrowful afflicted family. I immediately wrote letters to both of them saying all I could to comfort them in their great sorrow.

Emma's letter also stated that previous to the babe's death Ella had reced. the first letter from David written from Detroit & that she would copy and send it as soon as she could feel like writing.

[To Kanab with Her Father]

Pa returned from Logan on the noon train. It was decided that I should go South with him perhaps as far as Kanab, so I was kept busy preparing. Oh! how tired I am of packing, unpacking, and traveling around. That evening, pa, Charley, father Udall & family and myself were invited to Sister Bryan's to supper. We had a pleasant time. Sister B. presented baby with a dress pattern. They all expressed such kindly feeling for us. I am loth to part with such dear kind friends.

15th   We, pa, Charley, Sister Shepherd, Pauline & I, started for Richfield. Many dear friends were there to see us off. Mrs Lizzie Bryan brought baby a pretty knit Jacket while Mary Linton, and Etta presented her with muslin apron, bib, etc. It was agreed that father & Aunty should leave Nephi the following Monday overtaking pa at Navajoe Wells, oposite Kanab. We had a nice trip. Oh it seemed so good to travel with my own dear folks once more. I could not sufficiently appreciate it. The third day at noon we reached Richfield. Had a sad sweet meeting with my dear sister Bell. We had much to talk about & improved every moment. They procured two guitars for Bell & I to perform on. I found that during the year we had been separated Bell had become almost as good a guitarist as sister Anna. The first evening we spent at Celia's had music, singing, reciting by Edna & Charley, and as Tank and Charley were both Southern States Missionaries they gave us a true sample of Camp Meetings or religious revivals in the South, which was really first class. Charley called for mourners, Tank "getting religion" etc.

21st [20th] Tues.   We bade goodbye to all the dear ones and started on our journey to Kanab. Sister Bell joining our party. We came as far as Joseph City and spent the night with our old friends Bp. Gid. Murdock & family.[66]

Wed,   reached Mary's Vale. Bot hay and camped at Tripadore's.

Thurs.   Camped in an empty house at Keslers Ranche.

Fri.   reached Hillsdale.

Sat   passed the divide and camped in the timber. The mornings and nights were very cold for my poor little exile to be out by the camp fire, but she was a good patient baby and pa, Charley & Bell were so kind & handy in helping me care for her.

Sun.   One month from the day pa came up Kanab Canon, we passed down it. Camped that night on a wet sand bank in the Cañon, being unable to get out of the Creek bottom.

26th Mon.   The day baby was 7 months old we reached Kanab about 11 a.m. Were warmly welcomed by the Crosby family. Found

Martha Crosby all ready to go home with pa to visit her sister, Aunt Sade.[67] So I took her bedroom and she took my place in the wagon, pa having made arrangements for me to remain with Bro Crosbys family a few months. I went under the name of Frances Barnes by which I was called, and introduced every where.

2.8th Wed.   My dear ones left me. I felt lonely and forsaken indeed, but washing up all the dirty clothes baby and I had accumulated in traveling proved to be a very good remedy for the *blues.* Bro C.'s family consisted of himself and wife Sarah Jane, dear old white haired Grandma and four children, Bud, Willie, Lois, and Jakey. I never have seen such children for a baby. The boys nearly eat her up. They take nearly the entire care of her through the day. Ella's Aunt Macy, and sisters Jane Farnsworth and Luna Brown called on me. They were all very friendly.

Sunday,   I went to see Linda Marriger, who was confined with a baby girl. Another little refugee of the *femanine persuasion.* There is something remarkable about babies of this kind being all the same sex. Thursday [a] week after the folks started I got a note from pa written at the River. They had found Father Udall and Aunty waiting for them at the Wells and had made the journey that far and crossed the River in safety. They all sent me loving messages.

[Nov.] 13th   I have been at Bro Crosby's two weeks. They are all so good and kind and make me feel perfectly at home, but I am heartsick as mail after mail comes in and still not a word from Arizona. My dear Celia is all that has remembered to write to me. I feel very much hurt that the folks at home would be so negligent in sending me copys of Davids letters for I hear through others' letters that Ella has reced the second one from him some time ago. Poor health, I suppose is one great cause of my depression of spirits. I am afflicted similar to Job of old. My left hand is almost covered with salt rheum, and is so sore I can scarcely attend to my babe, or do anything else. While traveling baby got canker in her mouth, which effected my nipples so that for two or three weeks it has been positive torture for me to let baby nurse. Were not the dear folks I am with all so kind to me, I don't know what I should do. Sister Crosby gets the squaws to help her wash, and will not allow me to assist, although *baby* and I make a good part of it.

23rd   Reced good letter from Anna Tenney. She gives me good news from David & Ammon. Says they are permitted to occupy the same cell at night. I write David every two weeks & oftener, for I know he appreciates letters even though he is not permitted to answer them. Also reced letter from Anna Riggs, written in Ella's be-

half, receipting me for my letters and making excuses for not sending
Davids letters saying she had not felt like copying them. But I must
admit I am loth to accept the excuse she offered when there are so
many of the relatives they knew how to write and could have copied
them, if she did not feel like doing so.

26th   Baby 8 months old. Every body pronounces her a prodigy in
size, for her age. Her hair and eyes are growing darker which changes
her looks, and she boasts of one little pearly tooth, and a prospect
of more very soon. I am much improved in health consequently in
spirits. Jno' Stewart's remedy, (oat-straw ashes and lard) has cured
my salt-rheum, and canker medicine, afterwards glycerin and tannin,
has helped me in other ways.

[Letters from David in Prison]

27th   Today I have reced in one envelope the copy of Davids *three*
first letters written from Detroit. My fortune all comes at once. I was
deeply effected in perusing them. They seem almost like a voice from
another world. They read as follows:

> *Cell 148. House of Correction*
> *Detroit, Mich. Sept. 20th 1885*

My Dear Family:

*I arrived here 12 m. Sep 2nd   The officers treated me very kindly
while traveling. Was not put in irons until arriving at this Station,
when I was hand-cuffed to Mr Sterling (prisoner) and brought here.
Deputy Marshall [Bert] Foster promised me he would write you of
our safe arrival here. I hope he did so. I have received and not answered the following letters. (and will not be permitted to answer
them) Prest. Taylor's and Cannon's of Aug 20th   Express to them
my heartfelt thanks for their sympathetic and encouraging words,
as well as the timely aid they have contributed. Such assurances,
together with those of our many friends make the load light indeed
to what it otherwise would be. Three letters from father and one
from Aunt Rebecca. They are true to their boy. One from Bro J. T.
Lesueur. Tell him I feel well satisfied with the new board and Supt.
I would take every necessary step against fire, if the % is less annually. One from most worthy Gilbert D. Greer. Also one from Bro
Robert Holmes. His scripture was in place. One from Father and*

Wm Gibbons. I feel very much interested in the many items of local news. I have full confidence in their zeal and faithfulness in the labors required at their hands. One from Sister Celia Bean. I feel to thank them all for the deep interest they take in our welfare and may God reward them if we cannot. I have received one from Ella dated Aug 31st and two from Lois. [68] *These letters speak volumes to me, pen (nor pencil) cannot write of joy and light they bring to my lonely, and yet I feel angel-guarded cell. Then my Bro Josephs brotherly acts, and desires and father Hunts timely visit to you with the almost innumerable acts of kindness from brethren and sisters. I have not space to express my gratitude. It is joy to me to think of it. I am grateful. Send my letters (or copies) to absent members also carefully preserve letters for future reference.*

I left Prescott August 29th 6 a.m. Names of Marshalls, Bert Foster, M. Hickley, and A. E. Foote clerk of Court. Mr Sterling was my fellow prisoner. Have you seen any report of my being interviewed at Kansas City by News Reporter. If so what is it! This is why I did not write from there. I was very sorry to learn of the very serious loss of Crosby, Patterson, & Co. Parties owing for land must be looked after before going away.

For the first time I had the privilege of conversing with the brethren today. They have changed some. Ammon is some thinner. We mustered a laugh and had quite an agreeable visit. Bro J. W. Young [69] *called and seen us today. He gave us words of encouragement, also kindly gave us $50.00   I arrived here with $11.50. I am permitted to wear my garments. This I feel very grateful for. I am running a small saw, shaping timber for chairs. The cells are all 4 × 7 ft. We work 10 hours a day, from 7 to 12 and from 1 to 6. We bathe once in two weeks, have very good bed for a prison, clean sheet and pillow slip once a week. I change shirt and underclothes once a week. I have light so that I can read every other night. The prison and fare is as good or better than I expected. There is very strict discipline of necessity, still the officers are gentlemanly.*

I have felt very much concerned about your health. Poor little Mary and Erma. What a hard time they have had! I pray that they will be better. Then what a hard time you have had in looking after them in all the wretched hours of the last few months. What a trying time it has been. I am glad you can bear it as well as you can. Excuse this letter. I have had but a short time to write it in. It is now too dark for me to see the lines. You must all be of good cheer. Good will come out of the present chaos. I feel that I am standing it well considering. Will have the privilege of writing once a month. Kiss the children for papa. Bless them and you is my constant prayer. Write often.

Your Affectionate husband   D. K. Udall

Cell No 101   *Detroit, Michigan. Oct 5th 1885.*

My Dear Family:

Joseph's telegram of Oct 3rd received this afternoon. Sweet little Mary is dead! It does not seem possible! Oh why this sad calamity! It looks like the Evil one was not satisfied with what he had done for us, but had to reach out the grim hand of death, and take one of our number. Oh God! why hast thou permitted this? How well I remember her dear little form as she was on your lap when we parted. My Dear Ella, how I have pittied and prayed for you. I have felt sure that sickness and sorrow was at home, and then for you to have to bury one of the sweet little ones, without my presence and support, how great the trial you must have endured. I pray God to comfort & bless you. I have full faith in his overruling Providence. Today the clouds are dark and gloomy, but behind them there is a dark cloud that will banish every cloud from the horizon and we will yet have a time of peace and joy. We have this to comfort us. We know that our child has gone to our father and mothers and the God that gave it life, where there is not the pain and sorrow and wickedness that abounds in this world. That she is worthy of all the blessings of the new & everlasting Covenant. There is no question, therefore take consolation and be comforted. It will not do for you to give way to continued sorrow in your present condition, and then also for the sake of the children and me you must try & bear up under this severe trial.

I have been dreading to hear from home, for several days, fearing what has now come. Last Thursday night I dreamed I had sweet little Mary playing with her. I thought she was fleshy like she was before the summer complaint started on her, and more beautiful than I have ever seen her. I had heavenly comfort with her, and when I awoke, I feared the news that has now come. I told Ammon of my dream and my fears, on Saturday night when we were both put in this cell, to occupy it together, which is a great satisfaction to us. It makes prison life much pleasanter. For this great privilege we will be under a life-time obligation to Mr Wolfer the Deputy Supt. Considering the strict discipline I feel that the officers are exceedingly kind

to us, for which may God reward them a hundred fold. I have reced.
several letters of late, but my mind is too much weighed down with
sorrow, to remember just now who they are from. Kiss Pearly, Erma,
and Pauline for pa. They must be good children. May the angel of
health be with you that our lives may be spared to meet again.

God bless and strengthen you for every trial. From your husband
and father,

David K. Udall.

House of Correction, Detroit, Michigan
Oct 18th 1885   10 a.m.

My Dear, loving and sorrowful Family:

How hard it is in such times of sickness and death, not to be with
you to aid and comfort you. Your many trials, hardships and wan-
derings I keenly feel, and earnestly pray that you, one and all may
have strength according to your day. The Lord is having a record
kept of every trial you pass through which will redound to our exal-
tation and will weave a heavenly thread or chain around our hearts
(through our faithfulness to each other and our God) that never will
be broken. The joy I have in thinking of my devoted family, their
purity & virtue, and their fidelity to me, the thoughts of our religion
our Saviour, and our God, strengthens and bouys me up when at
times the heaviness of the atmosphere and attending circumstances,
strongly tend to crush the hopeful spirit I have nearly always enjoyed. I thank God that we have at least a portion of that faith that
inspires our leaders, and that our fathers and mothers have and do
enjoy. This world and its joys sink into insignificance compared with
the joy in this faith. The strength we receive now is a partial reward
for faithfulness. I cannot as yet feel fully reconciled to the sufferings
and loss of our dear little Mary. May God grant that the rest of you
may be spared to a good old age. May peace and health be with you
my family, is my constant prayer.

Ella and Lois, how I feel for you in these sad hours of deprivation
and trial. With the spirit of death that has been around and over
you, in your almost homeless and wandering condition. May God be
merciful to you. I know that we have thousands of as true friends as
ever lived, who will befriend you, but my organization is such that
these circumstances touch a very tender place with me. I cannot
write all I would be thankful to. Space will not permit. You know
me well enough to guess pages from these few lines. I ask of you not

to neglect a known duty if it is in your power. Take great care of your health. You are not strong. Teach the children to pray. Pearly, Erma and Pauline must go to Primary as they get old enough, and be good children. While in the South if Lois could go and work in the Temple it would be a great blessing. I would like to answer all your questions but I cannot. Ella you must not worry over business matters too much. Take the world as easy as you can. Be hopeful and take courage.

I am glad to know that Joseph and Emma are taking such a great interest in our welfare, as well as our many friends. Cheer and comfort Ammon's family all you can. It is a great help for us to be together although the cell is very small for two of us, 4 × 7 feet. We have all the reading matter we have time to read. Read 41st Chap. 10th verse of Isaiah, and I would like Bro Gibbons to have the 37th Chap of Psalms read in meeting. I am glad to hear of the fair crops and improvements at home.

I hope that the way will open so that you can settle all of our accts. Do not forget to pay the taxes. Write [J. C.] Herndon and see if they can not have my Polygamy Case dismissed this term of Court. I expect you had better take legal steps to collect from Wall, if he will not make some kind of a settlement. Be very careful about fire. Are steps being taken to appeal my case? This should be looked after immediately.

I have received letters from the following brethren and sisters. H. & E. Goldsbrough. J. W. Smith (Snowflake) J. T. Lesueur, two. Henry Fowles, W. F. James, Bro Hunt, Alof & May Larson, Apostle W. Woodruff, Joseph and Emma. Three from father. Sep. 14th 21st & Oct 1st. E. N. Freeman two. One from Sister Eliza and four from Lois Sep 6th, 21st 28th & Oct 11th. Many thanks for each and all. Ella I take the will for the deed. With best love I remain devotedly Your husband & father

D. K. Udall

A kiss for the little girls. I think best for Ida to remain where she is, for the present. Please write Bro Woodruff for me.

D. K. U.

Dec 3rd 1885 Reced the first letter from Aunty after reaching St Johns. She speaks in the highest terms of pa, Charley & Bell as traveling companions, and says her trip to St Johns was one of the pleasantest trips of her life. She gives me such hopes in regard to Davids pardon that I feel happier than I have for months. Apostles Snow, Young & Lyman were there at the time of writing and they were full of hope. In case the pardon failed to come, every step had been taken for a new trial.

4th Reced good letter from Sister May, three sheets closely written. She gives me all the news. Tells of the 5 days visit and good meetings held by the Apostles in Snowflake. Bro Lyman had pulled 5 teeth for Sister Annie, one for Sadie & one for Martha [Crosby]. Sister Minerva Snow was with them and talked to the R. S. S. [Relief Society sisters] Bros Snow & Lyman had gone through the eastern part of the Stake while pa accompanied Bro B. Young through the Tonto Basin; would be absent ten days.

I am busy cutting, fitting, sewing and writing, so that the time flies swiftly to me. Lon Stewart has insisted on my accepting a $10.00 coupon on the Kanab Coop Store from him. I felt loth to do so, but nothing would do him but I must, so I am trying to return the kindness so far as lies in my power by helping his wife Alsade with some sewing.

6th I Reced a good long letter from my dear cousin Celia from which I briefly quote.

Richfield. Dec 3rd 1885

My Dear Cousin

I have felt very anxious about you since receiving your last letter and very sorry to learn that with all your other troubles you must be afflicted with bodily ailments. I hope and pray you are well er'e this, and have a sufficient portion of the peaceful influence of the Holy Spirit, that you are feeling contented and happy, and able to banish the blues and look forward to the time when the pure in heart and the meek shall dwell with the Lord and inherit the earth, and from the vindictive and blood-thirsty spirit exhibited towards our people every where, I cannot think our enemies will be long in sealing their damnation. And when you read the noble sentiments expressed in your husband's letters and contemplate his unselfish and true Christian character for such a husband you can suffer much. His companionship for a few days is worth more to a faithful member of the church, than a whole life-time spent with a person of a lower order of mind. My testimonies of the beauties and happiness of the plural order of marriage, has increased within the last month quite materially. I have not a doubt that if Ella (with such a husband) would try, she could be far happier than if David were at home with her only and not so whole-souled in his religion. I am perfectly satisfied that the nearer a man and woman live up to their duties and serve the Lord the closer and holier the bond that unites them, becomes. xxx Albert and Ida started for St George last Wednesday. They went off in good spirits. I do hope you will get here for their reception which will be between Chris'mas & New Years. Roy has written several letters to Aunt Ida to tell her to come back & bring little Pauline. He wants to kiss her. May the peace and blessings of heaven attend you.

Your loving Celia

Dec 7th 1885 Reced copy of another letter from David, written Nov 15th. The time passed as pleasantly as they could hope. They were well, and kindly treated by the officers. Spoke of a visit they had just received from Bro James Dwyer of Salt Lake City. Poor boy! said he was getting used to his work so that it did not tire him like it did. Feels that the Lord is blessing them exceedingly. Begs of Ella and I to be united in our feelings. Tells E. he has not reced a word from her since the 29th of Aug. Feels very anxious to hear from home.

I wrote to him that night, which made five long letters I had sent him since coming to Kanab. I cannot neglect writing often, although it is poor satisfaction to address him merely as a brother. I spend my time writing, sewing and caring for my little one.

13th [12th] Sat Eve. I was very much surprised and delighted to receive a letter directly from Detroit directed to Lois Pratt. Extracts as follows

(Cell No 101) House of Correction
Detroit, Mich. Nov 29th 1885

Mrs Lois Pratt
Kanab, Utah.

My Dear Sister:
By special favor of the Deputy (Mr Wolfer) I am permitted to write to you today which I joyfully and thankfully do, but how I wish I could talk instead of write. I have instructed Ella to forward you my letters (or copies) from time to time, but I fear it has not been done as promptly as it should on account of the great trouble she has passed through of late. In consequence I know your great disap-

pointment, and I have felt to grieve over the lack of opportunity to inform you of my condition and offering a few words of appreciation and comfort to you in your lonliness.

I have received and read with joy and thanksgiving your dear letters, written one from Kanab, one Beaver 2 from Richfield and three from Nephi since I last wrote you, and the heaven-born feeling manifested in them for my welfare, reminds me of the integrity and devotion of Martha and Mary to their Lord in his many trials. God bless you my dear Sister, with that sweet babe. I feel that no sister could be truer to me than you have been. It is the devotion of a true wife. May your husband be as true to you as you are to your dear ones. When you see Father and Aunt, let them read this short letter that they may know I appreciate their parental care and journeying for the comfort and happiness of my loved ones. I feel powerless to express but I know God will reward them and all who have aided in the happiness of me and mine. I hope that my future life will be such that my parents, family and friends will be at least partially rewarded for the helping hand they have extended, and the great abundance of sympathy and good will they have showered upon us in this hour of trial. I have received such good and inspiring letters from Celia [Bean], Aunt Mary Pitchforth, and Bro & Sister [Henry] Goldsbrough. Thank them for me. I reced a piece of Harry Pitchforths wedding cake. It was very nice. xxx Thank Bro and Sister [Taylor] Crosby, also Grandma Crosby for their great kindness also give my kind regards to my many dear friends in Kanab, especially Aunt Macy [Stewart], Lou, John, Laurence [Mariger] and their families. I hope some day to meet your true friend Celia. Her letter to me was a credit to her sex.

We are all in pretty good health. We have plenty of reading matter, D. News, Herald, Juvinile, Mil. Star, Church Books and a good library in the Hall that we can go to.[70] Bro Kemps letter to the News is ok. Of course prison life is a continuation or repetition of humilliations that I will not attempt to describe, but the Officers are very considerate of our comfort and welfare when we consider the strict discipline of the institution.

Atty F. S. Richards writes me from Washington D. C. that I can expect my pardon by the last of this month, which may God grant.[71] I feel that I am standing imprisonment well for a beginner. Ammon often speaks of you and your good letters, neither has he forgotten his old friends in Kanab. He sends love. Follow the dictates of the Holy Spirit and the advice of your true friends and your family matters will be overruled for the eternal happiness of you and yours.

Hug and kiss the little daughter for me. God bless and comfort you.
With love and devotion as in days of yore,

David K. Udall

Dec 16th   At noon, on Wed. Father Udall and Aunty with Sister
Mary [Stewart] and her five little ones reached Kanab. They had been
greatly blessed with good health and fine weather, and had made a
quick trip. Father thought best for me to go on to Nephi with them,
so I commenced at once to prepare for the journey; The dear Crosby
family doing every thing that love could suggest for mine and baby's
comfort on the road. I can never repay them.

17th Thurs.   We all visited together at Bro [Laurence] Mariger's.
Aunt Mary telling us all about the folks in Arizona. Bro Mariger was
very kind indeed. He gave me a knit Jacket, and every little necessary
he could find out I needed from the store.

[Presidential Pardon]

18th Friday   We were all ready; team hitched up to start when
the following telegram was reced.

Chicago, Ill. Dec 18th 1885   Received at Kanab 9.15 a.m.

To Lois Pratt, Kanab.

I received Presidential pardon yesterday.

D. K. Udall.

Oh! what a world of joy those few little words brought to our
hearts. To think that our dear one was a free man once again, seemed
too good to be true. Father telegraphed to Nephi that we would be
home in eight days, and we bade our dear friends, and poor sister
Mary a hasty goodbye and resumed our journey.

[Return to Nephi]

That day we had quite a serious time getting up Kanab Cañon. The
creek was a solid glare of ice, so that the horses being smooth shod,
could not stand up. Once we had to unload every thing and carry it
to the bank and while Grandma held baby, Grandpa and I whiped

and halooed to get the team out. We had rainy, foggy weather all the way to Panguitch, but traveled from daylight till 7 or 8 oclock every night. At Mary's Vale we stopped at a Gentile house, Mr Wright. I slept on the floor in the house and poor little baby was so sick all night, I scarcely slept at all. She had a burning hot fever, and a dreadful cough like an attack of pneumonia. I sat up in bed with her nearly all night, and oh! how I dreaded to take her out into the freezing air at sunrise. But there was no help for it, and she seemed none the worse.

That night how thankful I was to reach Richfield where my dear Aunt & Cousins helped me to sweat, bathe and doctor her. The next morning after Father & Tank had administered to her she was like a new baby. The folks wished me to stay there, but as we heard both by telegraph and the papers that David was expected in Salt Lake we hurried on thinking he would come to Nephi. At Richfield I learned with great sorrow of the death of my dear sister Annie's little fat baby, which died on the 7th of Dec with inflamation of the bowels. It was just one year old this month and they have all written what a sweet angelic child she was. Left Richfield at 9 a.m. and traveled till 8 oclock that night camping at a farmhouse two miles from Gunnison. Found comfortable lodging but no Santa Claus came in the night, although it was babies first Christmas.

25th   Christmas morning 1885 at Sunrise found us traveling through Gunnison. Baby is well enough to smile & play a little this morn. Where and under what circumstances will another Christmas find us I wonder? God grant it may be in a home of our own shared by the husband and father that we have been so long seperated from. My little one travels south with one Grandpa & north with the other. It seems she is entitled to most anyone but a papa. We took dinner at "the bend" and had fried chicken in honor of the day. At dusk reached little Salt Creek where we were warmly welcomed and entertained by Sister Sarah Jane & husband.

[In Nephi]

26th   Traveled through deep mud all day reaching Nephi just after dark. The Linton girls had been and swept up and made a fire, and we were prepared to enjoy a warm house after our long cold trip. Aunt Elizabeth sent for us to come up there to supper which we did, and there found a letter from David just reced. written from Navajoe Station. So he had gone directly home, having to borrow money and pay his own fare. All the old friends and neighbors called in to congratulate us on his freedom, and our safe arrival home. Reced note from Chicago from Dade saying the House gave him a good suit of clothes on leaving, and that he weighed nine lbs more when he came out than when he went in!

Jan 1st [1886]   New Years Day, Aunty and I went up and took dinner with Sister Bryan & Aunt Julia. It was a very cold day. At night, in company with Mary L [Linton]. I disguised myself what I could, and went to the Theater to see "The Lady of Lyons." Aunty kept the baby. We had an enjoyable time.

3rd   Dear friend Emma Thorpe Ashworth, who had been staying here several weeks with Etta, started home on the train. She has such a sweet baby girl, Beatrice, the picture of her pa. While the Beaver Woolen Mills are shut down for the winter, she will accompany Wm. to St George & work in the Temple. What a nice time she will have. Reced letter from David written 7th from Albuquerque, descriptive of Prison life. I will enclose a copy of the same. Following day reced letter from St John as follows.

St Johns, Ariz. Jan 1st 1886   9 p.m.

My Dear Ones:

I have desired to write to you ever since my arrival home but seemingly I have had no chance. My dear, how I have wished for you both to be with us in these times when friends have done all they could for our happiness. I trust that you spent Christmas pleasantly with true friends and may God grant that 1886 may be a year of victory over our enemies and happiness to you though at present in exile. I greatly miss our little Mary. Kiss her little sister born in the patriarchal order of marriage for me. How I have learned to prize my offspring and the dear ones who have had the pain of bearing them. We remembered and talked of you in our sociables and prayers. Ella mourns and cries so much of the time over little Mary. Poor girl! She has been greatly tried, and she is so sensitive. She says for me to wish you a Happy New Year for her. She feels as though she cannot write. Ella feels different to what she did for which I feel to praise the Lord. When I learn where you are at Kanab or Nephi I will send your Christmas presents.

I arrived at Navajoe on the 22nd where I found sister Eliza [Udall Tenney] & Bro Wm Gibbons waiting for me. You can imagine the meeting. We arrived home 4.30 on the 23rd. Ella and the children, Joseph & family, Ammon's family, Bros [Elijah] Freeman, [John B.] Milner, Moor & others came out a few miles to meet me. In the *evening a reception was given me in the Assembly Hall which was crowded to it's utmost. Picnic, speeches songs etc. was the order. Ida, what true and good friends we have! I was overcome so that I could not refrain from shedding tears. So different to what I have had in the cold hard prison and world. If you could have been with us and the brethren released from Detroit how happy I could have been. I received nice Christmas presents from the Xmas Tree. From the Relief Society 1 pr Suspenders and a nice handkerchief, from the Y.L. Association a clothes broom in a beautiful case. From the Primary a Mottoe "Welcome." Also two $500.00 notes I had signed and was owing on the Wilhelm debt. My Bro Joseph has been a true brother to us in this trying hour. To redeem notes $300.00 from Lopez that he paid for the house and lot in town. $300.00 from Prest [John] Taylor, T.O. [Tithing Office] order and the remainder $400.00 in freighting & grain. I cannot express my surprize and joy. The Lord has surely blessed us in that regard.*

We had Ammon's family, and Jos & Emma [Udall] to Christmas dinner with us, and went to the dance in the evening. Your pa, Sister Annie, Martha Crosby, and Bro Wm Flake came over last Sunday from Snowflake to see me and spent the day with us. It hardly seems possible that I am worthy of so much attention and kindness. We had a very pleasant time. Gentiles and Mexicans seem glad to see me. We were at two surprize parties last week. Jno Pattersons and Bro Joseph's. Today we have enjoyed a nice time at Sister Jensens.

Dear, you have taught me a lesson about writing. I will try and be more punctual in the future. Goodnight! I hope you are both well. With best love I am devotedly Yours

David.

The effect of these two letters upon me can easily be imagined, the first made me fairly sick with horror. To think of the one dearest on earth to me having to suffer such injustice and indignities. I cried the remainder of the day and dreamed about it all that night. Very many of the old friends and neighbors came in to hear it read, the last letter telling of his hearty welcome at home, brought the reaction. How I rejoiced that he was once more at home among friends, and that they manifested their love for him so plainly, for I know how worthy he is of it. But oh! how lonely and homesick it makes me to think I can join in none of the rejoicings over the return of my *own husband*. The poorest meanest Mexican in St Johns is more highly favored than I, for he has the privilege of looking upon the dear face

I am so hungry to see. I have felt that his *liberty* was all I could ask, but now that boon is granted, the desire to see his face absorbs every other thought. Oh! what have I done that I should be thus cruelly exiled, banished from all that is nearest & dearest to me except my babe. Her sweet bright little face is the only thing that serves to cheer the flight of the weary days, weeks, and months. O Lord, help me to be ever mindful of the blessings I enjoy, and to bear patiently and humbly every trial thou seeest fit to send upon me.

Jan 18th   Deep snow. We visited Sister [Ellen] Lintons in a sleigh. Also visited Bro Goldsbroughs   That day reced note from David also pair of cuff buttons for Christmas present. He was busy night & day settling Tithing & Store business for the year. All well at home.

Jan 24th   Quarterly Conference. Apostle John W. Taylor here to one meeting. Sunday evening Mary L. proffered to keep the baby if I would put a veil on and go to the meeting which I did. Heard a splendid sermon from a Bro Goss, also beautiful singing by the choir, both of which served to inspire me with new courage.

25th   Mrs Lizzie Bryan brought my beautiful new guitar from Salt Lake. I had sent $14.00 which Charley and Bell left to get an instrument, in place of mine which they have. Mrs B. said she could get none for that price that she would take so she brought me a $25.00 guitar which she got as a bargain for $19.00. She said I was to accept it and give Lula lessons; (as I had been doing for some time) for the difference. I was delighted with it for it was the best instrument, and the sweetest toned I think I ever played.[72] Mrs Bryan also came and practiced herself for several evenings. I learned her "Sweitzers Song of Home" with guitar accompaniament to play in the "Ticket of Leave Man," in the Home Dramatic.

26th   Reced letter from David saying the Lord had blessed them with another sweet little daughter, born the morning of the 18th of Jan. Grandpa Udall's 57th birthday. Mother and babe both doing nicely.[73] Sister Eliza [Udall Tenney] was staying with them.

Jan 31st Sunday.   Mr & Mrs Bryan, Mr & Mrs Adelbert Cazair & Sister [Mary E. S.] Neff, all came by Aunties invitation and spent the afternoon and evening. We had singing, and pleasant converse interspersed with the reading of David's letters which they expressed a desire to hear. Their visit was a treat for me, not being permitted to go into company much.

Feb. 5th   I attended in company with Bro & Sister W. A. C. Bryan, Morris's Concert, which was very nice. Among other things little Lula Bryan sang "Come Birdie Come" with guitar accompaniament. Her parents feel very proud of her progress so I feel that I have done a little good since coming to Nephi.

7th Sunday. I reced letters from pa & David. All are well and prosperous at Snowflake. Bell & Charley have moved to their own home across the corner from pa. Orrin & Annie have exchanged their house & lot for one only a block from pa, so they are all there together, and pa says he is buying a place that will make a nice home for me when I am permitted to return. O I pray that the time may speedily come when I can go and enjoy it. The time never dragged so wearily to me before. The days seem like weeks and the weeks like months. David says in his letter dated Feb 1st that Ella is up and around looking as well and rugged as ever, the little new comer is christened Luella for her mother, and looks more like her than any of the children. He had just got through settling tithing and sent off reports. For the year 1885 the ward paid $4388.01. He longs to see his little exile, sympathizes with me in my loneliness, Says he will go to trial again in June, and if the Lord will open the way he will at least pay us a visit before that time. I answered immediately and begged of him not to think of coming; to go to trial first, before he did any thing to arouse suspicion, on the part of his enemies. By so doing I have faith that the Lord will help him to rid himself of this weary polygamy case, and I tell him I can better endure this cruel seperation, than I can see him come, make a hasty visit, and go back again without us. The thought of *parting* seems to far overbalance the joy of seeing him only for a short time.

Feb 10th 1886 Bro Harry McCune called and spent the forenoon. He had just returned from a mission to New Zealand, where Bro Tommy Stewart is President. He speaks of Tommy in the highest terms. Says he enjoyed his labors with him very much. We had a very pleasant visit together. He inquired all about David & his unjust imprisonment. I sang & played for him, he sang bass, etc. that p.m. We called on Jno & Ida Wright in their new home, to see their new baby.

11th My dear friend Mary's 21'st birthday. We spent the day at Sister Lintons in company with the Sisters Bryan, & Millard. I presented her with an autograph album & wrote her a birthday tribute as it is my first attempt I will copy.

"A Birthday Tribute"
Dear Friend Mary:

1 Thy natal day again has dawned,
  And we, thy friends assembled here
  Would wish thee joy and peace & health
  Throughout the coming glad new year.

2 How proud thy parents on this day

Their eldest daughter's twenty-one.
A noble type of womanhood
Her life of good works just begun.

3 Their loving care through all these years
Is now repaid and amply too,
By seeing her all they could wish
A faithful saint, Just, kind and true.

4 In looking forward they foresee
A home she'll someday call her own
Which in declining years will seem
Haven of peace and rest to them.

5 Their prayer that none but God's elect
Shall ever hold a claim on thee,
In fancy now they feel the clasp
of Grandchildren upon their knee.

6 Blest Girl:
Thou look'st around thee and can see,
All that thy heart holds dear.
No blighting sorrow yet has come
To fill your soul with gloom or fear.

7 Father and mother kind and true,
Brothers and sisters welcome you.
Friends known and loved from infancy
All join in this brief jubilee.

8 We dare not hope your future years
May pass as smoothly as the past.
Tis not the fate of mortals here
Much less of those whose lot is cast
Among the lowly saints of God
Seeking the path that Jesus trod.

9 But this we pray, whate'er betide
May strength be given as thy day
That every footprint made by thee
Be found within the "narrow way."

Thy life a symbol of true worth
That father, mother, friends will say
We bless the hour that gave thee birth
God bless our Mary's natal day.

Ida Hunt.

Feb 21st   Aunty and I visited at Sister [Mary] Pitchforth's in company with Bro & Sister Goldsbrough & Mrs Dr Atkins a young M.D. from Tooele, who has come to Nephi to practice in her profession. She seems a very nice young lady, of 26 years. Was born & raised in Utah but graduated in the medical Colleges in the East. Is very stylish.

22nd   Went in the evening to call on dear friend Kate Love who is home for the first time since last March. She has a sweet little daughter just five months old. There seems something strange about these little refugees all being of the feminine gender. Kate has merely come to tell her nearest & dearest friends goodbye before starting on a long journey. The arrest of Prest George Q Cannon and his treatment by the court officials, together with the constant imprisonment, one after another of the best men among us, seems to cast a gloom over the entire people.[74] When will these dark times change.

Feb 23rd 1886   Reced letter from Bell & Charley saying Sister May was blessed with a sweet little daughter born on the 2nd. I am so glad to hear that she is safely through her trouble and all is well.

26th   Pauline is eleven months old. She is a very large child for her age. As I write she is laying in bed, going through all the preliminaries of going to sleep for the night, laughing, talking, & biting her toes. Occasionally she will rise or sit straight up in bed and look over towards the writing table, to see if her mamma is still an occupant of the room, and then lie down again perfectly content. I have never before seen a child so strong, active & full of life at her age. She is never still a moment when awake, and wants to be on her feet walking about continually, and as she can scarcely go alone yet it keeps me busy all day long, the hardest kind of work too, looking after her. Were she not a good sleeper, I dont know how I should stand it. Dear little "refugee." How she would love her papa if she could ever have the privilege of making his acquaintance. But how utterly she is exiled from his heart, for it is impossible to love a child whom you never see, as you do those whose sweet, cute little looks & ways are constantly before us. I feel sometimes that my babe's beauty and sweetness is all lost, when her father knows nothing about it.

28th   Sunday reced good long letter from Sister Annie and Bro Lewis which had been delayed. Poor Annie is staying with May during her confinement and it makes her feel the loss of her own dear babe so keenly. She says the two months since its death seem the longest ones in her life. Also reced letter from David dated 22nd which I had been looking for so long. It was in answer to two long letters of mine. He says if I only knew his circumstances I would have great charity for him. I think the same in regard to his carelessness or neglect of writing to me. If he could realize my lonely situation, he would at least give me the comfort of regular & encouraging letters. He said they were all well. Prest. [John] Taylor had sent him a $600.00 T.O. [Tithing Office] order to help him in settling his law-suits. He felt very grateful for their thoughtfulness. In regard to coming to Utah, he said my suggestions had weight with him, still he was undecided. Prayed the Lord would direct him aright.

March 3rd   Have just been down to bid friend Kate [Love] good-bye. She is starting in company with her husband, Prest. Paxman on a mission to New Zealand, to be gone perhaps for years. He will take Bro Tommy Stewarts place as Prest of that mission.[75] Kate was also blessed and set apart by the Apostles for a mission among the Maoris. They have both been on the "Under Ground" for over a year, and what a happy change this will be for them. I only had the chance of seeing Bro P. for a moment, as they only dared visit at home very secretly. May God speed them & help them to make their exit from this "land of Deputies" undetected.

4th Thurs.   We have spent in fasting & prayer for the deliverance of Poor Brother Ammon, & his brethren in prison. I reced a letter from Sister Eliza a short time ago. She sent some nice verses Ammon had composed & sent them. Also says that the decision of the Supreme Court in their cases will be given March 5th and wanted us to remember the time and have faith with them that the Lord in mercy will soften the hearts of those Judges and cause them to reverse that unjust decision. We have tried to make that desire a special subject of prayer on this fast day. Ammon sent his last family letter by this way and wished me to copy and send to Bro [Wilford] Woodruff & others who had been so faithful to write to him. I did so immediately and then we forwarded the letter to St Johns. He was feeling well, but said Bro [Peter J.] Christofferson was sick. May God bless & comfort those poor prisoners and also their devoted families.

March 6th 1886   We found about 10 inches of snow on the ground this morning. Are having winter again. Father has abandoned the field and in company with his counselors has resumed his labors as Bp. visiting and catechising the people. This is my dear mothers 49th birthday. Sammy Linton came by with the team taking Mary to the Store, so they all pursuaded me to get in and go up to Sister Lintons for the day. I did so and had a pleasant time. Baby has also had a fine play with the children.

7th Sunday.   Aunty is making funeral clothes as she was one year ago today. Ellen Chase has lost her baby with diptheria, which is the second case in one week. All meetings, schools etc. are suspended for two weeks to prevent the spread of the disease. Bro [Charles] Sperry spend a pleasant evening with us.

8th   Monday my twenty-eighth birthday. Cold snowy weather. I reced. a good encouraging letter from my dear father. Aunty gave me a picture frame, Sister [Lizzie] Bryan a box of Stationary, Lenora Hartley a quaint little water pitcher, and Mary Linton a gold pin. The last named Nora & Mary came in to supper & so the day passed by very pleasantly. I feel very grateful for the good kind friends I enjoy.

9th   The 53rd birthday of my father and the yearly anniversary of my poor mother's death. I spent in weeping & prayer, lonely & sad, thinking what a sorrowful day it would be for my dear ones at home.

11th   We were invited to visit & take supper at the home of Bro Harry McCune, in company with Bro & Sister [Charles and Emily] Sperry, Sister [Margaret J.] Paxman & the Grace family.[76] Had a very enjoyable time, looking at all the curiosities he had brought from India, China, New Zealand and the different countries he had visited. In the evening after partaking of a sumptuous repast, we formed a band, violin, picolo, banjo, guitar & bass horn, discoursed such fine music that the guests all went to dancing. We had music & singing till half past ten when we adjourned. What pleasure is equal to the association of nice agreeable, refined people. Still it snows, snows, snows.

Sunday 14th   Sister Bryan & Pitchforth just returned from Salt Lake to Ladies Mass meeting.[77] They bring a kind invitation from Sister [Jennie] Whipple to come and visit her at the Desert [Deseret] Hospital.[78] Were it not for the baby, I should be delighted to go. Jos. B. took Sister Bryan and I in the wagon to spend the day at Lizzie's.

[Continued Disappointments and Misunderstandings]

Sun. 21st   We visited at dear Sister [Mary] Neff's. Quite a nice company there. Before going there I wrote long letter to David and received one from him and from which I quote. Unbeknown to me Aunty had written him a few lines taking him to task for neglecting me so long, so the poor boy thought he was *catching it* on all sides.

Snowflake. A.T. March 12 1886

My Dear Wife.

Once more I take great pleasure in writing to you. I feel sad to read your letter to Sister Annie. It is so blue and censurable of me.

I know if you knew my heart and the circumstances under which I am laboring you would be very charitable. Dear, I will not blame you for your reproof knowing your love and integrity for me, also the great trial you have passed through for your husbands liberty. You have left home and loved ones for my sake which I will appreciate through time and eternity and in days to come I will be permitted to prove to you that I am not as careless in my attention and affection as I appear to be now. I yearn for your love and presence and feel that it will be the happiest time of my life when you can be made comfortable under our own roof when I pray that love and peace may abound in all the house-hold. Ida, dear, I cannot explain by letter how I am tried by the state we sometimes get into. I have forgotten to tell you that our little Luella has red hair. It is a strange freak in our families. Ella blames me with it, and I have a good rig on her over it. The poor little thing has the colic two or three hours every day.

Bishop Preston[79] *and Bro Thurber of Richfield arrived in St Johns last Tuesday. Remained two nights and one day. We had an excelent visit with them. I got many many idea's from the Bp. on the lesser priesthood, tithing matters etc which will be a great help to us. He seemed well pleased with the tithing office, grist mill etc. I expected to get a threshing for the large expenditure in building office, barn & yard, and so expressed myself to the Bp. but he said I had better be whipped for doing something than doing nothing. xxx I arrived here in company with Bro Preston Friday noon.*

Sunday evening 14th   Conference has adjourned. We have had a very agreeable time. You were released from presiding over the Y.L.M.I. Associations, and Sister M. E. Freeman of St Johns was appointed your stead. I learn from the folks here that you have urged this release. My dear, I regret that the Young Ladies of this Stake have not had the benefit of your experience and knowledge. You are amply qualified for that position.

Prest [Jesse N.] Smith informs me that if he and I had been at home the last time Apostle E. Snow & party were here they would have organized another Stake making me President.[80] *He says it will be done, there is no doubt in a short time. He recommends it. Bro Smith is very friendly. The brethren feel that I have suffered enough, and that I will not go to prison again, which may God grant. I reported some of my experience to the Conference.*

I have been looking at the Turley place. I tell father to buy and I will make him safe. By some little Improvements it will make a pleasant home. I take it for granted you would rather live in Snow-

flake than any other town. I presume it will be some time before we can all live together as we have done in St Johns. Until then my dear girl feel assured I will do all that lies in my power to make you a comfortable home.

Dear I would rather suffer imprisonment than to know of your being unhappy. I received Aunts short letter in with Josephs. These letters seem to tell a sorrowful story. I would to God I could remedy it. No one knows the anxiety I have felt for you. Do not think I am unfaithful if letters do not come as often as desired. I make an attempt to write many times to my long absent loved ones, when I am interrupted. You do not understand my burdens. You may say there is no excuse for a husband to neglect his family, in the main this is verily true, but sometimes it seems there are circumstances when our loved ones and those dearest pleasures of life have to be neglected and sacrificed, to attend to the things of the Kingdom. May God grant unto us grace and patience for every hour in the day. I go until sometimes I am about worn out. I have been to Sister Mays, Annie's and Bell's to take meals, and made short visits. They seem happy and contented which I am pleased to see. They are all very kind to David, as they have always been. xxx

Kiss my little chunky girl for me. How I wish you could both be here. What a happy time we would have. Dear, how the love and sorrow of the past has made me feel since I have been here. It seems so strange. I do not see some of the dear faces that used to welcome me, and how lonely it seems. The little girls are growing to be nice little women.[81] The Seventies meeting is just out, so I guess I will have to quit. I have remained home tonight to think about and write these few lines to my long-suffering and true ones. For my sake be of good cheer. I beg of you not to lose confidence in the heart of Dade. A kiss for both of you. Goodnight.

David.

I wrote him a good long letter in answer to this which I hope will cover the wound I had made. Poor boy! how hard it seems that I have to be so far from him that I cannot understand his circumstances, without explanation, and that I am unable to render him the least assistance in his labors, or lighten his burdens in any way, and because I cannot do this, I make his life still more miserable, by complaining about it. How selfish and ungrateful, poor mortals are prone to be! I pray for strength and grace.

Mon. 22nd   We were invited to Wm & Lizzie Bryan's to a grand "soiree." As I was expecting to go to Springville soon, I thought I could go out in public with safety. The "elite" of the town were there, and I think it was the most enjoyable affair I have attended for some time. We spent the afternoon visiting, and after dining sumptuously at 5 p.m. spent the evening in music, singing and even dancing on the parlor carpet. The guitar seems to be something new in Nephi, and the company insisted on my singing and playing a great deal during the evening. As the guests did not retire till midnight I concluded to accept Mrs Bryans invitation to stay there over night with baby. The next day I came up to Bessie Sparks' and had a good visit with her and Sister Neff. Thursday I was invited to a grand party at Mrs Alma Hagues. Mrs Bryan told me they had fallen in love with my music. But I excused myself from going there.

Friday March 26th   My baby Pauline is one year old. How I thank and praise the Lord for my beautiful, bright healthy babe. She can walk alone, and can understand nearly everything I say to her. When we ask her where papa is she will reach both little arms towards his picture which hangs on the wall, and kiss at it, as though she loved any thing that bore the dear title of *papa*. Her Grandma gave her a silver spoon, and her little companion Lillia's Teasdale presented her with a china cup and saucer for her birthday. At 4 p.m. Cousins Tank and Albert [Nageley] came along on their way from Provo where they had been as witnesses. They only stayed an hour or so, but we had a pleasant little visit. That evening I wrote a pen picture of the baby to her pa.[82]

Sat   Wrote letter to Springville.

28th Sun.   On the strength of leaving soon I ventured out to meeting. Aunty kept the baby, and I enjoyed it very much. Took supper at Sister Jeffries, after which the grandma's again kept the babies and Bess [Sparks], Lizzie B. [Bryan], *Mame* C., Sister Neff & I went to a Presbyterian Revival or Conference. The singing was nice but oh! what primary doctrine. Monday. We washed. Tom Wrights wife called, gave the baby a pink gingham dress. Reced a long long letter from Sister May. All well at home in Snowflake.

Wed. March 31st   Baby and I took train for Springville. Cousin Mary and her husband, Cyrus N. Sanford met me at the depot & gave me a hearty welcome, as did my dear Aunt Lydia & Cousin Gilbert [Hunt] whom we found at the house. Marys family consists of seven children, two girls and five boys. They one and all loved the baby and were so good to help me tend her. For three days after I arrived there the baby was very sick and fretful and I could not tell what ailed her, but on Sunday the mystery was solved when she broke out thick with the Chicken Pox.

On that morning April 4th the Semi Annual Conference of the Church was convened at Provo, six miles from Springville. Mary and Cy went but the baby was too poorly for me to accompany them, which I very much regretted. When the folks returned that evening Cousin Ina Bean from Richfield was with them. She had taken advantage of the Conference rates, to come up and be treated by Dr Pike for a disease of the kidneys she suffered very much with. Monday morning I wrapped baby well and went to meeting. Enjoyed the carriage ride in the bracing morning air. Was surprised to find the Tabernacle at Provo such a spacious building. Bro John Nicolson and Apostle J. H. Smith delivered eloquent and touching sermons.[83] Met Mary L. and many dear friends from Nephi and better than all my dear friend Bro Willard Farr from St Johns. He had seen and talked with my dear Dade only the Monday before. That night I spent in Provo at Uncle Jim Beans with Ina. Bro Farr went up there with us and we had a good visit. He told me his business to Utah. Sister [Mary] Farr had come with him but remained with her mother in Ogden. He was expecting to be joined by Miss Minnie Romney in a few days when they would take a trip north. He would leave both *sisters* in Ogden for the summer and return to St Johns alone. Poor man! I admire his courage, but I fear his peace is ended, for some time at least. Prest. [John R.] Murdock and wife from Beaver were also guests at Beans.

Tuesday morning baby was so cross I did not go to meeting but attended in the p.m. and heard the reading of the Epistle from the First Presidency.[84] That night returned to Springville.

Wed.   Hap and Dilsey Sanford proffered to keep the baby and let me take comfort in going to meeting one day. I gladly accepted their kind offer and was disappointed when the Conference adjourned with the morning session. I bade Bro [Willard] Farr, Brother [Lorenzo] Hatch and many friends goodbye.

Thurs 9th [8th]   Sister Mary Kent from Bountiful made us a pleasant visit.

Friday.   Reced a good letter from pa. Went to a surprise party at Cy's sisters Aunt Celia Johnsons. Had a pleasant time, a splendid supper. Left baby till 2 a.m. with Dilsey.

Sat 10th   received good letter from David written on leaves from his note book while down in the field.

At the Farm. St Johns   March 30th 1886

My dear wife:

Your loving and very encouraging letter of March 21st reced this morning. I thank God for your true heart and devoted love. I well knew you would repent the hastily written words to Eliza [Udall Tenney]. I sincerely hope my little sweet Pauline is better now. Hug & kiss her for her pa. Learn her to pray as soon as she can lisp. In the path of humility and prayer is safety, and we should learn our children this while young. How pleased I am to hear of your pleasant times among our kind friends. Dear you must make the best of every opportunity, enjoy life as well as you can. I am watering. We have 45 acres of small grain in and with good luck we ought to have a good crop. Sundown. I was hindered and did not get down till noon. Will have to walk home, do chores and then go to Arbitraters meeting in the Mexican town. We are trying to settle our water trouble with the Mexican people by arbitration.

31st 2 p.m.   I was up late last night, and this morning I visited the sick so I did not get to the field till late. Ben Richeys wife and child died ten days ago and there is a great deal of sickness in town. xxx Prest J. N. Smith and Bp Thurber spent last Sunday with us. We had a good time. Have gone to the upper Country and will be back next Saturday. They will organize a Prayer Circle on their return. xxx

Since I last wrote you the District Court has convened here Chief Justice Shields presiding. He is only about 26 years old, is quiet so far as the Mormon question in concerned. Old [Sumner] Howard was here, he is practicing law. [J. C.] Herndon, our lawyer is Asst. prosecuting Atty. now. I had a talk with him. He still expects to defend me according to contract. He is sanguine that Ammon and the brethren will be released shortly. xxx

It must indeed be a poor Saint who would desire Prest. Cannon to go to prison. I thank God he done as he did.[85] After a Servant of the Lord has served the people as faithfully as he has then for some to refuse to pay any more Tithing. O folly! just as though the Lord wanted such peoples tithing. He is not poor. What such people appear to have belongs to the Lord, even the Earth and the fullness thereof. This unholy crusade is developing the true saint and putting the hypocrite to flight, and I feel to say let the good work go on, and O Lord give me and mine strength to endure every trial that may come. It is the even steady course that wins. These trials we are passing through are for our perfection. Let us try to bear them patiently.

My dear wife I want you to be encouraged. There are brighter days ahead. I must quit now. In writing this afternoon I have been up and down to turn the water half a dozen times. I may not get this off in the morning, as I have another arbitration meeting tonight.

April 1st 3 p.m. I came down to the farm early this morning, then went home to fast meeting, and came back at 2 p.m. I have a Priests meeting to go to tonight, Arbitrators meeting tomorrow night and Teachers meeting Saturday night. It seems like my work is like a womans, it is never done. The horse that will pull has to work.

You say if I took pleasure in writing to you I would find time. Dear you argue well, but from a false position. Our surroundings and circumstances are such that we cannot always do those pleasurable acts and duties that above all earthly things we would prefer. God and His Church first, families next. In this I find enduring happiness a conscience void of offense. Though at times it may appear that I neglect the dearest ones to me on Earth, still my heart is full of love and tenderness now as when we made those solemn covenants over the alter and in the presence of God and His Servants. Dear I ask you not to doubt me. Time will prove that I am that devoted husband of your ideal fancy. The Harvest is great and the laborers few. I have it in my heart to write you often but I have so many hindrances I cannot tell you them all. I beg of you not to postpone your writing and only write as often as I do. Your letters are a source of joy and encouragement to me. Do not deprive me of that boon, and return evil for what appears to you to be evil in me, but return acts of love and kindness for what appears to you to be evil in me. This course will bring joy and peace to you. It will indeed be a happy time when we can have a home of our own unmolested by our enemies where joy and peace will abound and may this day speedily come. I pray that this may find you both in good health. I have a bad cold and am not feeling well. Love to Father, Aunty, & all. Yours devotedly,

D. K. U.

Tues. April 13th Ina [Hunt Bean] came over from Provo. We all spent the evening at Miss Alice Johnsons. Met Hannah Grieve nee Friel for the first time. Had a pleasant musical *soiree.* Came home in a wet snow storm.

Wed 14th Through the courtesy of Mrs. Finely, Ina and I were permitted to attend Prof Hamil's elocution class which I enjoyed very much. On our return home found a surprise party in honor of Cousin Gib [Hunt] had taken possession. One of the jolliest crowds ever assembled. Games, songs music by Mr. Perce on the guitar, interspersed with a hot supper was indulged in till 4 in the morning.

Friday April 16th 1886   We all spent a pleasant evening at Bp [Nephi] Packards.

Sat.   had a family visit at *Ma* Sanfords. Ina & I stayed all night there.

Sun.   Hap [Sanford] & I went to meeting. Dark rainy day.

Mon.   Ina returned to Provo.

Tues.   Cousin Gib started for Dixie. We received a letter from Ida saying that on the 14th of April Celia [Hunt Bean] had given birth to another bouncing boy. Both doing splendid. I could not help being disappointed that it was not a girl this time as Celia needs some help so badly.

Sat. 24th   Commenced weaning Pauline. Visited Clara Packard.

Sun 25th   Attended Sunday School, and in the p.m. wrote long letter to sister May.

26th   Received short letter from David saying their dear little Erma had the scarlet fever, which many of the children in St Johns were afflicted with.

Wed 28th   Baby still frets over the loss of her dinner. She shows all the spunk imaginable. Poor little Pauline. This is her first cross in life. Cousin Pam [Bean] came from Richfield. I accompanied him to Provo on the 29th. Found Ina at Uncle Jim Beans where we stayed that night. Went from there to Ina's Uncles Abe Conovers to visit. Baby slept all the afternoon and Pam took Ina and I in the buggy to see the large Asylum, Provo Bridge & all places of interest.

Sat. May 1st   We returned to Springville. Ina was still very poorly. Dr Pike would not consent for her to return home with Pam so started Sunday morning without her. Mary [Hunt], Ina and I attended meeting. Bishop Bromley was the Speaker. His sermon was very touching   he expected shortly to go to prison for the sake of his belief.[86]

Tues May 4th   I made up my mind to have the remainder of my back teeth out, as there was a dentist in the family, my cousins brother-in-law, Bro Nephi Packard. I engaged him to come to the house and took brandy, but it did not work as it did before. I was very sick indeed and yet realized the pain. My jaw came out of place for the third time and had to be set. I vomited all that day and night. My dear Cousins Ina, Mary, and the Sanford girls did all they could for my relief and comfort while Dilsey looked after Pauline   for the first time in her little life she slept away from me. I did not recover from the effects of the operation for several days.

Thurs. 6th   Ina went to Provo. Fast day & Mary attended both meetings. I received good letters from dear friends Mary Ashworth and Mary Linton also from my dearest Husband from which I quote.

At the Farm. St Johns   April 29th 1886

My Dear Wife:

Your newsy and affectionate letter written from Springville April 11th & 12th received some days ago. It is a pleasure to me to know you are trying to make the best of your circumstances and I feel assured that if it is in the possibilities you will adapt yourself to your surroundings. This is one of the great secrets of life and you are blessed with it as well as many other noble qualities that I greatly rejoice in.

Kiss my precious babe for me. I sincerely trust she has entirely recovered from her chicken-pox and cold. Your beautiful pen-picture of her & the cheerful letter accompanying it came duly to hand   many thanks for them. They are such a comfort to me. Dear I can see you are a devoted mother, and I bless you with a husbands blessing for your devotion. It seems impossible that you are the mother of a child that can walk and almost talk. You remember how we used to pray for this great boon.

Little Erma is recovering nicely from the scarlet fever. None of the rest of our dear little ones have taken it and we think they will not unless it is brought from the neighbors. Bro & Sister Joseph Patterson buried their oldest son yesterday which leaves them without a child. How sad! Sister Beards children all have the fever and the poor woman is so destitute, which is the case with many in the ward, Ammons family among the number. I will soon have to see that they have help. I do earnestly pray that the brethren will soon be liberated. What a travesty upon Justice are these sham trials and rehearings. The Lord must surely come out of his hiding place. I am informed five years more will wind up the scene spoken of by the Prophet Joseph. I trust we will not be found wanting. We must struggle to keep oil in our lamps.

I enclose $10.00. It is a small pitance. I would send more but money is very scarce just now, but I have full confidence the Lord will open the way. I do not want you to fret over not being able to earn means of support just now, and, my dear, you are under no obligations in the least for what little I have been able to do for you. It is as much yours *as* mine. *"They twain shall be one flesh." This I* *feel with all my heart, and you know my loved one it is one of the strongest desires of my heart that you should have a joyful time and a comfortable happy home on Earth and in Eternity and I feel to make you this promise that the Lord will grant unto you and ours every comfort that your heart can desire. You may feel that it is slow in coming yet it will surely come. xxx*

We are now planting the corn and preparing ground for the pota-toes. We expect to go to Erastus next week and put in cane and lucerne on the Wilhelm place.

May 1st   when I came from the field Thursday evening I found Erma very sick with cold, fever, etc. We did not have any sleep till near morning and I had to stay home most of yesterday on account of it but thank the Lord she is much better now.

Bro J. T. Lesueur and myself have taken two mail contracts one from Navajoe Station to St Johns, the other from Holbrook to Fort Apache. The Contracts will last for four years. The mail is carried six times a week. We think we have a pretty good thing of it as we get our money direct from the U.S. and have no Barths to deal with. We get $9000.00 year besides some $3000.00 per annum for express and passengers. What do you think of it? I did think I never would go into the mail business again. The third time ought to be the charm with me. May the Lord cheer and comfort you is the constant prayer of your devoted one. Goodbye.

Dade.

Sun. May 9th   We visited at Ma Sanford's. The next day I reced letter from Bro [Willard] Farr asking me to meet him at the Depot, but it had been detained and he had gone by the day before. I felt much disappointed. Busy sewing.

May 14th   I reced Deseret News containing account of the acci-dents of Brethren at Detroit, also "Era" telling of the serious illness of dear little Pearl with scarlet fever. My heart is sick with fear & dread.

15th   I wrote letters to David and Ella, also to Mary Ashworth and Celia, and

Sun. 16th   I wrote letters through the day and attended a Joint session of the Y.L. & Y.M. Associations in the evening.

Mon. 17th   Ina came over. We all visited at Sister Lib Woods.

21st   Reced a letter from Aunty with one enclosed from David written May 8th. He says Erma had been very sick with bold hives. Pearl had had a very severe attack of scarlet fever. The little girl living with them had the fever, and Ella was nearly worn out, but he was thankful to say they were all better. Described his nicely fitted up new tithing office and his fine garden. Reced good long letter from Sister May dated the 14th. On the 5th she had celebrated her 26th birthday and at pa's urgent request my dear mothers clothing, keepsakes etc. were divided among her children, and the family. They had lain in the trunk since her death, and it made us all very sad to handle and hear them mentioned over. May said Apostle [Erastus] Snow and part of his family were visiting them and David happened to come on mail business while Bro S. was there.

23rd   In company with Mary and Ina attended S.S. [Sunday School] and meeting.

24th   One year from the day I parted with my dear husband. I wrote to him. It recalled many sad recollections.

25th   My wedding day I celebrated by taking a ride up in the canon with Grandpa Sanford and the girls. Felt disappointed that Pam did not come as Ina and I both expected to go south with him.

27th   Ina's birthday. We rode out to the Factory with Sy. [Sanford] on a load of wool. Had dinner at Ma Sanfords   on our return I was real sick with kind of cholera morbus.

28th   Pam arrived and they went to Provo. Got good letter from pa with money enclosed from my interest in the Coop' herd to get my teeth.[87]

Sat 29th   My dear friend Edna Shepherd from Beaver called to see us in company with Hannah Friel with whom she was staying. Edna had accompanied her father that far on his way to prison, sentenced 6 months for unlawful cohabitation. I was pleased indeed to see her.

Sun 30th   We went out to Bro Friel's visiting. They have a lovely situation between Springville and Provo and enjoy one of the finest views of the whole country. We had a very pleasant day spent in conversation and music. Kate [Love] and I displayed our talent on the guitar and Edna and Hannah on the organ. Edna returned with us and stayed over night, and the next day

Mon.   the Friel girls visited us. That evening Pam, Ina and Alta Conover who was going home with them arrived and we spent a pleasant evening.

Tues June 1st   In company with them I bade goodbye to my kind friends and relatives in Springville and started south. After a long hard days ride we reached Nephi just at dark. Found Grandpa and Grandma well and glad to see us, also good letter from David dated 22″ telling of his visit to Snowflake, meeting Apostles [Brigham] Young & [Erastus] Snow, getting the Willis boys of that place to run that part of the contract, etc. He also told me that he expected to start for Prescott the next week to stand trial for Polygamy. In regard to it he says "I feel hopeful that the case will be dismissed, although I have suffered imprisonment, still I am thankful to our Heavenly Father that I can feel as unconcerned as I do, over the result. I know that He will overrule for our good if we will do right." All well at home.

June 2″ Pam & Ina started home. Mary Linton, Sisters Neff and Bryan called to see me.

Mon 7th Old friend Tom Wright called and presented me with $5.00 which he said he had intended to do for a long time. I feel very grateful to him.

June 13th 1886 Sun. Bro John Stewart passed on his way to Salt Lake to meet Tommy and Clarence [Stewart] just returned from New Zealand. Reced letter from David dated the 6th in which he copies letter from his lawyer, Judge [John A.] Rush apprising him that he need not appear in Prescott at the beginning of the term but they will send him word when he will be required. Cautions him to arrange it so that *Ida* may not be found as he thinks dilligent search will be made for her. David tells me of the folks and doings at home. Says

so far as I have an intimation we are permanently located in St Johns. The sweet little curl of Pauline's hair came safely to hand. God bless the little head from which it was clipped. How I pray that she may soon know her father. How soft and silken it is, and seems about the color of yours. I will find a neat little place for it in my wallet with baby's picture and her birthday letter, which I nearly always carry with me and look at often and show to my nearest friends. Why don't you send me one of your photo's. Can't you make a Temple apron? We cannot get the material here, and I stand much in need of one. Peace & Love be with you.

Dade.

June 14th Louise Udall helped me to make my black bunting dress.

15th Tues. I went to write, or copy in the Co. Records for Wm. Bryan, hired a little girl to help Aunty with the baby. Wrote all week.

Friday 18th attended a birthday party at Sister S. A. Andrews. Had strawberries in every shape, and a lovely time in general.

Sat. 19th The Stewart boys arrived from the north. It looked natural to see Bro Tommy once more. He had been gone three years, presiding over the New Zealand [mission]. The boys were in excelent spirits and had reason to rejoice over the honorable mission they had filled. In the afternoon I went with Tommy to call' on Sister [Margaret] Paxman and Bro [Andrew] Loves family to deliver letters and messages from their loved ones. Spent the evening looking at curials brought from foreign lands and in pleasant converse. Many people called in to see them.

Sun. 20th   They started south for home.

Tues 22"   Reced letter from David dated 16th saying there was no word from Lawyers yet. He had missed the Quarterly Conference on the account of hourly expecting news from them. All well at home.

Thurs. 24th   reced good letter from pa in which he hinted at the possibility of coming to St George with all the family this fall to do a work in the Temple while I was already in Utah. I am still writing in the office but poor baby is so sick and fretful with teething that I dread to leave her to the care of others, and it is too much of a task for Aunty to have the responsibility of looking after her.

Sun 27th   Aunty kept baby and I attended meeting.

28th   Finished what writing there was at the office at present.

Wed June 30th   I attended the Y.L.A. anniversary Ball, which was also an ice-cream and strawberry Festival, in company with Friend Bessie Sparks. It was a very nice affair and I enjoyed it very much. W. A. C. Bryan treated all the widows to every thing nice.

Thurs. morn July 1st   I attended fast meeting. In the p.m. six of the Udall family with a great many others were taken very sick, from ice-cream left from party, which had become poisoned by standing in metal vessels overnight. It was a very narrow escape for them. That day I reced letter from David dated June 23" Josephs 25th birthday. He and Eliza [Udall Tenney] were down to the farm where they lived, eating a birthday dinner. His letter was full of comforting appreciative words, but no word news had been received from the lawyers. He thought they were making an effort to have the case dismissed without his going to Prescott, but he seemed to feel almost discouraged about it. Also a letter three sheets long from dear sister May. She discusses the pros. and cons of their coming to the Temple this fall. It will be a great task to get them all ready for such a long trip, still they will do their best and trust in the Lord to open the way.

Sun. July 4th   Aunty and I took dinner at Sister [Ellen] Lintons. Julia [Linton] kept my baby, and we all went to meeting, after which we had cake & ice-cream. Bro L. Just home from an "Under Ground" trip to Philadelphia.

Mon 5th   They called the Holiday. Base Ball, Dancing etc. but

Aunty and I worked hard all day, picking peas, picking over currants for Jelley.

6th   Washed. Bro [Edward] Pugh & wife from Kanab stopped with us. Said Thomas and Clarence reached Kanab the Sat evening after they left here. On Monday the town gave them a nice reception. Sister Goldsbrough kindly took baby and I for a drive. I received letter from Celia [Hunt Bean] dated the 4th which was such a good one that I sent it to David.

Wednesday, 7th   I sewed for Vina Wright. Old friend Wm Ashworth from Beaver called. His wife Emma came on the Train from the north. We remembered in prayer poor Ammon and brethren in Detroit, the decision in whose cases is to be rendered today. Made white dress for Mrs Lizzie Bryan.

Sun 10th [11th]   Reced. letter from Sister Eliza [Udall Tenney] saying word had just come that the decision had gone against the poor prisoners at Detroit, and Davids case had been put off till another term. Nothing but vexation and disappointment. May the Lord help us all to be patient under these severe trials.

Tues 12th [13th]   Visited Bessie Sparks. Reced letter from David dated the 7th. He said so much bad news had almost disheartened him. The Pros-

[Editor's note: Two excisions have been made to leaf 201–2 in the journal, taking two lines at the top and one line at the bottom, each side. Ida was reporting David's discouraging letter. It is likely David did the cutting at a later date. Two lines of the text are missing here.]

Court would not hear to a dismissal of the case. He said when he thought of his dear ones who had been in exile for so long his heart failed him. Knew this news would be a great trial, but prayed that the God of Heaven and Earth would strengthen us, and also said he would try to come and see us in September, which lightened my heart wonderfully.

Sun. 18th   Went to meeting and took Pauline who behaved well. That afternoon I went up to Davids old friend Tom Wrights and spent the night and next day with them.

22"   sent the letter to Dade.

23rd   I reced letter from Brother Charley telling the sad news of the death of May's sweet little baby, who died very suddenly of cholera infantum. A great amount of sickness in Snowflake.

Sat 24th   Quarterly Conference Convened. Bro Morgan accompanied by Sister M. and their bouncing baby boy, arrived from Salt Lake to attend it.[88] I was delighted to see them. They staid most of the time with us. Sister M. said she came on purpose to see me and compare babies, as she had heard what a fine girl I had. Bro Morgan preached all through Conference with a splendid spirit.

Mon 26th Pioneers Day was celebrated in fine style. Nice procession and good programme carried out. Bro and Sis. M. attended, after which they took dinner with us and then took the 2 oclock train for home. That day I reced long sad letters from May and Annie giving full particulars of the death of Mays baby. Both little neices born and buried before I have the privilege of seeing them, and my dear sisters called to pass through a trial that I shudder to think of.

. . . [Three lines excised.]

July 29th Went to meet Aunt Kit [Conover Hunt] at the Depot. She was taking advantage of the cheap rates on the G.A.R. Excursion to visit her Sister in Oakland, Cal. She staid over till noon the next day, and we had a pleasant visit. Reced letter from pa telling of Bells confinement with a fine 10 lb son on the 23rd. All doing Well. I was rejoiced to hear the good news.

30th We went to Sister Goldsbroughs and had a pleasant visit in company with Sisters McCune, Cowan, Forrest and others.

Sunday August 1st We took supper with Aunt Millard: Reced splendid family letter from Ammon Tenney, in Prison. Part was addressed to Hon F. S. Richards & Jno Stewart. He wished me to copy theirs & send them which I did. He seemed to be feeling splendid in spirits, but the hot weather effected his health.

Monday 2nd Made dress for Aunt Millard. Reced following letter from David.

St Johns, Arizona. July 25th 1886

My Dear and Affectionate Wife:

It makes me heave a sigh when I attempt to write to you. This way of living, that we have endured for over two years would be hard indeed did we not have confidence that our Heavenly Father would overrule these trying times for our good. I received by register my Temple Apron, on Saturday morning last. It is a nice one. What did you say the price is? I have received no letter from you for over two weeks. I truly hope you are both well. Is little Pauline my baby girl, getting over the summer complaint. I pray so. We are all quite well at home. Still the girls are all quite delicate since they had the fever.

. . . [One line excised.]

Mon. Aug. 2nd 1886. Absent a week. The Sheep are at the mountain under the care of Father Arnold and John Extrum. I have bought

*3700 head of Nathan Barth paying him $1.75 for the old ones and
$1.00 for the young ones, in yearly installments of $15.00 with 10%
per annum. It will take five years to pay for them. If John Stewart
takes an interest with me (which I think he will) we will take 6000
head more at the same figure. I think it is a good layout. The wool
alone of the present sheep will pay the installments as they fall due.
The mail is running nicely. xxx The last news I have to tell you in
regard to the Brethren at Detroit is that there is fair prospects of
their receiving Presidential Pardon. Bp [Hiram B.] Clawson of S. L.
City has been to Prescott so he informs me by letter, and through
the influence of the Lord he has been enabled to work upon the
feelings of officials and citizens to that extent that the Governor,
Secretary, Judge [Sumner] Howard, Asst. Dist. Atty. & others wrote
strong letters to Washington as well as signed in connection with
many citizens of Prescott a petition asking the Prest to pardon them
on the grounds they were only guilty of unlawful Cohabitation. A
petition was also sent from here. Bp Clawson feels confident they
will be pardoned. May God grant it is my desire.*

*Your pa writes me of the death of Mays little babe as well as many
deaths that have occurred in Snowflake among children. I feel sorry
for poor May and Alof. Dear, write often: Your letters are a comfort
and strength to me. I anticipate their coming with that joy known
only to a true husband or wife. God bless and comfort you both.
With kisses and love*

Your Devoted Husband   Dade.

Tues & Wed 4th   Visited Tom Wrights and sewed for his wife.
They very kindly invited me to go to the Mountain with them, but
I thought my baby would annoy them too much, being sick & cross
with teething. She is so naughty about biting scratching and fight-
ing other children that I never take a bit of comfort when I am out
with her.

Thursday   fasted and attended meeting.

Mon 9th   Went up the canon for a ride with Ettie and Tillie Teasdale and their parents. The little refugees enjoyed it very much. Got
cherries, hops, and enjoyed the mountain air and a good dinner. That
night Cousin Gib Hunt stayed with us on his return from driving
cattle east. Following week did sewing for Sister Paxman. Wrote long,
long letter to David posted on the 11th. Told him of all my joys and
sorrows of the baby, etc. etc.

Sun 15th   Attended meeting then visited Bessie Sparks with Sister [Mary] Neff. Caught in a shower and had to stay all night.

Mon 16th   Reced long letters from David and Sister May, both dated the 11th. Mays letter told of so much sickness and death it made me heartsick. The death of Sister Adaline Freeman of Snowflake, Sister [James T.] Woods of Woodruff and her daughter Nela Cardon were all recorded, but I was thankful indeed to hear that Bell was doing nicely though she had had a serious time at her confinement. Davids dear good letter was written from Woodruff while there acting as one of a committee of five to settle Sunset United Order difficulties.[89] He was expecting Tommy & John Stewart in a few days, in the interest of the sheep business. Would take Ella and the children to the mountain with them to remain during the shearing time. Cautioned me to be very careful what Pauline ate this hot weather, and also prescribed a cup of hot tea for my own benefit every morning before breakfast. (Asked again if I could not get one of my photoes taken and send him.) Following week we spent at peaches, picking, cutting, drying and bottling, till I was tired of the sight of them.

Sunday 22.   Attended S.S. [Sunday School] and meeting after which Vina and Will Wright and I took supper with Emma Bryan.

Sun 29th   After meeting, Aunty and I went home with Mary and Sister Linton. Mary and I took a ride with Bro and Sister James Jenkins.

Monday   Sister Linton, Aunty and myself visited Ellen Chase but Pauline was too sick for me to enjoy it. Reced letter from Charley Flake. Bell was getting better and sickness abating at Snowflake. They had named their son Marian Lyman after Charleys old chum.

Tues 24th I called on Mrs Bryan at the Telegraph office. While there Bro [Charles] Morris leader of the choir came in. Begged of me to join the Choir baby and all, but it seemed too great a task. I could not consent.

Thursday, Fast Day.   I sewed for Mrs Neff. Cold rainy weather. Reced note from David written 28th of Aug. while down on a hasty trip from the Mountain. Had left Ella and her brothers at the herd and came down to receive Bro B Young, J. N. Smith and others on their way to Savoia. The boys were delighted with the country. Had bought 8000 head of sheep and would keep them out there. He said two or three words of love, then closed by telling me I had better burn the letter. I had looked so anxiously for a letter telling more about his expected visit in September that I must confess I felt rather hurt and slighted at this short hastily written note saying not a word in regard to it. I sat down that evening and penned a short cool answer, asking him if he had wished me to burn it because there was so little in it. Then I cried nearly all night and felt perfectly wretched. It seemed to me the longer our husband and father was away from us the less he cared to see us, and I prayed earnestly that God would give him strength and courage to do his whole duty by all of his family. The morning light dispelled some of my sadness, and I added a few more words to the letter which sounded more cheerful and posted it.

Sun Sep. 5th 1886   Attended meeting. Prest [Canute] Peterson from Ephraim preached a Temple Sermon after which funeral services of Mother Washburn were held.

Mon 6th   Sewed again for Sister Neff. Bessie was there to visit and we had a good time. How sweet it is to associate with dear congenial friends. I feel as though I had known those two all my life. The same with dear friend Mary Linton. We must have been associated together in another sphere.

Tues 7th   David 35th birthday. I dedicated a few lines to him. That day every body felt sad over the news of Jno Q. Cannon's transgression.[90]

Wed 8th   Reced good letter from May and Bro Lewis with a piece of poetry written by Nettie over which I had a hearty laugh. Grandma Pratts genius for poetry seems to be cropping out in the 3rd generation.

Friday 10th   I got some false back teeth put in for chewing purposes. Went to a birthday surprise at Sister Paxmans.

Sat eve.   was a beautiful moonlight night. Mary, Alice Linton, Miss Mollie Gilbert and myself took the guitar and went up to Bro [Tom or Will?] Wrights and had music in the back yard. They were having a Lawn Fete at our neighbor, Lou Hydes, so we all went and watched them dance awhile. It was a lovely sight.

Sun 12th   Reced letters from pa, Annie, and Celia. Visited down to Bessies.

Mon 13th   Reced letter from David written on his birthday, telling of their Conference just over at St Johns. Saying that Ella and the children had just started to Kanab with Ellas brothers. Would be gone till November when they would return with Tommy [Stewart] who expected to locate in St Johns. They had gone into the wool, hide, and pelt business. Would start to the herd that day, from there go to Sholow to buy rams for their herd and from there attend the Quarterly Conference at Snowflake. He was so full of business he did not know whether he would be able to come to Utah before November or not.

O! how angry this last sentence made me. He never said he was sorry to disappoint me, nor made any particular excuse, but talked as though it would be all right with me, whenever it suited his convenience to come. For months past I had wondered if I could possibly endure life till September, when he had led me to believe I would surely see him. Now when the time was nearly up, to have all my fond hopes blighted, without one word of palliation by the one I had thought so true and tender—O, it seemed more than I could bear. I sat down immediately and while I was still in a passion, wrote a most cruel reply, and took good care to send to post before I had time to relent. I told him he need not worry about coming at all on my account. That I expected to go south to meet my father in St George before Nov. and I thought I had fooled around long enough, for some one who did not care a snap for me, etc, etc.   also told him that I had written some lines for his birthday but was too *mad* to send them.

Who but the Evil One could have prompted me to write such words to one I loved dearer than life? I had so many examples, that I saw daily around me, where men professing to be the best of Latter Day Saints would send their plural wives away from them, and seemingly take no more care or trouble about them, than they would mere acquaintances, and the *law* furnished them a cloak under which to neglect and mistreat their families and break the holy covenants they had made. And I was ready to judge my husband by such men. I had no dear wise mother to council me not to write until I had got over being angry. Aunty only gloried in my spunk. Said he deserved a good going over, while Father remonstrated with me, saying that while to us it would appear that David was rather neglectful, we did not know his circumstances, and could not understand his motives. He knew it would all be made right some day. I never admitted to Aunty that I was sorry for what I had done but I felt very unhappy, and laid awake many an hour weeping and praying over the matter.

Afternoon of the 13th Mary [Linton] came for me at request of the Supt and I went to post books in the Coop Store, leaving Julia Linton to Pauline. Wrote two days. Mary told me the boss was much pleased with my work and would like me to continue but baby was so sick with summer complaint I had to stop for awhile.

Friday 17th   R.S. [Relief Society] Conference. Sisters Minerva Snow and M. A. Hyde in attendance. By request I sang "Stick to Your Mother Tom," Alice Paxman to play the accompaniament. O how I enjoyed those meetings. For the first time in my life I heard women testify that the Prophet Joseph had sealed them as plural wives to their husbands. We were all invited to Sister Bryans to supper, after which Nora Pitchforth and I attended Choir Practice.

Saturday   was the Y.L. and Primary Conference. I went to both meetings. We had all who had been to supper at Sister Bryans the night before to supper at Aunties. Enjoyed a good visit with all.

Sun 19th   Sister Snow and Hyde left for home. Aunty, Mary and I spent the evening at Sister Broughs.

Tues. and Wed. following   I wrote in the Store.

Wed night   Aunty was called to Sister Goldsbrough, who was blessed with another fine son. Aunt had agreed to wait on her through confinement, so baby and I were left alone. Mary staid with us at night part of the time.

Friday 24th   Cole's grand circus and Managarie visited Nephi. People came from all parts of the country to see it. I went in company with Mary and Mr [John] Brough. Saw all kinds of wild animals for the first time in my life. It took forty cars to bring them down; I enjoyed it all, but did not go into ecstasies as I should have done when younger at witnessing such a grand display. That evening old friends Henry and Hannah Baker of Richfield, also Mrs. Dibbie Goldsbrough, Mr & Mrs Jos. and Wm. Wright spent the evening with me.

Sat.   I reced good letter from Sister Eliza. She speaks of David boarding with her, and how Olive and Phebe [her daughters] had opened their eyes when they heard him pray for me and the little one. This was the first they knew of the baby. It seemed as though this letter touched my heart and made me realize the extent of the wrong I had done my dear one.

Sun 26th   In the depths of humility I wrote to David asking him if he could ever forgive me for the hasty cruel words I had written. Telling him how I had suffered with remorse but it had taken me all this time to thoroughly repent, and I now felt if there was any thing I could do to atone for that wrong, I would be glad to do it. I also enclosed the birthday lines and sent them off. That night our friend and neighbor Mercy Wright gave a birthday party for her husband Jos. I was invited and went feeling very sad, but there was such a merry musical crowd there, that I had to lay aside my sorrows and join in the merriment. I sang and played a great many times during the evening.

Mon 27th   I received a letter from pa in which he takes me severely to task for writing as I did to David. He had just returned from St Johns. D. had given him my letters to read and had also unburdened his heart to him, and pa was full of sympathy for him in his trials and lonely situation. I felt very guilty indeed but was glad pa had taken D's side instead of mine. I wrote and told him so, at the same time calling his attention to the fact that I had some just and sufficient reasons for writing as I did. It was a very natural thing that I should look at the cases I saw around me daily where men pretending to be good saints would send their plural wives away out of sight and seemingly take no more trouble about them, the Edmunds Law furnishing them a cloak to mistreat and neglect their families, and thereby break the sacred covenants they had made. A very easy matter to look at such examples and judge my own dear husband by them! O what trying gloomy times those were. I prayed to the Lord with all the earnestness of my soul that my husband might have the strength and courage to be true to all parts of his family.

Wed 29   Reced another letter from pa saying that David expected to start for Utah in a few days. Would probably be here by the 2nd of October. So my heart was full of joy and hope once more though the news seemed too good to be true. Posted books at the Store two days. Little Mary Anderson kept baby. Father boarded with me so it was not so lonely. Mary L. [Linton] kept me company nearly every night.

Oct 1st   She, baby and I went to Mr Geo Andersons Gallery to sit for our photographs. That day 3 p.m. Mrs Bryan brot me a telegram reading as follows.

Holbrook. A.T. Oct 1st 1886 To David Udall: Am unavoidably detained. Will not be in Salt Lake as anticipated. Will write.

David K. Udall.

Next day I reced the following letter which explained the telegram.

St Johns   Sept 26th 1886

My Dear Wife:

I leave here tomorrow afternoon to pay you a visit. May the Lord grant that it may be entirely enjoyable. I will go by way of Holbrook to Snowflake. Then back to Holbrook. Leave there on Thursday, and arrive in S. L. City on Sunday evening or Monday morning. Expect to travel with Prest J. N. Smith & Co. I desire you to meet me in S.L.C. on one of the above dates, if nothing happens. Be sure and bring my little Pauline. God bless my little girl: I hope and pray that her health is improved. We will attend Conference, visit your relatives in Springville, remain a few days at Nephi, then go to Richfield by way of Sanpete and return to Nephi, and then I may conclude it best to bring you back home with me. I have been promising myself this contemplated visit and pleasure trip with you for many months and at last thank the Lord the time is drawing near. It is nearly two months since I reced a letter from you only those two cruel notes, I

Ida and daughter Pauline, Nephi, Utah, 1 October 1886.

referred to in my last. *I know you have repented them. If not I will lecture you when I see you as a lover does his sweet-heart. Inclose a letter to me in two envelopes, and address the outside one to Presiding Bishop's Office, S.L.C. Inform me where you will be in the City and you will find that I am a pretty good* hunter. *I desire to be a little quiet and reserved, while in Utah. I am afraid this will give you scarcely time to get ready to come and meet me, but I sincerely hope it will not detain you from coming. You must not let it; and prepare yourself for a long long story when we meet. I wish some one would put a flea in Wm R. May's ear(?) I remember my last visit. You must banish every evil thought of my unfaithfulness to you, for you will discover that I am* true, *and that I appreciate your sacrifices and devotion. I long for and impatiently await the time of meeting.*

I am your affectionate and devoted husband

Dade.

It seems from this, one of his letter have been lost, and being in answer to those two cruel letters the very one above all others I should most dislike to lose. I feel certain too, it contained money, as it [is] not like him to send for me to meet him in Salt Lake without saying how I should pay my expenses when he must know I was without money. One of my letters, the long one I wrote in August has also failed to reach him. What can the reason be? My disappointment is almost lost in the anxiety I feel to know what has happened to detain them. I hope and pray it is nothing serious. Also reced letter from Celia chiding me for not coming or writing.

Mon 4th   Posted books at Store. In the evening attended a pleasant social party at the residence of John Wright. Went in company with Will & Vina [Wright].

Tues.   Received the expected letter, stating that just as they were ready to leave Holbrook telegrams reached he and Bro [Jesse N.] Smith requesting them to remain where they were until further instructions reached them. Sent from Prests Office S. L. City. At 2 oclock Mary Linton went to Salt Lake for a week to visit her relatives. I wrote in the Store the ensuing week.

Wed 6th   Aunties 46th birthday. I sent my little girl over to Mrs Goldsbroughs with a plush satchel for her present.

Sat 9th   The joyful news came over the wires of the pardon of Bro's [Ammon] Tenney, [Peter J.] Christofferson & [Christopher J.] Kempe from the Detroit House of Correction. What joy those few words brought to the heart of every true Saint, and especially would their sorrowing families be made to rejoice. Reced letter that day from David saying he was back to St Johns again and very much disappointed to find the letters that had come to him during his absence which he knew were from me, had been returned to Nephi as he had instructed. He wished them sent back immediately, and I returned them unopened. Poor boy writes as though he was heart sick and discouraged, and my heart aches in reading his letter knowing that I had been the one who had added the last bitter to his cup. He still thinks of coming to see us, and says after the instructions reach him he will telegraph what day he will start.

Sun 10th 1886   Attended meeting. Also helped Sister Pitchforths in washing & changing their poor daughter Alice who was very sick with milk leg. Cold bleak day. My baby was very sick for two days with teething and worms. Will Wright being away from home Vina and I took it turn about sleeping at the others house.

14th   The Bean cousins from Richfield passed on their way to Salt Lake to prove up on their land. They invited me to go home with them and I made preparations to do so.

Tues. Thurs. and Friday I wrote in the Store but suffered very much with cold.

Sat   Quarterly Conference Convened. I attended all the meetings which I knew would be my last in Nephi for some time at least. Apostle H. J. Grant present. Sunday evening Aunty gave me a very pleasant surprise by inviting my dear friends Bess, Lizzie, Mrs. Neff, Leonora and Mary to take supper with us and spend the evening. Bro Grant called on purpose to see my baby he said, and he stayed for supper so we spent a very pleasant evening.

Sat 16th I received the following letter from my dear husband, also a $50.00 P.O. Order.

St Johns   Oct 7th 1886   10 p.m.

My Dear Wife and Child:

It is with exceeding joy and pleasure I have read and reread your truly affectionate letter written August 5th 6th 7th & 10th that came to my hand this evening, after lying months in the Store office. Bro [John T.] Lesueur has several times assured me that he had not reced. the letter, and has looked through his papers several times and did not run across it till today. I felt very cross over it.

After reading your true letter, I feel as though I had been in a trance the last few weeks. It cannot be that you have changed since then. It was in an evil hour you wrote those two last letters. They did not speak your heart. The one now before me contains the sentiments and expressions of my dear Ida. *The letter is old but it sounds natural. (It does not sound manly for me to say that I have shed many tears of joy over this letter but I have.) I thought I had passed through enough during the last few years to make me hard hearted, but of late I find soft and tender spots and I thank God for it. My pen can never tell you what I have endured since I last saw you. You mistake the true man when you think that time and absence weans away the love of husband and father. You mistake me if such are your thoughts of my devotion and love for you and our darling babe. I remember you in my thoughts when you knelt with me, in your maiden purity, before that Holy Alter, when we made those solemn covenants, before you knew many of the trials of life. I remember your self sacrifice in those months and years of daily trial in that mexican town, when your words were full of strength and love that greatly helped me to bear up under many untold trials. I remember the lovely babe in all its purity, as it lay on its mother's lap or by her side, when it could not sense the presence of its father. My Dear it seems to me I would be worse than brute to be untrue, after the experience we have had and beholding the devotion I have seen in you. You have misjudged human nature.*

I am surprised to hear of Father's weight. Can it be that family cares are weighing that heavily upon him? I am truly sorry to hear that the children are not more considerate of him. I did think that for my years of hard labor until I was 23 years of age, in helping Father to make a living for them that they would certainly in their turn be kind and considerate to our father in his old age. These are the evil results of what I have witnessed many many years ago, envy, jealousy, selfishness and giving way to the evil one. What my poor father has endured for the principle of Plural marriage will go a long ways towards exalting him.[91] *God bless him for his integrity to his family and his religion.*

I have wondered often if you were not greatly tried over some things you speak of. You have never mentioned it before, but I have feared it for a long time. If I do not come to Utah this month, I will send you money to go by train and Stage to St George, where you can await the arrival of your father and family and in the mean time work in the Temple. I will make a desperate effort to have my case tried or dismissed at this term of Court. If I gain my liberty or remain under bonds I will come and meet you at St George or Kanab and have a good visit.

Oct 9th   No mail from Box B. S. L. City yet. Instructions are slow coming, but I got a letter from Judge Rush in answer to one I wrote him. It will be expected of me to be in Prescott to attend court the first Monday in Nov. This being the case and the fact of my being detained here waiting for instructions makes it appear out of the question for me to visit my dear ones before going to trial. I have earnestly prayed that it might be otherwise but it seems that fate is against it. I inclose a money order on the Nephi Post Office, drawn in favor of David Udall for $50.00. I desire you to use this money in making you both comfortable, and to bear your expenses to St George, as heretofore indicated. Use it with joy, my dear. O, if I could but do more for your comfort and happiness. I have sent your recommend for the Prest's signature, to be forwarded to Father at Nephi.[92] *I desire you to proceed to St George without delay, where I feel satisfied you will be happier than you have been for some time. 3 p.m. The mail is about ready to start so I will close. God comfort my lonely and loved ones that have been in exile among strangers so long. Why is it thus? May the Lord preserve us in purity till that happy time when our enemies will have no power over us, and God speed the day.*

With love and kisses for both, I am your devoted husband,

Dade.

Mon 18th   Wrote letters to Mary Sanford, Celia and the folks at home sending them my photos. Took supper at dear Grandma Bryan.

Tues 19th   The Salt Lake Tabernacle Choir came on an excursion to Nephi. Gave a concert that night. In the afternoon of that day Aunty and I visited for the first time our neighbors Lou Hyde and wife. Their Aunt Mary, an old friend of my parents, who had just came from Colorado, was there to supper, and we had a pleasant visit. I promised to visit her next day at her daughters Mrs Schofields. That evening Aunty kept Pauline, and Mary [Linton] and I attended the concert. The singing was delightful only that we could not hear the words. The instrumental music, especially that of Young Professor [Ebenezer] Beezly was first class.

Wed.   I washed. Spent the afternoon at Mrs Schofields. Visited with all the Hyde relatives there. Reced long loving letter from David from which I excerpt.

Oct 15th   St Johns. In speaking of my angry letter he writes as follows:

I forgive you with all my heart and soul and love you more than ever. Those hastily written words will go into oblivion never to be remembered against you. I beg of you not to think of them any more, and beleive me to be to you what I profess that is a true loyal husband. My Dear, my heart is full of love and compassion for you. In reading that appealing and pathetic letter, with those devotional and love-inspired lines, that you wrote on my birthday, I felt my heart would burst with joy. My wife I do not feel worthy of such. After these years of trouble it does not seem possible that it is in the human heart to have such love and devotion for me.

My dear Ida, forgive me too for every unkind act, word, thought and apparent neglect. Consider my surroundings and be merciful. I never have doubted you, but in these days when the Evil One has such power, I knew not during the long silence what could be the matter. I have been wretched indeed the past few weeks, but I feel much better now. xxx

I have a testimony that the day of deliverance is near at hand, and that we will have joy in the earth. The Lord will visit with blessings and not with cursings. For the trials and sacrifices you have endured for your husband and your religion I promise you eternal Glory with the sanctified, with husband and children if we will continue faithful. This life is but a span. O why should we give way to its allurements. Be comforted my dear one. All will be well soon, and we will have joy, and a home and the associations of our loved ones. What a happy time it will be! At times it seems to me that I cannot await the day. I ask nothing from you more than you have done. My forgiveness is unaloid. I forgave you without asking as my letter of Sept 21st will show if it is ever found. Go to the temple and rejoice before the Lord and He will hear and answer your prayers. The dead will be made to rejoice. And be assured that you have a husbands blessing.

How oft have I felt I must go to you to soothe your aching heart and speak a few words of cheer, to help to bridge over the months and years of loneliness that you have endured, but it has seemed like I could not. After I left you in May 1885, I expected to go to trial in June, but it was put off till August. Then followed those dreadful months of inprisonment till 17th of Dec 85. After returning home all eyes were upon me, and duty called me to settle the tithings of the Saints of this ward, as no one else understood the T.O. [Tithing Office] business here as I did. This took till about the middle of February 1886. About this time we commenced to put in our crops, and as we have to depend on the farm for a living, I felt as though it must be looked after, fully expecting that I would pay you a visit in May. This was not done for reasons you will understand. June came along and my trial would have taken place but was postponed again. In the latter part of this month Mr [Solomon] Barth made proposals about the sheep business. On the 10th of July I was obliged to receive some 4000 head or abandon the trade. August was agreed upon to receive the remainder, which was lived up to. In the meantime I had to have a close watch of the business until the Stewart boys came out. When they came they were not able to remain long. As soon as could I arranged for my anticipated visit in Sept. These and a thousand other things have tended to keep us apart for these long months.

I do not offer them as sufficient reasons, as I now feel that nothing of a financial nature should have prevented my going. I have suffered in my feelings sufficient as I feel (if you will but forgive me) to pay the debt of neglect. In it all I thought I was doing right. What I have done has not been through fear or favor but according to my best judgement but I now see the danger we have been in, and I regret my erring judgement. I wrote you on Sept 21st in answer to yours of the 6th & 13. I regret very much that you did not get the letter and earnestly hope it will yet come to light. It contains many sentences that are too holy for the ungodly. I also enclosed a $10.00 Bill thinking you might be short of means. This was the first money I had got hold of for a long time. xxx

I received by yesterdays mail your letter that was returned when I was away, dated Sept 26th also the birthday lines and yours of Oct 3rd 5th etc. with our true cousin Celia's letter enclosed, dated Sep. 30th. What these letters and verses brought to me I never can tell. I shed tears like a child my joy was so great. God bless Celia! She is a true friend. I must see her at the first opportunity. Send her a brother's love for me.

I want to tell you what shape my affairs are assuming, that I think will be for our future convenience and comfort. The mail business is proving a success. I can at any time take a run around from St J. to Snowflake free of charge only the R.R. fare from Navajoe to Holbrook which is $2.40. Then we expect to run sheep between Snowflake and the mountain south-east. In looking after these interests, that will call me away from here, I shall have many opportunities of being *with you. My dear, it seems hard to write this way, to think this way, that a man cannot own his families openly and above the board without being in danger of the "Pen." But such is the case and we will make the best of it until the day of deliverance comes which is surely near at hand. I have arranged it all in my mind for our comfort and happiness if the Lord will but bless and I am assured that He will. I feel that the way is gradually opening, and that I will soon be out from under bonds and be a* free man. *If it lies in my power I will have you a comfortable home in the place that will most suit you and our circumstances. (Snowflake)*

With you all we praise the Lord for the brethrens pardon. Don't know just when they will be home, but are preparing a pleasant reception for them. I can appreciate their feelings. Poor men! How they have suffered.

Oct 16th How are you both this afternoon? I am lead to wonder where you are and what you are doing. Received telegram from Ammon this morning. They left Detroit yesterday. Will probably be home next Tuesday. We have reced. advice from our true friends in Utah not to make any display on their return. You will probably not hear from me again for two weeks, until I return from sheepshearing.

My dear I want you to be happy, and have no remorses, and beleive me, that I love you with all my heart. Shun the very appearance of evil; be humble in prayer, and we will come off conquerors. Do not fail to write me often, as I feel much concerned about your journeyings. Take good care of yourself and sweet little dumpsey *Pauline. We will soon make friends when we meet. xxx Ida dear, excuse this long letter and give me the pleasure of a longer one, as part pay for my unworthiness. May the Angels of grace and peace be with you. With a husband's love I subscribe myself. Yours most truly,*

David King Udall.

Thurs 21st We moved in the stoves. I called on Emma Bryan who was confined with another daughter. That evening J. H. and Ann Eliza Brough came and spent the evening. Also Mary, Alice and Sister Linton. Mary was suffering so with toothache she stayed all night and the next day stopped from the store to doctor herself. Friday reced letter from Tank, to say they would be along Sat evening, so Sat I spent in packing and separating my belongings. I could not take more than half as I might have to go by stage from Beaver, so I bought a new trunk, and left all except the clothing I should need during the cold weather. Dear Aunty; she seemed almost sick at the thought of parting with her bonny little Pauline, and my heart ached for her in the lonliness she would feel when her little *racket* was no more heard about the still house. She and dear Grandpa could not do enough for our comfort on the road.

Sat 23rd   A beautiful day. Many friends called in to tell me Good-bye. Mr & Mrs W. A. Wright presented me with a velvet basque and a beautiful Book. Mary L. gave me a jersey and the baby a little white hood, and Aunty gave baby a sweet little velvet bonnet. That night the boys came.

[To St. George: Vain Expectations]

Sun Oct 24th   With a sad heart I parted with my dear friends. Father Udall, Aunty and Mary [Linton] and [I] started for Richfield in company with Tank, Pam & Uncle Jos Hunt. Camped two nights on the road. The baby was good and the boys did all they could to make me comfortable so that I quite enjoyed the trip. Found Celia well and delighted to see us. I rejoiced to be with the dear girl once more.

Oct 27th   Reced letter from pa saying that dear Sister Annie was confined on the 15th with a fine 10½ son. I felt to rejoice in the news.

29th   My Cousin Ida Nagely was taken in labor. Her dear mother and husband both being absent Celia, Ina & I felt quite a responsibility. After sixteen hours of suffering she was delivered of a nice little daughter with which she surprised her husband the next day on his return. Mon night I attended a nice joint session of the Y.M. & L. Assoc. with Tank and Celia. Played the accompaniament, and helped them sing a song. Spent the following week in visiting and calling on dear friends, writing & receiving letters from absent ones. Had good visit with Sister [Anna] Hepler.

Sun 7th   Started for Beaver, on half an hours notice in company with Ed Thurber and Bro Christiansen, who were going to give surety for their Brother Jos Thurbers appearance at Court, he being then confined in the Beaver Jail on a charge of polygamy. They took Pams large covered carriage so I had a very comfortable way to ride, and Bro T. [Thurber] was very kind in making friends with and helping me with Pauline. We faced a cold wind up Clear Creek Canōn, reaching Will Morrison's place at 8 p.m. I bought milk and hired bed.

Nov. 8th   Started at sunrise, reaching Beaver at 5 p.m. Were warmly welcomed by my dear friends Bro Wm & Sister Mary Ashworth, who also entertained over night the brethren who brought me, with their brother whom they immediately rescued from jail. The weather was so freezing cold we could not get out much, so Mary and I visited night and day at home. I went to see the Crosbys who were my only remaining relatives in Beaver, Aunt Louisa and family having removed to some unknown Territory.[93]

PART 5

Pioneering Eastern Arizona, 1887 to 1905

IDA'S JOURNAL ENDS on 8 November 1886 while she was in Beaver en route to join her Hunt family in St. George.[1] Ida's father had decided that while she was still in Utah he would take the opportunity to have his and Lois's older children sealed to them. (John and Lois had not been married in the Mormon rite of marriage until after the older children were born. Children born to a sealed couple were considered sealed to their parents.)

The Hunt family had planned to take Ida back with them to Arizona. The Hunts rented a house in St. George, where May, Annie, Bell, Lewis, John, Ida, and their father temporarily set up housekeeping. They fixed their own meals, took care of temple ordinances, and visited old friends. Annie wrote, "Ida . . . came down from Nephi, and we had such a good visit with her. Pauline was then almost two years old, and as pretty as a picture."[2]

David's polygamy case was dismissed on 3 December 1886, news that brought joy to Ida. Her happiness was short-lived, however, because David sent her a directive to return to Nephi. Explanations for the directive are missing. Did he want to go to Nephi, visit friends, and thank them for their kindnesses to Ida? Did he feel that he and Ida needed time together after these years of separation? What appropriate accommodations could he provide for her and their child, out of harm's way? Ida's crushing disappointment may have destroyed all desire to write in her journal.

Ida was embarrassed to return to Nephi after telling friends so often that she would be going home and then having to stay longer, and she did not return until 21 January 1887. On the way she visited her Aunt Ellen, now remarried to William McGary and living in Milford, and Ellen's daughter Nellie Jones and her family near Beaver.

Ida reported her arrival in Nephi to Nellie Jones: "I find I have made so many dear friends and acquaintances here, that it takes no little amount of time to receive calls from a great number, and try to return a few of them in which way I have put in my time since I got here."[3] Ida then addressed a note to her Aunt Ellen: "This is your birthday but I cannot tell what age you are without taking time to look grandma's journal over and see what year you were born. . . . The prospects are good that I will be here for some time yet, as I cannot travel alone."[4]

To Arizona

Early in March 1887 Ida received word that David was finally coming to get her.[5] He arrived for his daughter's second birthday and must have been surprised at her rejection of him. Jealous of his attention to her mother, she would not let the stranger touch her, crying, "Keep his hands off!"[6]

The three weeks of travel and camping between Nephi and Snowflake was the longest time Ida and David had spent alone during their almost five years of marriage. The journey from Kanab retraced the wedding trip over the "Honeymoon Trail," only this time the two-year-old was their daughter.

David did not take Ida to St. Johns. To do so would have been an affront to his non-Mormon friends who had helped get his pardon. Instead, he took her to Snowflake, where she and Pauline lived in a small house with her sister Annie, Annie's husband, their baby, and her youngest sister Loie. After her long absence in Utah, Ida was happy to be with her Hunt family and many friends. The guitar Ida had acquired in Nephi was used many times. Now not only Annie could play, but Bell had purchased Ida's old one and had learned to play. Orrin, Annie's husband, also played. They spent many pleasant hours teaching each other songs learned during the years of separation. Music became even more important in the Hunt family from this time on.[7]

Loie Hunt West remembered the family gatherings when Ida was living in or visiting Snowflake. Members would play their guitars, sing, give recitations, read their poetry to each other, and laugh about experiences, keeping alive memories of people and places where they had lived. May, who neither sang nor played guitar, entertained them with dialect readings. The family had such good times together that Loie said her friends would beg to be with them and just listen.[8]

New church callings made significant changes in the Udall family.

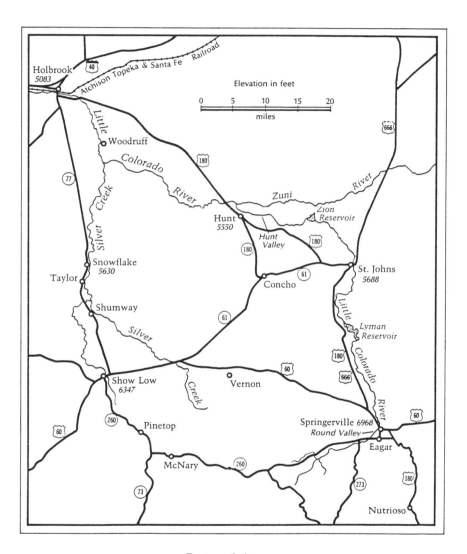

Eastern Arizona.

On 23 July 1887 David K. Udall was set apart as the first president of the newly formed St. Johns Stake, and he called Ella to be the stake Relief Society president.[9] No longer would David make frequent trips to Snowflake, as he had done while bishop to counsel with stake president Jesse N. Smith. Snowflake was in another jurisdiction, and thereafter he went there only on rare occasions. One such occasion was his visit on 25 December, three days before Ida gave birth to his first son, named Grover Cleveland for the president who pardoned David. (According to family stories, David was never present for the birth of Ida's children, though he always gave her a blessing prior to the birth of each child born in Arizona.)

Round Valley

About this time David and his brother Joseph, who were partners in the sheep business, used their herd of sheep as down payment on the purchase of the Milligan farm and gristmill near Eagar, two miles southwest of Springerville in Round Valley and about thirty miles south of St. Johns. Situated at an elevation of about 7,000 feet, it was just north of the mountain forests. The brothers planned to grow grain and run the mill, and they hired Orrin Kartchner, Annie's husband, to cut timber. In March of 1888 Ida and her two children, accompanied by Orrin, Annie, and their son Kenner, moved into an old adobe house on the Mill Farm, as it was called. Ella retained her residence in St. Johns.[10]

That summer Ida's father, his new plural wife, Happylona Sanford, and his daughters Bell and Loie visited Ida and Annie at the farm. David's permit to cut timber ran out while they were there, so Orrin returned to Snowflake with Ida's father to get his team and move his family. On his return he brought Ida's two milk cows and heifer calf. Annie's departure "left Ida very lonely on the big farm."[11]

Monotony was broken for Ida that first summer by two visits from Ella and her children. The women had not seen each other since 10 July 1884, four years earlier. Although Ida knew Ella's daughters Pearl and Erma, she had never seen Luella, nine months younger than Pauline, and David King, Jr., five months younger than Grover, and Ida's and Ella's children had never met. Pearl remembered that first meeting with Pauline: "I saw a shy little puss half hidden in the folds of her mother's skirts and reluctantly peeping now and then at three new sisters who were admiring her auburn curls." Pauline remembered it too, her disbelief as she watched Pearl and Erma sit on their father's lap and comb his hair and beard. Ella assured her daughters that Pauline was their papa's little girl too.[12]

That fall Joseph Udall, his wife Emma Goldsbrough, their daughter Nellie, and sons Joe and Harry came to Round Valley to help with the harvest. Ida had heard much about Joseph and Emma while in Nephi, and they developed a wonderful relationship. In later years when Joseph moved to the farm and Ella's family lived there, the Udall children had many happy times together, working and playing on the farm and in the gristmill. It was a children's paradise.[13]

It was here, however, that problems surfaced between Ella and Ida. It may have been that Ida's long absence in Utah and Snowflake suppressed those problems. When they were living far apart, it was easy to expect Ida to take care of most of her own needs. Once they began sharing a husband and his means on a day-by-day basis, it was hard for each of them. In her conversion to polygamy, Ida had observed the fair treatment Jesse N. Smith gave his wives, and she knew of her father's good treatment of his second wife, Sarah Crosby. Also, during her stay in Utah, Ida had observed many polygamous relationships, including those where younger wives were given equal and sometimes preferential treatment, which impressed her. Now, when Ida asked for a fair share, she found it was impossible for David to give it to her. He would not offend Ella. Nor would he stand contention in his family. His solution was to send Ida back to Snowflake to live at her father's expense.[14]

To Snowflake

In Snowflake, Ida lived with her two children in the house of her father's wife Hap, while Hap visited in Utah for six months. When Hap returned, Ida lived with her for another year. The long stay in Snowflake was a terrible blow to her pride. She wanted to confide her problems to her father, but feared that if she told him how she was treated he would insist on breaking her marriage. She had to decide if she loved David enough to remain married to him and accept her role as he dictated it. She made her decision on the basis of her love for David.[15]

That love had to be sustained through periods of David's apparent indifference. Ida's letters reveal her lonely neglect. From Snowflake she wrote Ella on 14 April 1889, thanking her for Luella's gift to Pauline and mentioning David's long silence:

> I have not heard a word from David since the 25th of March. Did not know that he had succeeded in getting off to Conference, until Bro F. [Frost] told us. I was sorry to hear you were feeling so poorly. Hope this will find you better. . . . I am glad to hear you are safely settled at the farm; Hope you will like living there, and that after getting acclimated

you will all enjoy good health. . . . I have an invitation to take a trip
with some of my folks, up in that part of the country in the course of a
week or two. I am tempted to accept, not only for the benefit it would
be to the children, but I could stop at the Mill on our return, and get
some of the things that I need so badly. Have not heard a word from
David yet. Don't know where he is, nor what his intentions are, but
I am satisfied I shall have to stay here long enough to need what few
summer clothes we have, very much, and this seems to be my only
chance to get them. Of course it is uncertain about going. . . . [16]

While in Snowflake, Ida answered an advertisement in the *Ladies
Home Journal* soliciting agents to sell books on "tokology" or mid-
wifery. She became an agent under the name of Lois Pratt and soon
received samples and had orders for thirteen books, even though the
times were difficult. She felt it was a "good mission to get these books
circulated among the sisters here."[17] Ella was the agent in St. Johns,
where Ida had become acquainted with the book.

Ida's second son was born on 23 August 1889 and was named John
Hunt for her father.[18] Ida remained with her children in Snowflake,
separated from husband for fifteen months, from Christmas of 1888
until March 1890, when she rejoined the family in Round Valley.[19]

Round Valley

Ida "spent a happy summer living with Ella and family" in Round
Valley, but in September Ella returned to St. Johns so the children
could go to school.[20] Ida had a lonely winter in Round Valley, caring
for the children and cooking for carpenters who were working on
the mill. In April 1891 she had a visit from Mary Linton Morgan,
her old friend from Nephi who had married John Morgan, one of the
church's general authorities.[21] This visit was a hint of things to come.
On a Saturday morning in June, Ida wrote Ella in St. Johns about
Mary's visit:

> Mary & I have spent half the time washing & ironing since she
> came. It is so unhandy on acct of water and with the men to cook for
> and babies to tend we don't progress very fast with sewing. . . . I send
> the first eggs I have got ahead, since we moved, and I don't make near
> butter enough for us or I would be glad to send you some. . . . Please
> send the milk can and egg bucket by return mail and I will try and
> fill them. . . . I send the bread-board and match safe, as I feel you need
> them and if there's anything else in the house you need please mention
> it, and I will send first chance as I know I'll only be allowed to take
> such things with me as I can barely get along with, and the things will
> lay unused here. . . . If you can get me a few green tomatoes to put in

with cabbage for a little chow chow for threshing time I would be so glad. Sister Lytle promised me enough cabbage for that. . . . It is uphill business here, with so many hungry eyes taking in every move."[22]

Ida was referring to federal marshals, deputies, and their agents, anxious to help in the prosecution of polygamists. Ida and Mary spent two months in Round Valley before having to flee to Snowflake, where they remained until John Morgan came for Mary in September 1891.[23]

Ida returned to Round Valley that September, and Ella joined her in November. The whole Udall family lived together "under one roof" the winter of 1891–92. That spring, however, things changed drastically for Ida.[24]

In September 1890 President Wilford Woodruff had issued what became known as the Manifesto, which called for the end of plural marriages in the church, and in October the General Conference of the church had sustained it. Much confusion followed as to whether the Manifesto terminated existing plural marriages considered illegal by law or only forbade contracting new polygamous marriages.[25] Direct evidence is lacking, but it is presumed that David decided to conform to what he considered church policy, and he ceased to live with Ida, at least for a time. He moved Ida from the Mill Farm into Eagar, where he checked on her occasionally, and she again supported herself.

Living away from the rest of the Udall family must have been like another exile for Ida, though her loneliness was lessened a little by work and church. While living in Eagar, Ida kept the Co-op Store. She was near church members and entered into activities she had been too busy for while on the farm. She taught Sunday school, sang in the choir, and served as a counselor in the Relief Society.[26]

A reverse change for Ida came when David took both wives and their children to the four-stake conference at Pinetop in the White Mountains in July 1892. There Joseph F. Smith and other leaders of the church met with the Saints, advocated new political arrangements, gave religious instruction, and performed marriages. Ida's Hunt family was there. Her father had transported the Salt Lake visitors from the railroad at Holbrook to Pinetop, and his wife Hap and daughter Loie cooked meals for them. Each night a dance was held on a pavilion built in the center of the camp. A highlight was meeting old friends and renewing spiritual activity. More important, church policy on the continuation of existing plural families was clarified to David. Shortly thereafter, he began living with Ida again, though she did not move back to the Mill Farm until the following spring.[27]

To Snowflake

In November 1892 Ida and her sister Loie, who was living with her, went to Snowflake for a family reunion. Ida's Aunt Jane Stoddard had brought her aged mother, Celia Hunt, from San Bernardino to live with the Hunts. May wrote that their grandmother looked about the same after eight years' absence, except for being a "little more wrinkled."[28]

While Ida was in Snowflake, her family suffered a great loss. On 8 December 1892 Charley Flake, Bell's husband, was shot and killed by a desperado he was arresting. Bell was left a widow at age twenty-eight and was expecting her fourth child. Ida remained that winter in Snowflake with Bell, helping with the birth of the son, Charley.[29]

Back to Round Valley

Returning to Round Valley the first of March 1893, Ida found Ella, David, and their children preparing for a trip to Salt Lake City to attend the dedication of the Salt Lake Temple and the General Conference. A dressmaker was sewing new clothes for Ella's family because Ella was going to stay in Kanab for six months after the conference was over. David led the group to Salt Lake and then returned alone to Arizona.[30]

For Ida it should have been a happy time, having her husband to herself; however, she was expecting a baby in June and had a difficult pregnancy. Her sister Nettie came to help before Jesse's birth on 24 June 1893 and remained most of the summer.[31] In May of 1895 Nettie came again to help with the birth of Gilbert Douglas, born on the thirteenth. While helping Ida, Nettie became romantically attracted to Joseph Rencher of Eagar and married him, becoming a member of the Eagar Ward on New Year's Day 1899. Ida had waited a long time to have a sister live nearby, and she enjoyed her companionship. They often combined their talents to put on programs for meetings of the Relief Society and the Young Ladies Mutual Improvement Association.[32]

When Ida first moved to the farm, she had found herself isolated from old friends, her family, and the church. It was years before she went to St. Johns, even on a visit. Of the fourteen years of David's enterprise in Round Valley, Ida spent several in Snowflake at her husband's request, or to help her Hunt family, or with Mary Linton Morgan, who was eluding federal marshals. Even in Round Valley Ida was forced to move quite often, which did not help matters.

Pauline wrote, "I should have become accustomed to this life of helping my mother move into another place to make a home at least every year. . . ."[33] During one move, Ida wrote her sister Nettie, "O how I wish you were here to move over there with me. It will be so lonesome I know I shall nearly die, but oh I long for more 'room to dwell.' "[34]

One happy experience her daughter Pauline remembered was a Fourth of July celebration in Nutrioso. David K. Udall gave the public oration of the day, and Ida sang "The Star Spangled Banner." It may have been one of only a few times that Ida was honored with her husband. Her sister May wrote that Ida did not take the Udall name for many years, because she was keeping a low profile.[35]

On 20 July 1897 Ida's last child, Don Taylor, was born. Ida's health was not good. Pauline wrote of her mother's life in Round Valley:

> The high altitude and cold winters told dreadfully on her health. She had never been too robust, and a heart affliction, due to bad teeth, preyed on her as she bore her six children. Her husband was away from home a great deal with his church and civic duties, which left the rearing and caring of the children mostly to her.
>
> She half-soled their shoes, barbered their hair, and made every article of clothing they wore until they were nearly grown. She made butter and cheese for sale, raised chickens and a garden each year, while at the same time cooking for hired men. It was a most uncommon thing to ever eat a meal to themselves as a family. Her husband ran a large farm, a gristmill, had freighting outfits, so as a result, there were many hired men around.
>
> She was a wonderful mother, whose government was that of love and firmness. She envisioned a goal for each child early in life and inspired each of them with confidence to attain it. Notwithstanding her frail body, the multiplicity of her everyday duties, she always found time for the refinement of life. There were petunias blooming in the window or mignonettes in the yard. On the wall hung pictures, the frames of which she had fashioned from pine cones. The Mexican house often ran tubs of water through its leaky roof, yet she never gave up the yearly going over its ceilings and walls herself with the whitewash brush. The rag carpet on the floor had taken hours of her time to make, but brought comfort and cheer to her home.
>
> On the Sabbath day, she was often seen in the cart with its shafts, drawn by one horse, accompanied by her children and their cousins on the way to the school house, one mile distant, or perhaps walking another time. There, a Sunday School class would be taught by her or a choir practice held. So her life ran on in this little mountain home, for fourteen years, scattering sunshine and cheer with her kindly words and beautiful singing voice. How common it was to see the hired men

Ida Hunt Udall and her family, Eagar, Arizona, 1898. *Standing:* John H., Pauline, Grover, and Jesse; *seated:* Gilbert, Ida, and Don.

and boys, rough and uncouth as most of them were, gather around the coal oil lamp, after the evening meal, and beg "Aunt Ida," as everyone called her, to play the guitar and sing for them. She would, provided this one or that would perform in turn. How she loved these big hearted mountain people and endeared herself to them.[36]

Ida's family, appreciative of her difficult life, was very supportive. In March 1898, while David was in St. Johns for conference or doing business as usual, Ida's brothers, sisters, and their spouses, knowing how lonely she would be on her birthday, got together and wrote her a long poem naming all of the men, young and old, who had been attentive to her or had proposed marriage. Ida enjoyed the poem and thought her family clever to put her romances together. She shared it with David, but he was not amused. He was likely insulted and felt guilty about not providing better for her. The last lines could have hurt:

> To your husband we wish to say
> He certainly won a prize,
> When he succeeded in winning you
> Who was coveted by so many eyes.[37]

Necessities were hard to come by and the fulfillment of dreams nearly impossible. Ida nurtured a dream for an organ and a sewing machine. Having taken organ lessons in Beaver and having a daughter who showed musical ability, Ida wanted an organ. David had bought one for Ella, and Joseph and Emma Udall had one. Ida, however, would have to pay for it herself. Fortunately, she was able to earn a little savings by substitute teaching. She finally got her own organ when a family moved away and offered theirs to her, for the exact amount of her savings. A sewing machine was another dream she had, knowing how much time it would save her in making her children's clothes. To earn the money for that, Ida sold subscriptions to *Woman's Home Companion* to her friends. She also made butter and cheese from the milk her own cows produced and sold it to the Becker's store. With these earnings she bought a "Superior" sewing machine in 1897. Ida altered Loie's and Nettie's dresses to make nice dresses for Pauline, but when Pauline began to date, Ida purchased some beautiful woolen material from the sale of butter and made her a lovely new dress. Ida never had a nice dress in those years, but the calico dresses she made for herself always had style.[38]

The time Ida spent in Snowflake over the years was often a welcome relief from her hard life in Round Valley. She and her brothers and sisters made their own entertainment and used any occasion for a get-together and good time—birthdays, anniversaries, arrivals, departures, conferences. As May put it, "We always have a good time when Ida is here."[39]

At one stake conference, George Goddard was present and preached on the Word of Wisdom. He sang his famous song telling the Saints to

> Take away the coffee,
> Tobacco and the tea;
> Cool water is the drink for me.

He had a wonderful voice and after stirring up the people, he got them to take the pledge not to drink coffee, tea, and liquor or use tobacco. Pauline reported that her mother stood and took the pledge, and from then on she lived by it. Earlier when her mother was not well, she would have a cup of something hot. When asked what it was she would say, "Oh, it is just a little frightened water." Thereafter there was no more tea, and no longer was there a bottle of brandy in her trunk for making a hot toddy when someone was chilled and exhausted.[40]

Another time, when Ida went to Snowflake to help care for her Grandmother Hunt, who had suffered a stroke, she attended a reform class on health for the women of the town, given by Ruth Hatch who had been called by the General Board of the Relief Society to teach practical nursing to the sisters. Ida took stenographic notes on the lectures, and after returning to Round Valley, she taught much of the material of those lectures to the sisters of the area. Minutes tell of her giving lectures on, for example, the danger of wearing corsets, especially while pregnant, and better ways of caring for the sick.[41]

When there were special events in Snowflake, Ida and her sister Nettie would often make the trip, join in the festivities, and visit with Hunt family members, all of which gave Hunt relatives a strong incentive to visit Ida and Nettie in Eagar. Annie wrote of the time she and Bell and their families visited, and Ida had a birthday party for one of the girls. Birthdays of the Udall children were always special events. These were times when Ida taught social skills to the children. Pauline remembered learning to dance at birthday parties. Pearl's fifteenth birthday was one all of the children remembered. Ida had each child contribute savings and ordered a ring through a catalog. She made a lovely pink dress for Pearl, and Ella prepared a delicious breakfast and served it on her Haviland china, used only for special occasions.[42] The years the two families lived together in Round Valley at the Mill Farm were, according to Pearl, "happy years of childhood to us, notwithstanding the toil and disappointments of our parents."[43] For the children of David Udall and his brother Joseph, the Mill Farm was "a land of enchantment." "The big goose, the old mother pig and her litter in the pasture on the other side of the foot-bridge across the mill race, the penstock, the creek and pasture . . . a child's paradise . . . our heaven on earth, our plantation. . . ." All created affectionate memories held fresh and dear in old age.[44]

For eight months in 1898 David K. Udall kept a journal, which provides a more detailed account of life on the farm.[45] "Mill Farm," he wrote, "This is where we live, and would be our home, if our debts were paid." He related the long hours devoted to plowing, planting, and watering the fields and repairing fences. On 17 May he noted he planted the last of the wheat, a total of ninety acres. On 10 June he wrote, "I have been sowing & watering Oats. I am working 4 men and 2 of my boys and 5 teams every day." Harvesting began sometime in September, close to the date of the first killing frost. Work on the farm was never-ending, and the debts on the farm were mounting.

Family finances were helped by his taking a U.S. mail contract. On 30 June he wrote, "Today ends my 4 years Mail Contract from Holbrook to Springerville. . . ." But the next day he reported, "Today I start on new Mail Contract from Holbrook to Springerville 100 miles for $2850.00 per year & from Springerville to Luna Valley 40 miles for $450 per year." From these sums he had to pay the drivers and buy horses, carriages, and feed. It, too, was a marginal operation.

At the same time the Udalls were farming and carrying the mail, the mill had to be moved, set up, put into operation again. There also were problems at home: the death of Ella's baby girl, Rebecca, and Ella's poor health. Ida had suffered with Ella two years earlier when Ella's fourteen month old son Paul died. When Rebecca became ill at six months, Ida told Pauline that it would be less painful to give up her own baby than to watch Ella suffer through the loss of another child. Rebecca died on 6 April. One month later David wrote, "My wife Ella is feeling very low spirited, indeed, it makes my heart ache to see her in such trouble, and it seems that I cannot say a thing to comfort her." No doubt Ella's problems were increased due to her poor health. On 20 July David wrote, "Yesterday & today my wife Ella had 27 teeth pulled. She has had very bad gums for many years. . . . I hope we will soon get her a new set." By August, Ella was still not feeling well enough to attend the conference in St. Johns. Instead, Ida, baby Don, and Pauline were there for the meetings, making it only the second time Ida had attended a stake conference in St. Johns since her return from Utah. Of the conference David wrote, "The

Lord be praised for the good feeling and prospering in the land. The St.s are being blessed & are prospering in the land. I don't call to mind an unpleasantness during the conference." However, two days later, on 24 August, he confided, "What a source of worry & anxiety it is to be in debt. At times I feel that my cares are more than I can carry. Our Father in Heaven can deliver us, and may it please him to do so is my desire & prayer."

That fall David borrowed money to send Pearl to Provo, Utah, to attend Brigham Young Academy. Her two-year absence was hard on all of the family, especially Ella; however, Pearl's experience led to hopes that all the children would be able to go to Utah for schooling. Ida encouraged her daughter Pauline to dream of following Pearl's example, but events would later conspire to thwart Pauline's dreams.

When the Udall brothers first bought the Mill Farm, it produced good crops, which enabled them to pay the principal and interest due on the mortgage, but successive years of drought resulted in their paying little more than the interest. With David's encouragement, Joseph withdrew from the partnership in 1898. In the fall of 1899 the holder foreclosed on the mortgage. Ida and her children moved to a small house in Eagar. Through the kindness of friends, arrangements were made to lease the mill and part of the farm for another year. In the spring of 1900, Ida returned to the Mill Farm, and Ella and her children moved to St. Johns to look after the mail and express business there.[46]

To St. Johns

In time Ida and her children also moved to St. Johns, living in a rented house. The first thing Ida did after arriving was to send her son Grover with their best milk cow to put in Ella's corral. David and Ella had lost everything; Ida, not considered a legal wife, had been able to keep her cattle.[47]

One bright spot in the dreary Udall picture came in September of 1901, when Ida's cousin Nellie Jones came from California to visit relatives in Snowflake. Ida spent a month with her family, entertaining Nellie. The sisters, Ida, May, Annie, and Bell, went camping in the Petrified Forest with their brothers, Lewis and John, before visiting friends in Joseph City, where they were entertained by the Tanners and Bushmans. One Sunday, Ida, May, Lewis, and John were the speakers in church. The following morning Nellie took the train for California. At Holbrook Ida parted with her sisters and brothers, taking the buckboard home.[48]

Although they were poor, Ida enjoyed her winter in St. Johns, being with old friends. She attended church and socials in her gingham dress, covered by her paisley shawl. That winter she also made costumes for an operetta the St. Johns Academy presented, and she and her daughter sang in the chorus.[49]

Part of the solution to the depressed financial fortunes of the Udalls came when Ida applied for and settled on a homestead in her own name in Greer Valley (later called Hunt Valley), ten miles north of Concho and twenty miles downstream from St. Johns on the Little Colorado River. By road, via Concho, it was about twenty-five miles from St. Johns. This homestead gave her a place to live and provided a way station for the carriers of the mail in the mail-contracting business David had engaged in, off and on since 1881, between Holbrook, St. Johns, and Round Valley.[50]

The Ranch at Hunt

Ida's homestead, named Hunt, was located in a flat, open valley covered with sagebrush and groves of cedar trees. The only resident was Thomas L. Greer, who had arrived in 1879 (giving the name Greer Valley to the place). It was a windswept expanse, vast and lonely, but the soil was fertile, and with water good gardens and crops could be grown. New wells produced only brackish water for household use. Good drinking water had to be hauled from Greer Springs. For irrigation water, David and his sons looked to the completion of their reservoir, ten miles upstream on the Little Colorado River. With prospects of plenty of water, other families joined the Udalls. By 1903 Elijah Freeman and Willard Farr of St. Johns had taken out homesteads. Still later Ida's father, John Hunt, and some of his children acquired land. Freeman built a lumber house, and Farr set up two large tents for his second wife, Minnie Romney Farr, and her children. These families, along with the Greer and Udall families, became the nucleus for a school district that Ida petitioned for and obtained and in which her daughter later taught.[51]

Ida's life on her homestead, which began in the spring of 1902, was one of monotonous hard work, long hours, and isolation from all church activities and all but a handful of scattered families. The years of hard work, medical neglect, and weariness began taking their toll on her health.

It was with enthusiasm, however, that Ida set out to build a new home. David and Ida's sons worked hard to build their reservoir (called Zion's Lake). She and her two youngest sons lived in a tent until a small house could be built, consisting of a large kitchen and living room, with a small bedroom on each side. Later a large sleeping room was built on the second floor, where all the boys slept.[52]

Another change for the Udall family came in May 1903, after Matthias F. Cowley visited the Snowflake and St. Johns stakes. Apostles Cowley and John W. Taylor were privately advocating the continuation of polygamy. On the trip between towns, Cowley told Ida and David of the circumstances of Mary Linton Morgan, Ida's old friend from Nephi who had visited her in Round Valley in the spring of 1891. Mary had been married to John Morgan, who along with his first wife had befriended Ida while she was in Utah. John Morgan had spent his life in church service and had not done well financially. He had died 14 August 1894, leaving Mary with three young sons and no savings. Mary had been providing for her children by working as a domestic, which left her three boys without supervision. Cowley proposed that David take Mary and the boys into his family. They could live at Hunt and learn to work along with the Udall boys.

Ida was willing and anxious for her dear friend Mary's companionship, but before anything could be done, Ella had to give her consent. She was not interested. Others must have put pressure on David, however, for he made the trip to Utah, and by the Christmas holidays of 1903 Mary and her sons—Linton, twelve; Harold, eleven; and Matthias, nine—had come to make their home at Hunt.[53]

Even after Mary came and with the help of Pauline, the work at the homestead was never-ending.[54] Cash income came from David's mail contracts but at a cost. Carts and later army buckboards carried mail between Holbrook, St. Johns, and Eagar, and Hunt provided a way station, where mail drivers could spend the night, eat, feed their animals, and prepare for the next day's trip. Their farm raised the hay and grain for the teams. Ida's home thus became a post office and a place for travelers to spend the night while en route to and from Holbrook. Ida never knew from one day to the next how many guests she would be accommodating and whether they would pay for lodging or be taken care of as friends. The house was expanded to care for them.

Ida always had a garden and kept chickens for eggs and meat. She raised pigs, had cows for milk, and made butter and cheese. Even before Ida was married, she had cattle in the church herd at Snowflake. Her father, seeing her difficult situation at Hunt, now began giving her a heifer each birthday as a means of helping her become more independent. He did the same for Pauline after she began teaching school at Hunt. In the winter the pigs and a steer were killed to provide meat for the two families.

Ida felt her lonely situation at Hunt, especially the first winter, when her daughter was in St. Johns attending the St. Johns Academy and living weekdays with Ella. Only on weekends did Pauline get home to help her mother, going down on the mail cart on Fridays and returning for Monday's classes. When Pauline was teaching school at Hunt during the winters of 1903–4 and 1904–5 (she taught the Farr and Greer children, her brothers John H., Jesse, Gilbert, and Don, and the Morgan boys), things were easier for the family, especially since she gave her earnings to build up the ranch. Much of it was spent on barbed wire fencing that had to be replaced after each flood. The Udalls were in a new situation at Hunt. The drought that had brought failure to the big farm in Round Valley was now broken, and the area was instead inundated with water. As President Joseph F. Smith had promised the Saints in 1900, when he dedicated the St. Johns Academy, "the rains would come and the land would become a place for ducks."[55]

Pearl

Ida's life was not the only one that had taken some unexpected turns. Tragedy had struck Pearl on 27 March 1900, when Gus Gibbons and Frank LeSueur of St. Johns were shot and killed by desperados that the young men had been deputized to arrest. Gus, an old family friend, was married to a young woman from Snowflake and only recently had returned from a mission. Frank was Pearl's sweetheart, and they would likely have married had he lived. Pearl was deeply affected, but she continued teaching school, until secret decisions led to a changed life for her, one that put her in close sympathy with Ida's experiences.

In September 1903 Apostle Rudger Clawson visited the St. Johns conference. While staying at the Udall home, he became interested in Pearl and asked David K. Udall for her hand in marriage as a plural wife.[56] The Udall and Clawson connection went back to Rudger's father, Hiram B. Clawson, who had tried to assist David in his polygamy and perjury trials and imprisonment. The apostle also may have attempted to help David's financial situation in 1900. Family history has it that David did not try to influence his daughter; rather, he left it to her to choose. She had to think it over. She later related that en route from St. Johns to Thatcher to teach school, she pondered and prayed about the proposal the entire trip. Apostle Clawson met her there on one of his visits that fall. During that year, Pearl decided to accept, and in the spring of 1904, when school was out, she went to Salt Lake City. There in the Salt Lake Temple on 9 May, she received her endowments, a step usually preparatory to marriage.[57]

At the April General Conference, President Joseph F. Smith had presented, and the church had voted to accept, what became referred to as the Second Manifesto, which absolutely prohibited further plural marriages on pain of excommunication. Notwithstanding this official pronouncement, the couple went ahead with marriage plans. According to Pearl's sister Louella, the marriage was performed aboard a ship off the Pacific Coast, outside the international waters boundary (evidencing the view that the Manifesto applied only to the United States). Clawson's biographers, however, state that his calendar did not allow that, but that the marriage took place in Grand Junction, Colorado, on 3 August 1904 and was performed by Apostle Matthias F. Cowley.[58]

Pearl's situation was most difficult. Because the marriage was neither legal in the eyes of the state nor sanctioned by the church—in fact, expressly prohibited—all circumstances of the marriage became shrouded in secrecy and silence. Clawson could not take her into his household or acknowledge the marriage. This would jeopardize his position and membership in the church as well as hers. She could not openly associate with Clawson or his family. Pearl would have to continue her life as a single person, rather difficult for an attractive woman her age. St. Johns was her home base, but the school year of 1904–5 she taught in Eagar. Anticipating a trip to Salt Lake City at Rudger Clawson's invitation, Pearl pondered her situation and wrote her mother on 1 February 1905, "And now mama use your ingenuity and see if you can think why I am going and why I stay when gone."[59] In fact, it was Pauline and Ida who, perhaps inadvertently, provided the solution.

Ida and Pearl: A Trip to Utah

Pauline could see the effect of the years of hard work on her mother's health and was determined to use some of her savings to send her mother to Utah for a visit with Ida's sister Lois and old friends, in hopes the change would restore her health. Accompanying Ida to Salt Lake City gave Pearl the cover she needed. There, Pearl would live with "tried and true friends," where Clawson could see her when he was in town.[60] She would also be visiting relatives and other friends.

Ida and Pearl left Holbrook by train for Salt Lake City by way of Pueblo, Colorado, following the route Ida had taken when she went

Ida Hunt Udall, Nephi, Utah, July 1905.

underground in 1884. This time it was Pearl who was going underground to be near her husband. Much of what Pearl was to go through Ida had experienced in her own way. The two grew even closer.

In Salt Lake City, Ida stayed with her sister Lois Hunt West, who was expecting a baby, and Pearl moved into the home of a couple named Thorup. Letters written home are rich in details concerning visits with relatives and friends and attendance at meetings, socials, and parties.[61] Ida and Pearl took excursions to Provo, Springville, and Nephi. Ida visited friends in Manti, Richfield, and Beaver.

Ida spent two days in June with Pearl in Salt Lake City. On Sunday evening they went to a meeting in the Second Ward, where they heard "a very fine discourse on the subject of 'Self-sacrifice' " by Professor Willard Done.[62] They were together again in August. On 11 August Pearl wrote her mother:

> . . . Aunt Ida . . . stayed with me last night, took an early walk to the park and had a lovely visit with A [Rudger Clawson] from five to nearly six o'clock. . . . A and I decided perhaps it will be better for me to go home and spend the winter with you, providing there is some work for me to do and that you and papa approve of the step. . . . why should I stay housed up here on expense seeing A only for a few hours once a week or longer time between visits and nearly dying with the lonesomes the rest of the time. Why not go home and teach school and be free and enjoy my folks? . . . if I felt like going home he had decided it would be best to go. . . . A is going off for a month's trip the last of August, and I have wondered how I would pass that long month. . . .[63]

During Ida's first visit to Julia and Philo Farnsworth's home one Sunday, she gave them an account of the Udall's hopes, work, and losses since going to Arizona. Sharing the experience with Pauline, she wrote, "He, like everyone that I have talked with since coming here thinks papa [David] should be called to a better country, but if we only had our prospect for water back that country is good enough for me. I saw far worse looking country between Provo and here. Alkali-saltgrass & bad lands minus the beautiful cedars."[64]

That evening after dinner they went to the Eighteenth Ward meeting. "It is the 'blue blood' ward of the city, Aunt Loie says, and Julia was so anxious for me to see everything." After hearing Arthur Shepherd play the organ and a choir of trained voices sing, they listened to talks. "Bro. Knight preached a sermon that Julia said was for my special benefit on the saints who would stay with their missions—come life or death. None others would get into the celestial kingdom." The next morning, after spending the night with the Farnsworths, they attended a ceremony at the cemetery where the Wells monument was unveiled. Ida later wrote her daughter, "Pauline, I want you to come back here and graduate at one school or the other. With a diploma you would be fixed for life. Don't count on anything else."[65]

In July Ida wrote of her social experiences:

> I find my *friends* are *legion*. Now does not that fulfill Bro. Woodruff's promise to me and papa's [David's] blessing time & again, that the Lord would surely *remember* me and bless me? Sr. Winder [Temple matron] told me yesterday in the Temple, she never saw a woman with so many *friends*. . . . Sr. [Emma S.] Woodruff—[Clara?] Cannon—[Maria] Winder—[Annie T.] Hyde—Aunt Mary Musser, & Susan Smith among the regular workers and yesterday thru request of Uncle Lawrence my name was called off and I was let out before any one else. He wished me to go to the Lake with their family party, which Aunt Loie and the little girls and I did. We enjoyed it immensely. . . . We went at four & returned at 8. . . . We had a nice lunch together after our swim in the *briny deep*. O it is the loveliest treat I have enjoyed yet.[66]

She also described another pleasant experience:

> On Tues afternoon I was the guest of Sister Winder out to Saltair which means she pays my way out & back, hires my bath suit and furnishes my dinner. . . . While promenading the pavilion at Saltair Sister Winder introduced me to Apostle Geo. A. Smith . . . he took off his hat and says, "Sister Udall I feel honored to meet you. I heard some of the prettiest things said about you the other day that I have heard for many a day." Well I was so abashed that Sr Winder answered for me, and told him it was *true* whatever he had heard. The next morning while walking to the Temple, Prest Smith's coachman came along and asked us to ride so I have had a ride in the Prest carriage. I tell you these things daughter to comfort you and Aunt Mary in your lonely hard life at the ranche. To show that people can live that way for years and still be remembered & honored.[67]

In October Ida was joined by her husband, her father, his wife Sarah Crosby, and her brother Lewis for the General Conference in Salt Lake City. One evening a party was held at Lois's home honoring her father. Many friends from earlier years attended, including President C. D. White of Beaver, Celia Hunt Bean of Richfield, Bishop John Bushman and James M. Flake from Arizona, and Richard S. Horne of Salt Lake City. There were songs, music, and speeches honoring John Hunt. After the conference Ida, Pearl, and David K. returned to Arizona. Pearl joined her mother, sister Erma, and brother Levi in Holbrook, where they were keeping a hotel. Ida returned to Hunt to resume her labors.[68]

The End of Indictments

While Ida was still in Utah, David had been arrested and indicted for polygamy. This was the work of U.S. Senator Fred T. Dubois, famous Idaho Mormon-hater, who had come to Arizona and brought pressures on Arizona officials to prosecute polygamists in northern Arizona. "Our local officials did not care to bother with it but were forced to do so," Joseph Fish remarked. A vast number of witnesses were obtained, and ten men were arrested, including David K. Udall. The men were taken to St. Johns, where they were required to give bonds. Attorneys were employed, at $150 a case, and it was decided that the men would plead guilty; the accused would not have to attend court. On 8 December 1905 their cases came up, and because of the "masterly way" the attorneys handled the cases and the clemency of Judge Robert E. Sloan, each was fined only $100.[69]

David's role in this episode is not altogether clear. He did "expect to plead guilty to the indictment." Apparently, he borrowed the money for his bond from a schoolteacher named Hinckley and accepted the "offer" of daughters Pauline and Luella to pay the note, for on 31 October he wrote Pauline as he was about to leave for Prescott, "I received a letter from Bro. Hinckley the other day. My note is due tomorrow Nov 1st for $200.00 and interest, in favor of him should be met. Could you not send the $100 as your part of what you girls kindly offered to pay, so that I will receive it on my arrival in Holbrook, that I may forward that Amt to Bro H. Luella will commence to teach school here next Monday Nov. 6th. As soon as possible she will pay the other $100.00. I will pay the interest. . . ."[70]

It would appear David was not able to provide fully for his family, nor did the future offer much hope for betterment. Ida continued her sacrifices, and Pauline was increasingly called on to give her mother more help, especially as Ida's health declined.

PART 6

The Ranch at Hunt and Ida's Last Years, 1905 to 1915

THERE WAS LITTLE improvement in Ida's situation at the ranch and small prospects of significant change. In fact, things worsened, and life on the ranch began to take a heavy toll on her health.

When Ida returned to the ranch from Utah after her six months vacation from the daily grind, she found herself in a new situation. Pauline, always her helper and confidante, was teaching school in Snowflake, saving money toward the long-dreamed-of chance to attend college in Utah. Ida faced the long winter without her daughter and with the prospect of a separation the following year when Pauline was to go to school in Utah. John H. and Grover drove mail. Ida found Aunt Mary "worn out."[1]

The winter of 1905–6 Ida had less help and more work than ever. Luella reluctantly agreed to teach the school at Hunt beginning in November, but she did not stay to help during the weekends.[2] Instead, she went to St. Johns on the mail cart and stayed with friends. In one of the winter's fierce storms she started off to ride horseback to St. Johns with her brother Dave rather than stay at Hunt.[3] That spring she confessed to Pauline that she had enjoyed herself "with the boys and mamas. They have surely been good to me and I'm afraid I havent done my part tho, and I know I've tried them all at times. . . . The boys have all been good as could be all winter and I believe they had done pretty well in school."[4] Pauline was no doubt happy to hear about the boys, but Luella's behavior could hardly have pleased her.

While teaching at Hunt, Luella became aware of the small herd of cattle Ida and Pauline were accumulating. When she reported this to her family, feelings were aroused, and David, to minimize contention in the family, went to Hunt and told Ida that the cattle would have to be turned in to the Udall family. Ida and Pauline accepted the decision and complied.[5]

In addition to Ida's other obligations, she helped in the business end of affairs. Her writing ability and her business sense were not lost on David, who had her write his correspondence, both church and business. He used Pauline as a scribe when she was teaching at Hunt, but Ida continued to manage the finances of the ranch. She wrote business letters seeking the best prices on farm implements and seeds and kept all the accounts for her enterprise. She used the money earned from overnight travelers to provide for her family's needs, and when there was extra, she purchased furnishings for the ranch house. Her meticulousness is reflected in a letter to Pauline, asking her to make a purchase for the house: "Take time to purchase us a good cupboard in Holbrook and get some freighter to bring it up. Go to every store in town and see where the best washers and cupboards, chairs, etc. are."[6]

Winter Storms, 1905–6

The winter of 1905–6, long remembered for the terrible snow-storms, exacerbated the continual strain Ida felt from having the boys out in the snow, rain, and floods and increased her work load. She often stayed up late at night waiting for them to return so she could feed them, even though she had to be up by 4 A.M. to get breakfast for the driver and to arouse a son to water and feed the horses before harnessing them to the mail cart or buckboard.

Ida's letters give graphic pictures of the work load, the loss of sleep, and the strain she was under. In late October 1905 she wrote Pauline that "the boys and I have made a cheese, churned and chopped three gals of chow today. Yesterday we did the biggest two weeks wash so you see your mother can work yet, but my fat will soon go." A few days later she noted, "I have made four [cheeses] since Aunt Mary went to St. Johns. She will be home tonight I guess."[7]

On 23 November 1905 she told Pauline, "We have had a snow storm. The first snow in November for 10 years. . . . We have had the same old feelings over the mail boys, for David had to wait at 7 spring for the flood to go down, and poor H. is out tonight. There is no sound of him at 10 Oclock and wind is so very bad. But I feel very thankful that we have things in so much better shape than last year. . . . H. got in at 10:30 dug mud all day." On 24 December Ida reported to Pauline her continued anxiety over the weather and the boys driving mail:

Last Thurs morning poor David got lost in the blizzard and came back that night at 5 oclock. O how thankful we were to see him, but I worried all night about my poor H. who did not get here till 10 oclock Friday. As good fortune would have it Bro [Willard] Farr chanced to be with him so they each rode a horse and a big mail sack from the Petrified Forest home. They shivered around a Mexican camp fire from 10 oclock till 4 a.m. during the night because they could not keep the road, but the weather was not so cold then as it is now. Grover started out Friday morning & made it thru to Woodruff. . . . Snow is over a foot here & 18 inches at St. Johns. Don't worry but have as good a time as you can. I can hardly get over the disappointment of your not coming. Pray for us all.[8]

Because of the storms, Pauline could not make the trip from Snow-flake to Hunt to be with her mother at Christmas. On 30 December Ida wrote to Pauline:

I have not written you one real Christmas note even and here it is Sat. night 5:30 before I sit down for a moment this day, and we have to set the alarm at 4 a.m. every morn in order to get Bro [Isaac] Thomas off about an hour before daylight, but the weather has been so very cold for the last two weeks we have had to bring every thing in the house and get the drivers breakfast on the heater. . . . Today the air has been loaded with frost all day making our old Cedar grove simply beautiful. We must have had 16 or 17 inches of snow fall here and it seems like it has scarcely melted at all so you can guess what a wintry scene we have had here. The boys got their skates, which you sent them and that is about all their Xmas but the whole family have enjoyed them. . . . We have got out the guitar in the evenings and sing songs till the mails come. . . . Sr [Julia] Farnsworth wrote me a nice Xmas letter and sent me a beautiful copy of Hawthorne's *Scarlet Letter* for a present.[9]

In Ida's next letter, dated 7 January 1906 at 5:30 A.M., she confided:

I have been so homesick to see you for a week past I hardly knew how to stand it, but the good long letter reced the night of the 5th partly dispelled the feeling. O I think it is too bad when I have only *one* girl that I should have to be separated from her *so* much of the time, and I wonder why it is that two people who dearly love to go to meeting as Aunt Mary and I do should be banished to a lone ranche for months at a time. I have to think it is for the good of our boys to be able to stand it at all, for I had far rather spend my whole life here than to have one drinking smoking boy. . . . O we do have some good boys! Lin [Morgan] has gone to bed at 7 p.m. and got up at 4 a.m. to feed horses & get mail off, all thro the Dec nights but since he has had the tooth ache (He got a fall on the ice Xmas day, and had to stay in by the stove and be up in the night sometimes all thro the Holidays), Jesse has been getting up and seems to do it just as cheerfully as Lin. This morning the alarm went off 10 minutes to 4. I called Jesse & he got right up made the fires, fed horses & we got *slow* Johney off at 5:30. . . . Grover staid home to celebrate his 18th birthday, but he coaxed pa to kill old Peter, for beef, so he worked like a good one all day. (Sent hind quarters to Aunt Ella & we kept fronts.) In the morning we talked over the subject of his having a heifer on the promise I had made them. He said he had never tasted whiskey nor bot 5 cts worth of tobacco & thought any of the boys would be entitled to a heifer if they kept their promise as he had, so Jesse made the motion and put it to vote, and every boy held their hands high as they could for Grover to have Rosy's brockled face heifer. She will be 3 years old in the spring and is a beauty. . . .

On Saturday, 13 January 1906, she declared that "when spring comes . . . we want to do big business—that is getting our farm, chicken ranche, and dairy in shape to live without this old mail line. . . . It is quite certain that Bro. W. W. Berry and Uncle Jos. have the mail line for next time. . . . Yesterday is the first day it has thawed since the big storm. Isent this cold freezing weather remarkable for Ariz? . . ." A few days later she took time out of her busy schedule to write to her cousin Nellie Jones: "I realize that your birthday is very near at hand and I must write a few words in spite of the work there is staring at me . . . I have men-folks galore to do for. . . . I have been two or three days at this, as I had too much work in the day and too sleepy at night, as I have to rise at 4 a.m. to get the first mail off. Then I have had passengers the last three nights to do for. . . ."[10]

During Ida's years at Hunt, she got away from the loneliness and work of the ranch only for special events. She went to Snowflake occasionally and once in a great while to St. Johns. As the winter of 1905–6 began to break and travel was possible, Ida made a trip to Snowflake. Back at the ranch by 23 February, she was thrown again into the hectic routine of daily demands on her.[11]

A Paralytic Stroke

The long severe winter, her anxiety over the boys, the almost daily visitors, the increased work load, little help from Luella and Aunt Mary, few breaks from the monotonous loneliness, and medical neglect all combined to take their toll on her. Her blood pressure rose dangerously high, and in March 1906 she suffered the first of three strokes. The attack came one afternoon as she sat at her sewing machine. Don saw his mother attempt to stand and nearly fall as her left leg gave way.[12]

Most of her life, Ida had suffered from bad teeth, which may have contributed to a heart disease. Although she had her teeth extracted in 1904, her heart condition remained. Symptoms had shown up while she was in Salt Lake City the previous year. In October 1905 she had mentioned her health: "I have been so I could not sleep much at night ever since I came back to Salt Lake. My heart has hurt me almost constantly. Perhaps it is overwork." After another long day of working in the temple, she had written, "O it was a grand day but I was completely exhausted. . . ."[13] The pains continued after her return to Hunt. On 30 December she confided to Pauline, "My *heart* gets so bad some nights."[14] On 16 March, after the stroke, she revealed to Pauline, "I have had a strange experience during the last few days, but papa [David] says I must not think nor talk about my sickness, so I am going to do as he says, and only through the blessing of the Lord and the administration of the Elders we have been saved from a dreadful calamity; and I thank and praise Him for it. . . . Well Pauline there is a passenger tonight and such a crowd I can't write more." Two days later she added, "My head feels clearer all the time, and I begin to feel quite myself again. Folks say I look so much better. . . . My little boys never looked so sweet and good to me as they did that night when I thot perhaps I might not be able to wait on them more." On 21 March she wrote that "I am gaining every day," but sometime in April she remarked that "my nerves . . . have been surely strained during papa's absence."[15]

The family thought that she had a miraculous recovery from this stroke, but according to her memory she suffered "a long seige" of it.[16] At any rate, her letters clearly indicate that soon she was fully back into the old routine, with no relief.

David was frightened by the stroke, and he became apprehensive about what might happen to Ida in the future. Having no means to do anything about it, he wrote Pauline asking her to give up her plans for schooling in Utah and to return to the ranch to teach the following year. He also asked her to purchase a home in St. Johns for her mother, using the savings she had acquired toward her schooling. She could pay half the cost this year and the other half the next year. The house David chose for Pauline to buy for her mother was a three-story house, owned by J. B. Patterson. It was soon dubbed the "Air Castle" because of its height and the fact that the outside air circulated so freely through it, particularly the top floors.[17]

To pacify Pauline, her father let her and Luella go to Utah for a couple of months so they could attend the University of Utah summer school. While they were gone, three nieces of Ida took turns staying with her at Hunt and helping out. In Salt Lake City, however, Pauline and Luella attended less than one week of school, because Luella developed a gathering (abscess) on her throat and had to be hospitalized. Afterwards they went to Nephi and visited relatives before returning to Arizona, where Pauline assumed her role of providing for her mother.

That fall Ida was moved into the Air Castle with her sons Grover, John H., and Gilbert and Mary's son Linton Morgan. The mail contracts had been relinquished to others, and the Udall boys were at last free to go to school. Pauline taught school at the ranch: her younger brothers Jesse and Don, the Farr and Greer children, and the two younger Morgan boys. She went to St. Johns on weekends when she was needed.[18]

That school year, 1906–7, while living in St. Johns, Ida served as president of the Primary, attended Relief Society when her health permitted, and sang a solo in a stake conference. At a conference, she gave a lecture on "The Duty of Parents to Children," giving good advice on deportment. She thought that parents should attend the dances and know how their children behaved and that parents should teach their children ballroom etiquette at home.[19]

A Second Stroke

At the end of December 1906, Ida suffered a second stroke, though light, and she recovered as she had at Hunt earlier in 1906. On 5 January 1907 she wrote Pauline, "Grover is chief cook and he does it so nice and easy, and scolds me if I go in the kitchen. If the house would only keep its self tidy we would get along all right and my being sick would be a blessing to the boys, I think. But oh I hope I am not going to have a long seige like I did before. Shall take care of myself and doctor up the best I can."[20]

The summer of 1907 Ida was at Hunt, and nieces from Snowflake came to help while Pauline attended eight weeks of summer school at Flagstaff. That fall the family moved back to the Air Castle, and Pauline taught fifth and sixth grades in the St. Johns school. Ida was grateful that her daughter was again able to enjoy some social life, even with the demands of teaching and caring for the family. With the Air Castle paid for (Pauline remembered the sum as $700), Pauline now saved for her plan to study domestic science at Utah Agricultural College in the fall. But first came a long-awaited trip to California in the summer of 1908.[21]

Trip to California: The Third Stroke

It was with great anticipation that Pauline took her mother and Ida's sister Annie Kartchner by train on the visit to their Aunt Frances's home in Anaheim, California. There they saw where Ida's grandfather, Addison Pratt, had lived his last years, died, and was buried in 1872. Luella and Pearl were also in Los Angeles at the time. Luella was working for Ida's cousin, Nellie Jones, and Pearl was attending the Los Angeles College of Osteopathy. Pearl began the three-year program in 1907, graduating in June 1910.[22]

Pauline settled her mother and aunt and then left for Los Angeles to be with Pearl and Luella. Two days later Ida suffered a third, more severe stroke that left her a semi-invalid for the remaining years of her life. Pauline, Pearl, and Luella went at once to her bedside. After a few days, they took Ida by train to Baker. They were able to put her stretcher in the baggage car and remain with her. At Baker they were taken to the home of Nellie Jones, Ida's cousin, daughter of Ellen Pratt McGary. Later they moved to a rented apartment in Los Angeles.

After regaining consciousness, Ida had tried to get up and take care of herself, but at that time the doctors believed that remaining in bed was the best therapy. Pearl interrupted her osteopathy schooling to help care for Ida. She taught Pauline how to give her mother massages and devised some physical therapy exercises helpful in Ida's partial recovery. Because of Pearl's personal experiences, she had great empathy for Ida and considered it a privilege to be with her at that difficult time. Pauline took full financial responsibility for her mother's care, writing to her father for an advance against her savings to use to rent hospital equipment and to pay doctors' fees and other services.[23]

Ida's stroke was a terrible blow to everyone. Ida was only fifty years old at the time. Her left side was paralyzed, including the muscles of that side of her face, which sagged down. Her beautiful singing voice was gone. No longer could her family hear her singing as she did her work. She could not play the guitar. She could no longer manage her long auburn hair that had been her crowning glory. Nor could she care for her own needs or those of her children again. None of her children was married, and her youngest son was only eleven years old. Pauline would now have to shoulder the physical as well as the financial responsibilities of caring for her mother.

Back to Arizona

After about a month of care, they returned to Arizona. Ida and Pauline stayed at Hunt for awhile before going to live again in the Air Castle in St. Johns. Pauline was prepared to devote all her energies to care for her mother. From her mother's bedside in Los Angeles, Pauline had written her father, "It looks as though it is not the right thing for me to go on to school. I am willing to give up all for mama's sake if she can only be spared us in good health. I want to do and be whatever and wherever the Lord wants me to."[24]

Only after Ida learned to walk again did Pauline take on outside work, at first three hours a day teaching English, math, and church history to a group of men preparing for missions. Each day Ida would be waiting for her daughter's return. They both realized that a dramatic change had taken place. The daughter now played the role of mother in the family, not only to her brothers but to her mother as well.[25]

Ida was pleased when Pauline received a proposal of marriage from Asahel Smith, son of her friend Augusta Smith and stake president Jesse N. Smith. Although Pauline had had suitors in St. Johns, Round Valley, and Snowflake, her situation had changed with the care of an invalid mother. Asahel, however, felt it would be a privilege to help Pauline care for her mother, a woman he had admired since his childhood.

Ida spent Christmas 1908 at Hunt with Mary Morgan, while Pauline went to Snowflake to complete the wedding plans. At the end of March Ida went to Snowflake to stay with her sisters while Pauline was on her wedding trip and honeymoon. Asahel and Pauline were married 2 April 1909 in the Salt Lake Temple.[26]

Still on the Move

Pauline returned to Snowflake and with her husband set up house-keeping in an upstairs apartment of his mother's home. Ida lived with them, spending time also with her sisters. The following September, David rented two rooms from Ida's brother Lewis in Snowflake and moved his three youngest sons—Jesse, Gilbert, and Don—to live with their mother and attend school. John H. was in Thatcher attending the Gila Academy, and Grover was on his mission to West Virginia. Pauline went each day to help with cooking and laundry and to care for her mother's hair. The Hunt family members were all attentive to Ida.[27]

Ida Hunt Udall and her family, Snowflake, Arizona, January 1910.
Standing: Gilbert, Jesse, and Don; *seated:* Ida and Pauline.

The last of January 1910 Ida's first grandchild, named Rudger Grant, was born. Ida was delighted with him. Three weeks later, Asahel received a call from Church President Joseph F. Smith, no doubt on the recommendation of Stake President David K. Udall, to serve as bishop of the Hunt Ward, consisting of Saints at Hunt and Concho. This put Pauline and Asahel right where they could best care for Ida. They accepted the call, and by the first of April Ida and her sons were en route to Hunt with them. At the beginning, Ida and the boys lived in her home, while Pauline and her little family occupied a sturdy tent with wooden sides and a floor.[28] In time, however, Pauline convinced the family that a tent beside her own should be set up for her mother. This would take Ida away from the noisy Udall establishment and save Pauline from walking the distance and carrying her baby each day to take care of her mother. This was done, and Ida's sons could now visit her at night. She was free to read her favorite books, and Pauline and Asahel could continue their loving care.[29]

With the coming of cold weather, Pauline took her mother, baby, and younger brothers to St. Johns, where again they lived in the Air Castle. Asahel freighted and visited when he could but otherwise bached at Hunt, taking care of his church duties by visiting his congregations on a rotation basis. Ida's younger sons were in school. Her health was not good, but the family managed. Ida never blamed anyone for the stroke that was surely the result of her years of overwork and strain, nor did she complain about her lot. Instead, she tried to make people happy, and as a result she was a blessing to her family.

The hurt of it all, her weakened condition, and her dependence on her loved ones did not go unnoticed, however. Pauline shared in a letter to Asahel, written 16 November 1908, "Sometimes it touches my heart to the core to see the sad expression that passes over her face at times." Most of the time Ida's brave front shielded her emotions from public view, but in November 1910 Pauline wrote of coming upon her mother when "she was so lonesome and blue she had to go to the neighbors and have a cry. When I walked in and surprised her she broke right down. She never was so glad to see anyone."[30]

Ida's stroke, tragic as it was for her, became an unexpected blessing in the relationship between the two wives. Because Ida was no longer any competition or threat to Ella, she was at last accepted by her. One of polygamy's greatest obstacles was removed. Ever after, Ella was loving and gracious to Ida and her children.[31]

Even so, Ida could pass on to others a lesson of her life, as she wrote on 12 August 1910 to her cousin Nellie Jones: "I beg of you as I do all my sisters not to overdo your bodily strength in doing work that worries and tries you day after day. . . . save all the energy possible for your old age."[32]

The next summer, 1911, Ida and Pauline were back at Hunt, this time in a house. By fall the Udalls began building their dream home in St. Johns. The boys helped haul building materials from the railroad, helped make the cement bricks, and did carpentry. Pearl left her practice as an osteopath to cook for the builders.[33]

While the big house was being built, 1911–12, most of the Udall family lived in the Air Castle. Ida, her sons Gilbert and Don, Matt Morgan, and Ella's sons David and Levi were all there. Jesse, Grover, and John H. were at Hunt harvesting or freighting materials for the house. Ella underwent a serious operation in Los Angeles, and Pearl went to nurse her. That left Ida in St. Johns, though she wanted to be at Hunt with Pauline, who was expecting her second baby, Andrew.

Ida's letters provide a glimpse into the lives of this diverse family. In writing to Ella and Pearl on 28 November 1911, Ida said:

> Beatrice says if I will stay here she will do her best to cook for the boys & look after the house. . . . Aunt Mary would stay but papa [David] thinks they need her worse at Hunt, and no doubt they do for he has been on such a strain lately that he got so during Conference that he could neither eat nor sleep and more surprising he did not get sleepy during meetings. The weather has been freezing cold both day and night for over a week, so you must enjoy sunny Cal. all you can and be glad you are not in the "air castle" during such weather.
>
> David and Levi are well and are the same sweet boys, working on the house which is showing magnificent proportions more every day now. . . . Gilbert and Matt started to Snowflake at 4 oclock in the morning. Prof [M. O.] Poulsen is going to chaparone the crowd and is sanguine he can beat both Flag. & S.F. [Flagstaff and Snowflake] teams. . . . Papa has been talking to Erma this morn and all are well there but the thresher is not in running order yet, so Jess & Harold are gone to Holbrook for freight. Grover & H. are killing pigs at Hunt. . . .[34]

On 7 December Ida again wrote to Ella and Pearl:

> Beatrice has been a brick to stay with us. . . . Bea thinks our boys the most wonderful helpers in the world. Perhaps we have misjudged them! . . . They have got nearly all the shingles on the house now. It is a dreadful job because of the nasty smelling paint they have to be dipped in before tacking on. . . . The school boys dip them at noon & night. . . . But oh! these are lonely days for me without any of our dear girls. When the threshing gets done and papa can come up once in awhile it will cheer me up some I hope. . . . I would take the first train for Hunt only that Beatrice would not stay with the boys without I staid with her, . . . I must find my own [Pauline] to stay with. . . .

Well here come the five boys with Pearls good letter & card bearing
the good news that you have moved from the Hospital! Joyful news to
all of us.[35]

By January 1912 Ella and Pearl were back in St. Johns in the Air
Castle. Ida wrote to her daughter that since there was no comfortable
way to get to Hunt, she was going to Eagar with David to spend a
week with her sister Nettie and Emma Udall: "There is such a crowd
of us here and not a drop of water only muddy well water to use, so
I think its a good time to go visiting. Every tap in town is froze up
and many of them burst open. . . . No washing done since Xmas, so I
will have to take my clothes up to Aunt Nettie. . . . Aunt Ella gains
slowly, but fast as we could expect her to in with so much confusion
and sleeping in the front room at Holiday times."[36]

Along with the expenses of building the big house came the bills
for Ella's surgery, followed by disasters. The dam at St. Johns broke,
and all the improvements made in ditches were destroyed. Then there
was a fire at Hunt, started when a traveling salesman left his hot
footwarmer in the granary. The fire took the granary first and burned
up the lumber and windows Pauline and Asahel had stored there for
their dream house. The fire also spread to the stables and burned
valuable horses. It all made David "feel like we were going to the bottom in a hurry," Ida wrote. "Poor man when will these times come
to an end."[37]

Besides the financial problems, Ida had concerns for the safety of
her sons. Jesse, while freighting a load of lumber from Whiting's Saw-
mill to St. Johns, narrowly escaped being killed when he was thrown
to the ground just before a plank struck the spot he had been occupying. Jesse was also often exposed to dangerous weather conditions in
his work. In Ida's November letter she told of Jesse's driving through
a stormy night to get Sister Charlotte Sherwood from Hunt to Snowflake so she could make connections to go to Cibecue to nurse a
family member who was near death. Jesse considered himself blessed
that he got through the cold night safely with his passengers. Then
John H. was nearly crushed between loads of hay sometime in early
January.[38]

Ida was no doubt concerned about Pearl as well. Pearl's relation
with Rudger Clawson appeared increasingly futile, compounded by
his call in June 1910 to preside for three years over the church's European Mission, headquartered in Liverpool, England: "Pearl was in a
state of uncertainty and turmoil. She had been married to Rudger
now for eight years. During its entire course it had been a clandes-
tine marriage of secret meetings and long absences. It was illegal

and increasingly at odds with the church, and it was a marriage of joys and sorrows of which Pearl could share only with her immediate family."[39] Rudger's wife Lydia had remained in England with him only until September 1911. Pearl and Rudger were corresponding. In February 1912 Pearl's brother David went to England to serve his mission. The following October Pearl traveled to England, ostensibly to research her ancestral lines. During the three months she was there, from 17 October 1912 until 17 January 1913, David arranged several rendezvous. Rudger and Pearl discussed their relationship, and by the time Pearl left England, Rudger had released her from the marriage. Pearl was free at last.[40] Her medical practice took her to the Gila Valley, Mesa, Holbrook, St. Johns, and ultimately Salt Lake City.

The Family Home in St. Johns

Meanwhile the new Udall house was finally finished, and in the spring of 1912 the family moved in. For whatever reasons—whether financial, legal, or health—Ida deeded the Air Castle property to David on 19 March 1912.[41] David had estimated the cost of the new house the previous November: "Our home will not cost less than $7,000.00," plus $1,000 for furnishings. Whatever the cost, the Udall home was a monument to family cooperation.[42] It remained one of the distinguished landmarks in St. Johns and served as a center for the family. A first-floor room was given to Ida. Thereafter she was based in St. Johns, though she continued to spend time at Hunt with Pauline, in Snowflake for visits of several weeks at a time, and in Eagar with her sister Nettie and friends.

The Udall home, known today as the Elm Hotel, also became a home for the unmarried sons, when they were not away working or at school. That year John H. and Grover both married, and they established their own homes in St. Johns. Levi took his bride, Louise Lee, to live in the Udall home while he studied law, and Luella and her husband, Garland Pace, lived there after he completed his medical training and began his practice in St. Johns.[43] Udall nieces and nephews from Eagar also lived in the home while attending the St. Johns Academy. All were helpful to Ida, especially her daughters-in-law, Dora Sherwood, married to Grover, and Ruth Kimball, John H.'s wife. Ida loved being near her grandsons: Grover's Sherwood and John H.'s Nicholas.

Ida's health was now better than it had been. She walked with more confidence, as a result of the exercises Pearl developed for her left leg. Walking on uneven streets or uphill was a problem, however.

While she was in Snowflake, her young Hunt nieces served as her crutch; Ida would place her arm around a niece's shoulder while the niece held her waist.[44] With this help she could go visit her many friends and relatives quite freely. While on her visits, she always had good help with one of her biggest physical problems: taking care of her heavy hair, which was usually worn on top of her head in a coil or a bun and in a single braid at night. There was no way she could take care of this alone, inasmuch as she never recovered the use of her left arm and hand.

In St. Johns, when Pauline was not there, others had to help. The wives of Grover and John H. were on hand. A cousin from England, Alice White, lived with the Udalls for some time, and she became very devoted to Ida.[45] There was also Joseph Udall's daughter Joyce, who lived in the home while attending the St. John's Academy. She helped with Ida's hair and at times slept with her on extra cold nights to keep her warm. Though Ella never took personal care of Ida, she was always kind to her.[46]

The events that took Ida to Snowflake were conferences, the dedication of the Stake Academy, her father's birthday celebrations, or the Twenty-fourth of July celebrations honoring Utah and Snowflake pioneers. Ida was always a favorite with the Hunt family, and her affliction only enhanced their love and service to her.[47]

The letters Ida wrote after her stroke appear as beautiful as those penned before, but they were hard for her to write. On one written shortly before her death, Luella wrote a note telling of the hours it had taken Ida to write it and expressing the hope that the recipient, Nellie Jones, would prize it. As difficult as it was for Ida to write, she took care to try to keep up her correspondence with her family. When Ella was in Salt Lake City attending a conference in April 1914, Ida made sure to write her, reporting that Erma's children were recovering from whooping cough and that the rest of the family was getting along well, news Ella was no doubt pleased to hear. Ida also wrote to congratulate Luella and Garland Pace on his having passed his state osteopathic medical board exams in Arizona and the birth of a son.[48]

After the Udalls moved into the big house in St. Johns, they instituted the tradition of having a family dinner during the Christmas holidays. Ella, a gracious hostess and good cook, served a meal all of the Udall children and their spouses looked forward to. Ida wrote to Pauline in Hunt on 27 December 1914, saying, "So we won't give up the hope that you'll be at the family dinner yet before the season is over."[49]

Now that Ida was in such poor health, it was particularly important for her to be with all the members of her family. David later recounted that Ida's "love for all the children recognized no apparent difference between her own and Ella's. This was exemplified the night following an election in 1914 when her son, John H. and Ella's son, Levi, had awkwardly been placed as opponents on different tickets, each running for the same office. (Clerk of Superior Court.) I came home in the early morning hours after the election count had been made and going to Ida's room said, 'Mother, your son is elected.' Rousing herself she sat up in bed and asked, 'Which one, father?' When it proved to be John H., she was so glad that Levi was only a few votes behind."[50]

Ida continued to be troubled by the financial problems that always seemed to plague the Udall family. In December 1914 she wrote to her aunt, Louisa Pratt Willis, who was then living alone in Idaho, "It would be such a joy to me if I only had a $10.00 or $20.00 bill to send you for Christmas. But to tell the truth, dear Aunty, finances have been very close with us for the last few months   I have not had the heart to mention money for any thing, but we hope for better times. . . . my son John H. has been elected clerk of the Superior Court of Apache Co. which is a four years job at a good salary."[51] Ida, always interested in receiving any news about her family, closed her letter by asking her aunt to let her know how she passed the holidays and how she was doing.[52]

During February 1915 Ida's health deteriorated, and Pauline was called to come from Hunt. Taking her baby David to St. Johns and leaving the older boys with her husband, Pauline cared for her mother under the direction of Dr. Garland Pace. In March Ida nearly died, and her father, brothers, and sisters were called to her bedside. She was so overjoyed at seeing them that she got better for a time.[53]

In early April 1915 the Lyman Dam broke south of St. Johns, and the ensuing flood washed out dams at Hunt, Woodruff, and Joseph City. Lives were lost, and the land was ravaged by the floods. Knowing that she would not live long, Ida wanted to see her ranch at Hunt once more. With David in the Ford, driven by her son Don, she made the trip to Hunt. Pauline went ahead to prepare for her coming.[54]

Home to Hunt

Ida had seen floods at Hunt before but nothing to compare with this one. It looked "like the destroying angel had passed over."[55] Roads were out, telephone lines were down, and water covered everything, but at least Ida was home again.

On Sunday evening Ida asked the family to play organ music and sing her favorite songs. Before retiring, she exercised her arms as she always did each night, using rope and pulleys attached to the back of a door, hopeful of bringing back some use of her left arm and hand. Late in the night, as was her custom, with Pauline's help she got into a chair to read, promising to ask for help in returning to bed. When Asahel was up with a crying child, Ida appeared fine, even offering the child one of her crackers. But later when Pauline checked on her, she found Ida had died, apparently without a struggle. It was early Monday morning, 26 April 1915.[56]

Gilbert, who was at the ranch that year, was awakened to ride the ten miles by horseback to Concho to telephone his father in St. Johns. The Hunt family was also notified. David and John H. arrived with Dr. Garland Pace in his car by 8 o'clock that morning. Soon John H. and Gilbert were on their way to St. Johns, with their mother's remains in a wagon. Pauline, in writing the details of her mother's death and burial to Pearl and Loie in Salt Lake City, quoted John H. as saying, "She was with them all the way. . . . like she was telling them what to do."[57] While returning to St. Johns, David K. met his two sons Jesse and young David, each with freight outfits. Taking Jesse in the auto, he left David with both teams. A car was sent for Pauline's family and Mary Morgan.

Pauline wrote:

> Even after the ride up she was a most natural and beautiful corpse. Ruth and Dora with others made a beautiful, simple slip and dress . . . then Ella dressed Ida in a beautiful model temple suit that she had brought from Salt Lake City the year before. . . . Oh! she did look beautiful. The shoes and all fit perfectly. . . . The coffin made under Grover's direction was so pretty with white plush and silver handles with little oak leaves in silver for trimming. Oh how happy and proud she must have been to have for her pall bearers her own five handsome sons aided by one just as near as could possible be her own, Levi. . . .
>
> While she was being buried that very same mocking bird that has sung for her so many mornings when others' ears were closed in sleep was there so close giving the same song. . . . She had talked of the lilac just coming out and us not seeing it, so many times after she came down here. Father placed a huge bouquet of them on her grave which was just covered with flowers.[58]

Ida's father, brothers, and sisters (except Loie, who was in Salt Lake City) were present at the funeral in St. Johns, coming from Snowflake and Eagar. The speakers praised Ida's devotion to her family and her church.[59] One unusual feature of the funeral was the opportunity for friends to stand and pay tribute to her. Five men responded. The choir sang the opening and closing numbers. There was a double mixed quartet, and Thurza Brown sang "In the Time of Roses," and Josephine Patterson sang "One Sweetly Solemn Thought."

John W. Brown paid tribute to Ida's love of music, flowers, and poetry. As a polygamist, he spoke of the difficulty in living that principle and praised the Udall family for their success, giving credit to Ida for the love she had always shown Ella's children.

In his funeral sermon, George H. Crosby, Jr., who had known Ida for thirty years, remarked:

> Her ability to make friends was most wonderful, for I have seen people who have seen her but once and gone away who say they liked her better than anyone they ever knew. I have been in her company perhaps two hundred times and I have never heard her say ought against anyone, and never have I heard ill spoken against anyone in her presence but that she has defended that person. She did not need offices to make her great, her strong sentiments and thoughts of doing good for all and her affection and kindness was shown in her whole life. She had musical ability. How often have I found pleasure in listening to her sweet guitar. She also had literary ability and I have never heard more beautiful thoughts than were those penned by Aunt Ida. When I was teaching in Eagar I shall never forget her loyalty to me, her loyalty to Eagar, and her loyalty to the family. You could not tell from her treatment which were her children and which were Aunt Ella's. I couldn't see any difference.[60]

Brother Crosby then quoted a poem she had copied while in California that he said was a requiem of her life. He ended with "Ida Hunt Udall never lacked a friend because she was a friend to everybody. They say that the world loves a lover. Ida Hunt Udall has love in her heart for everybody and consequently everybody loved her."[61]

PART 7

The Legacy

AFTER IDA'S DEATH and burial, David made the trip to her home in Hunt to take care of her effects. There he read her journal and wept as he was reminded of the many sacrifices she had made for him, especially while living on the "underground." As he mourned her passing, he wondered aloud to Pauline what he was going to do now that his peacemaker was gone.

The family had not ceased mourning Ida's passing before death called again. John H.'s wife, Ruth Kimball, died unexpectedly on 27 May, only a month after Ida. A year and a half later, on 5 October 1916, John H. married Leah Smith, who became the mother of ten children.

In June 1916 Mary Morgan moved from Hunt to Utah to live, bringing an end to her active involvement with the Udall family. Mary's sons were on their own: Lin was a law student in Washington, D.C., and Harold and Matthias were married to young women from St. Johns and Snowflake. In Utah Mary worked and was assisted by monthly checks from David for as long as he lived.[1]

Ida's three unmarried sons continued attending school and working. In June 1917, within a week of each other, Jesse and Gilbert were both married, Jesse to Lela Lee of Thatcher (whom he met while attending the Gila Academy) and Gilbert to Sara Brown of St. Johns. Don served a mission to the Eastern States Mission from 1917 to 1919, and in 1922 he married Emily Patterson.

Ida's influence as family peacemaker carried on after her death. She had always told her children that nothing hurt her as much as hearing them say anything unkind about Aunt Ella or her children. Ida's nature was to adjust to the problem and solve it by having her family give up anything that caused bad feelings. Not long after Ida's death, however, her children stopped following her example. In July an open conflict emerged between Pauline and Luella over who would get to teach in the school at Hunt.[2] Luella needed income to help her husband get his M.D. degree; Pauline wanted to teach at home for much-needed cash. Sides were taken, and the discord might have spread had David not taken action. Realizing that much-feared contention was coming into his family, he told his children that if they did not stop their quarreling, he would renounce them all. To make good his threat, he went to Thatcher, "visiting with the [W. W.] Pace family." A reporter noted, "He is looking into conditions with a view to locating here if things are favorable."[3] By the time he returned to St. Johns, Ida's children had gotten a clear message, and, remembering their mother's example, made peace. This peace and friendship continued among the Udall brothers and sisters through the remainder of their lives. Only when Ida's children were with each other did they speak of Ida's and their own sacrifices for the family. Then they were almost reverential in speaking of their mother's efforts to maintain peace.[4]

Pearl had unusual insight into the Udall family—the hearts and minds of brothers and sisters, a keen appreciation for father and mothers, and what each went through in life. As early as 1909 she expressed the spirit of the family in a letter to Pauline: "Who can say my dreams were not my 'prophets'? For where do you find a family who has taken more real comfort together than we have? There have been disappointments in finances and college ambitions, but so far, we have been true to each other and happy when together. . . . despite our weaknesses and shortcomings and ups and downs, we have lived and loved, and oh may the love grow stronger as our lives and interest broaden. . . ."[5]

Pearl's hopes were realized. As the years passed, the brothers and sisters grew closer in love for one another. All the children came to appreciate fully the sterling qualities of their father David and their mothers Ella and Ida.

After thirty-five years of service as president of the St. Johns Stake, David was released on 30 April 1922. At the same time, Ella was released as president of the Relief Society. Five years later, they were called to serve as first president and matron of the new Arizona Temple, where they served for seven years.

The children of David K. Udall and his wives made names for themselves. In 1916 Pearl opened her medical office in Salt Lake City, where she carried on a successful active practice the balance of her life. She married Joseph Nelson, a widower and prominent Salt

Lake entrepreneur, mothered his seven children, and was the special aunt to a generation of Udall nieces and nephews.[6] Erma married
Will Sherwood and in time made her home in Holbrook, Arizona.
She was active in the Parent-Teacher Association (P.T.A.), serving as
state president. As mentioned earlier, Luella married Garland Pace, a
physician. They made their home in Salt Lake City and Provo, Utah.
Ida's only daughter Pauline reared a large family and at the same time
served for seventeen years as stake president of the Primary in the
Snowflake Stake.

Levi set an example in studying law and passed the bar in 1922.
He was followed by Don in 1923 and Jesse in 1924. Each of these
men served as superior court judge, Levi in Apache County, Jesse in
Graham, and Don in Navajo. After Levi was elected to the Arizona
Supreme Court, John H.'s son Nicholas was elected judge in Mari-
copa County. Four Udalls thus served as judges at the same time.
Three were Ida's: two sons and a grandson. In 1960 Levi died suddenly
while serving as chief justice, and the governor named Jesse to suc-
ceed him on the court. The following November Jesse was elected to
that court and in 1964 served as chief justice. He served on the court
eleven years before resigning. In addition to these positions, three of
Ida's sons—John H., Jesse, and Don—served in the state legislature.
John H. was twice the Republican nominee for governor, at a time
when Arizona was strongly Democratic. He was later elected mayor
of Phoenix, as was his son Nicholas, who served several terms.

Important church callings also came to the Udall men. Levi, at
the age of thirty-one, succeeded his father as president of the St.
Johns Stake, serving twenty-three years. Three of Ida's sons, John H.,
Jesse, and Gilbert, served as bishops. Don served as one of Snowflake
Stake's presidents of Seventies, a missionary arm of the church. Jesse
served as president of the St. Joseph Stake at two different times. (He
and his brother Don were called into active duty as lieutenant colo-
nels in World War II.) At the end of the war, Jesse was again elected
judge and called to be stake president, positions he held until called
as president of the California Mission.

The Udall men kept their interest in land. Grover spent his life
as a farmer and stockman, and he served as president of the Lyman
Water Company. He and his wife also purchased the Udall home and
turned it into the Elm Hotel. John H. maintained a cattle ranch at
Hunt, and he, Jesse, and Gilbert also had farms. David and Gilbert
followed their father's example of taking mail contracts and each sold
life insurance.

The Udall name became well known throughout the state. In

later years, two of Levi's sons—Stewart and Morris—gave the name national recognition when they were elected to the U.S. House of Representatives (Stewart also served as the secretary of the interior during the Kennedy and Johnson administrations, and Morris later ran for president).

Tributes to the Udalls, and to Ida particularly, came in many forms. Ida's sisters, affected as much as any others by her passing, did much to preserve her memory. May, who kept a voluminous journal, completed Ida's unfinished memoir of her early life, Ida's journal of her 1877 trip from Utah to New Mexico, and Ida's birthday book to 1915. Ida's brothers and sisters told her children and grandchildren stories about her talents and life experiences, lamenting her untimely passing compared with their longevity. Lewis died youngest at eighty-one, May and Bell were eighty-three, Annie was eighty-four, and John was eighty-nine. Nettie was two months short of ninety-five and Loie was ninety-six-and-a-half when they passed away.

Could David have been thinking of Ida's life span compared with that of her sisters when on his deathbed he confided to Pauline his concerns? He was troubled not about dying but about meeting Ida again. "How can I face your mother again after the things I had to do to her?" Pauline, knowing better than anyone what her mother had sacrificed for the Udall family, assured her father of the great love Ida had for him and of how happy she would be to see him, her husband and the father of her children. Reassured, David died peacefully.

That was on 18 February 1938 at St. Johns. Ella had died nine months earlier. David, Ella, and Ida are buried next each other in the St. Johns Cemetery.[7]

Even before their deaths, there were special occasions for well-earned tributes. On 1 February 1925 David and Ella celebrated the golden anniversary of their wedding in the Jade Room of the Hotel Utah in Salt Lake City. Many distinguished church leaders were there and paid tribute. President Heber J. Grant spoke of his close contacts with the Udall family over the years. Elder George Albert Smith of the Quorum of the Twelve told of his visits to the St. Johns Stake and the Udall home:

> It was an eventful thing to be welcomed into the home of President Udall and to be made to feel that I was an honored guest there, and to realize the real friendship that was in the hearts of his two good wives. It is a memory that I treasure among the other memories of my life. I saw the children in his home coming and going, but I could not for the life of me tell which was the mother of the children. They were all the same. As has been said here tonight, the one good woman has finished

her work and gone home. I wonder if she can look down upon those she called dear tonight, and if she can realize how much she contributed to making the success that has been attained by our good brother and sister in whose honor we are meeting tonight.[8]

He and many of his generation like him knew the significant role Ida had played in the Udall family. Her life ended in 1915, but her memory is very much alive in her descendants and all who have known her through letters, journals, and biography.

APPENDIX 1

Genealogies

Addison Pratt and Louisa Barnes Family

Addison Pratt   +   Louisa Barnes
1802–72   1802–80

Ellen Sophronia	Frances Stevens	Lois Barnes	Ann Louisa
1832–95	1834–1909	1837–85	1840–1924?
Md	Md	Md	Md
William McGary	Jones Dyer	John Hunt	Thomas Willis
=	=	=	=
Addison	Addison	Ida Frances	Tillman
Aurora	Harry	May Louise	
Nellie, Md Will Jones	Frank	Annella	
		Christabelle	
		Lewis	
		John Addison	
		Nettie	
		Lois	

Jefferson Hunt and Celia Mounts Family

Jefferson Hunt + Celia Mounts
1803–79   1805–96

Gilbert	Nancy Ann	Marshall	Jane	John	Harriett	Joseph	Jefferson	Hyrum	Parley	Mary
1825–58	1827–1920	1829–1915	1831–99	1833–1917	1835–1918	1837–1916	1839–41	1840–80	1845–47	1845–1930

Md
Lydia Gibson

John — Md
1 Lois Pratt
2 Sarah Jane Crosby
3 Happylona Sanford

Joseph — Md
Catherine Conover (Kit)
=
Celia, Md George Teancum Bean
Ina, Md Epaminondas Bean
Ida, Md Albert Nageley

Hyrum — Md
1 Emily Knowles
2 Sarah Elizabeth Henderson

John Hunt and Lois Pratt Family

John Hunt + Lois Barnes Pratt
1833–1917   1837–1885

Ida Frances	May Louise	Annella	Christabelle	Lewis	John Addison	Nettie	Lois
1858–1915	1860–1943	1862–1946	1864–1934	1866–1947	1869–1958	1872–1966	1875–1971
Md	Md	Md	Md	Md	Md	Md	Md
David K. Udall	Alof Larson	Orrin Kartchner	Charles L. Flake	Della Ann Willis	Mary Ellen Cross	Joseph A. Rencher	Joseph A. West

David King Udall and Ida Frances Hunt Family

David King Udall + Ida Frances Hunt
1851–1938   1858–1915

Pauline   Grover   John Hunt   Jesse Addison   Gilbert Douglas   Don Taylor
1885–1968   1887–1950   1889–1959   1893–1980   1895–1981   1897–1976

Md   Md   Md   Md   Md   Md
Asahel H.   Dora   1 Ruth Kimball   1 Lela Lee   1 Sarah Brown   Emily Patterson
Smith   Sherwood   2 Leah Smith   2 Lillian Cluff   2 Lucinda Mortensen
                                                    Jenkins   3 Mildred Glazier

David King Udall and Eliza Luella Stewart Family

David King Udall + Eliza Luella ("Ella") Stewart
1851–1938   1855–1937

Stewart   Pearl   Erma   Mary   Luella   David King, Jr.   Levi Stewart   Paul Drawbridge   Rebecca May
1878–78   1880–1950   1882–1966   1884–85   1886–1952   1888–1960   1891–1960   1894–96   1897–98

           Md   Md   Md   Md   Md
           [Rudger   William W.   Garland H.   Aurora   Louise Lee
           Clawson]   Sherwood   Pace   Meriger

           Joseph
           Nelson

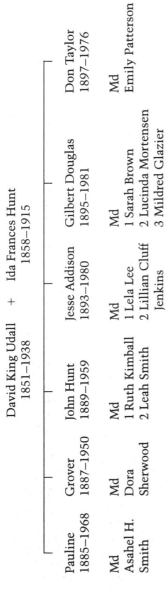

APPENDIX 2

Selected Letters

THE COLLECTION of over seventy letters written by Ida between the years 1879 and 1915 add much to her life story. She was a skillful writer, with an ability to provide interesting information. The following letters are examples taken from the Ida Hunt Udall Papers.

Letter 10: To David, 26 March 1886

Babie's letter for her papa

Nephi, Juab Co. March 26th 1886

My Dear One:

As this is the first anniversary of the natal day of our dear little one, I feel that before retiring tonight I must give you a brief pen picture of her, which I hope will afford you as much pleasure to read, as it does me in writing it. How I grieve to think you could never have seen her in her bright beautiful baby-hood, after she was old enough to know and love you. That season is already past, and she seems a great big girl. Can understand a great deal that we say to her. She was one year old at half past 10 this a.m. She weighs 23½ lbs, and can walk half way across the room alone, which is quite wonderful for so heavy a child. Her cheeks are so red and the rest of her face so white that her countenance appears like two roses in the snow, crowned with her sweet auburn hair which begins to turn up in little drake's tails all over her head. When we ask her where her papa is, she will reach out both little arms (which feel like a pair of white rabbits they are so soft and fat) towards your picture which hangs on the wall and kiss at it, just as Erma [Ella's daughter] used to the original. She seems to know by instinct that she is entitled to a pa, for she nearly worships that bit of wood and pasteboard which bears the dear title. O she seems to me like a royal little queen, with her stately perfect little form. How thankful I am for that, and her robust health. I think it is Dr Fowler who says that in order to aspire to any thing great and noble we must first become a *perfect animal.* So I have great hopes for her. It seems a luxury to her to live, breathe, eat and sleep. Now I have told her beautiful good qualities, I must tell you of her bad ones, for which I know the child is not responsible although she often gets blamed for them. She is the most restless uneasy child I ever saw. She is perfectly happy and good natured so long as someone is leading or carrying her about the house or garden. Out doors is her specialty. She has always been just all that I could carry, and how often have I walked and worried with her until I was so tired and discouraged I could sit down and cry, and I need not tell you how I have longed in vain for a dear kind papa to *rest* me occasionally. I know very well her restlessness is caused from circumstances under which she was born. When I reflect that during the whole time I carried her, I was never once at home nor felt settled and at rest, I cannot wonder that my child is perpetual motion. Still I thought she would be just the other way, that she would dread leaving home & wandering from one place to another as badly as I did. I pray that the Lord will kindly overrule all these things, and I believe she will outgrow this *mania,* still it is very fatiguing just now. Her grandma gave her a little silver spoon, and her little companion Lillia Teasdale gave her a china cup and saucer for her birthday. Her "cousin-uncles" Tank and Albert from Richfield, passed this p.m. on their way from Provo where they have been witnesses for nearly a month. They pronounced Pauline a "real daisy," and say she gets prettier every day. Oh I know how her papa would love her, and she would love him. May God speed the day when they may meet to part no more. I was going to wean her awhile ago but Granpa was so opposed to it that I gave it up. He thinks I should nurse her all summer but I don't think I could live through it.

    With a kiss from her, I will say goodnight

Letter 11: To David, 1 July 1886

Nephi, July 1st 1886

My Dear Boy:

    I must try and write you a few lines this p.m. although Miss Pauline objects—She comes and jerks the paper out of my hand with an exclamation that says plainly she considers it my duty to give my whole attention to her as I left her at home and went to fast meeting this morning. I have been thinking for several days past that I would write you for if I remember rightly the last letter I wrote you on Joseph's birthday the 23rd was a little blue. I remember I felt very homesick at the time. And now your dear sympathizing missive written the same day has just been handed me I must surely do so. Poor boy! how long the time must seem to you, hourly expecting word to go and yet none coming. It seems so strange that your lawyers do not write once in a while even if they have nothing to tell. Thats what you must do my dear one. It would be far pleasanter if you have some good news to tell, but when you have none, it helps me to bear this weary suspense to hear from you often. I hope dearest you will understand my situation well enough to make allowances for my homesick letter and not let it trouble you. I believe it is impossible for one dependent as I am, to always keep cheerful. But through the help of the Lord I do pretty well, and one of the greatest consolations I have, dear, is the thought that you would never have it thus if it could possibly be avoided, and just so soon as the Lord opens the way there will be a change. But if you care in the least for my happiness never mention going to prison, for I shudder yet every time I think of the dark cloud that hung over me and weighted my spirits to the very earth, all the time you were in the wretched place. God forbid that you should ever enter in its doors again. Rather let me live this way all my life dear one. It would be a pleasure compared to the sacrifice you speak of. As you say our portion has been *wait wait* for so long I dare not set my heart on the case being dismissed, still I feel to say the Lords will be done.

My work in the office was completed for awhile last Monday. I copied some 80 pages in the County Records, which is all there is for the present. It has not been looked over nor appraised yet. I am glad it is through for it is too much for Aunty to have the responsibility of looking after the baby when she is so sick and cross with teething. I must stay and take care of her myself. I am thankful to tell you that she has three large double teeth through, and considering this dry sickly time of year is tolerably well, but her little flesh that used to be so plump and solid has grown soft and transparent and there are deep blue circles round her eyes like Pearl [Ella's daughter] had when she was teething. Oh Dade when I gaze upon the sweet face and perfect form of our darling, I feel a thousand times paid for all the hardships I have had in the last two years. (on the 10th of this month will be the anniversary of our home leaving) I beleive that the Lord in mercy sent her to cheer and comfort me during this weary exile, and well she performs her mission. She kisses me fifty times a day, and what do you think. She sits in the same little chair that used to be her pa's. Father says it was made about 32 years ago. Joe [Udall] gave it to Edward Richey when he was a baby and now he is a grown man it comes back to this poor little refugee. Do you remember it?

Yesterday was the anniversary of the Y. Ladies organization. They had an ice-cream and strawberry festival. Bess Sparks bought a ticket and insisted on my going with her. So I went and took babe and it was just fun to see her enjoy the music etc. I took my own money along for extras but I was treated so much I did not have occasion to spend it. Will Bryan is so thoughtful of the widows & orphans. O. my dear how I wished you could have had some of their ice-cream and berries, they were splendid. Mary L. [Linton] was there looking lovely with Isaac Gad just returned from a mission her devoted escort.

I have just had a long letter from May [Ida's sister]. She talks quite favorably about Pa and all the family coming back to the Temple this fall while I am here. You see there are part of us that must be adopted, and we are all so anxious to have it done. She thinks they could not come till 1st of Nov. and oh! how can I wait that long. I should have to meet them at St George as they could come no farther north.

Dear I know this delay is wearing on you. You write as though your spirits were about flagged out. Be of good courage. The Lord has not forgotten you.

Ida

Letter 13: To David, 7 September 1886

Nephi, Juab Co. Utah   Sept 7th 1886

My Beloved Husband:

It is nine oclock p.m. Our little one has just closed her eyes in peaceful slumber for the night, and before following her example, I feel that I must dedicate a few of my thoughts and good wishes to her dear papa whose thirty-fifth birthday it is. Where are you and what are you doing tonight is the question uppermost in my mind. No doubt participating in a little merry making over the happy event. If so do you give one thought to your poor exiled girl, who feels that she is dying for one sight of your face?

How grateful I feel to the proud happy mother who clasped you to her heart for the first time, thirty five years ago today, and more especially to the merciful Father who blessed her in giving you birth, for without that birth how incomplete would be my existence at present.

How vividly I recall the different birthdays you have passed since I had the pleasure of being intimately associated with you. The first I remember was the thirtieth anniversary. Being in your employ at the time I was a boarder at your house, and participated in the pleasant surprise which your wife gave you. Your 31st birthday found me lately returned to your home, not as an employee, but as your fond loving wife and secretly cherished as such, although on account of religious persecution, to all outward appearance I held the same position as before. On your 32nd birthday Sisters [Mary] Freeman and [Mary A.] Farr proposed and assisted Ella and I in making you a nice party which was a surprise for you on your return from a hard days work in the field. Your 33rd anniversary found sister Eliza [Udall Tenny] and I refugees at Snowflake. Fled from home and the hands of our enemies to avoid testifying against our loved ones. It was a bleak windy Sunday in keeping with our spirits. Your 34th birthday alas! you were a lonely prisoner in the far away House of Correction at Detroit, and I, a heart broken wife and newly made mother, trying to write to you from my old home, Beaver. O what sad and happy changes can be brought about in one year. Although I have never seen you since that dreadful time, I have the blessed assurance that you are a *free man*, enjoying the blessings of *liberty, home*, and *friends*. For this I thank and praise the Lord & may another year bring about still happier changes is my constant prayer.

God bless you every day and hour,
   My husband tried and true!
Its truest, best and holiest love
   My heart still keeps for you.

O, say your love has not grown cold,
   Does absence break the chain
That bound our hearts so firmly once
   Er this sad parting came?

My heart grows faint at thot of all
   The weary months gone by,
Without one sight of your *dear* face
   One glance from love-lit eye.

But we'll be true, yes we'll be true,
   And may God speed the day
When free from *Courts* with our loved ones
   We'll live in peace alway.

                        Ida

Letter 17: To Lois Hunt, 8 November 1894 (in the Journal of Lois Hunt West)

Springerville, Arizona   November 8, 1894

My Dear little Sister Loie:

If I can keep my eyes open a few minutes, I want to say some words of congratulation and appreciation to you on this your 19th birthday. I have been thinking about you so much today.

How well I remember 19 years ago tonight we were all packed up ready to move onto the Sevier. Had gone over to Aunt Kits [Conover Hunt's] to spend the night, where we were expecting to leave our dear mamma for a month or so. Celia [Hunt] and I had been out to a literary meeting in company with "Big John Murdock." On our return at 11 p.m. our escort seemed quite talkative and inclined to spend the evening. Aunt Kit was on pins, and had to work several dodges to get him to take his leave. The next morning when he called to bid us good-bye before our starting for the Sevier, and found a little stranger had made her appearance, since his departure the night before. I know he felt rather cheap. So you see the very first day of your life, you were called upon to part with some of the dear ones whom you had just come to bless. Pa, Bell, John and I going to join May, Annie and Lewis on the Sevier, and leaving Ma, Nettie and you in charge of dear Aunt Kit and the girls, who were all devotion to the whole of you. They had a nice comfortable adobe house, and Aunt Kit was such a good nurse, that dear Ma was well cared for and always said her last was her easiest and best confinement. You must have enjoyed it too, (while your elder brothers and sisters were having such a hard time helping build a new home in the wilderness) for when you were a month old and Pa went back after you all, you were the sweetest, best natured little kitten of a babe, one ever need wish for, and we all loved you nearly to death. Now, although so many great changes have come, it seems impossible that you are 19 years old. May you have as many more birthdays as your heart can desire, and each one find you richer in wisdom, knowledge and all the graces, to say nothing of this world's comforts and blessings. How I wish I could be home tonight. I know you are all together having a good time somewhere. I hope dear Aunt Jane [Stoddard] is with you and that you will kiss her dear old face for me and give a thought to the absent ones who would like to be with you.

Letter 21: To David, 24 May 1905

Salt Lake City, Utah   May 24–1905

My Darling Husband:

As this is our twenty-third wedding day I am going to write you a few words to tell you how much I thank the Lord for you, and to tell you how I spent this wedding anniversary which has been one of the happiest in my life. Even though I am far from you I can think of you with joy and know you are "true to the core."

Last night Loie and I went to the [Salt Lake] theatre and today I have been dreaming of the play. I enclose a bill. As I looked over that brilliant audience last night I thought with joy that my husband and sons and daughter would compare favorably with the handsomest of them. All we lack is the money and cultural opportunities—and we will have them some day. I felt very thankful that I was able to appreciate the theatre to the fullest extent. My senses have not been blunted by seventeen years in the desert, so that I cannot tell a good thing when I see and hear it. Every strain from the orchestra was the sweetest music to me and the acting was very good.

X X X X X Kisses and love. Good night and sweet dreams

Ida

Letter 23: To Grover Udall, 16 July 1905

Nephi, Utah   July 16, 1905

My Dear Son Grover:

I dreamed last night of kissing and loving you and best of all you returned my love. It made me very happy, for I felt that you would be glad to see your mother once again. These scorching hot days make me fear for you and papa who have been so much effected by the sun.[1] I think of you in that old buckboard and wonder if you have a shade of any kind over it. Please write me a few lines Grover, and tell me how you are getting along. How is business generally? Do you ever take time to study and read and above all do you remember to pray for me and all of us? I gained five lbs. while in Salt Lake so I am going to have my photo taken and send you. They take them very cheap in Nephi. I don't know how good they will be. I came to Nephi on the 7th of July. Found dear old Grandpa and Aunty [Udall] better in health than they were in Arizona. Tho Grandma's sight is failing

very fast. They remember their nice visit in Arizona and ask about
all their grandchildren and I am so glad to be able to give them a good
report of them. We, Grandpa, Aunty and I, are going to Manti Temple
on Tues. next and work there one week. If cousin Celia [Hunt Bean]
is there I may go on to Richfield but cannot tell. You can direct a
letter to me at Nephi, Juab Co. and I will get the P.M. to forward it to
me if I go on. Tell Aunt Ella and the girls I am glad they have such a
good business but sorry they have to work so hard and are deprived
of meetings ec.[2] It seems to be a great worry to papa in the letter he
wrote me since the 4th. I hope you boys are good and thoughtful to
help them all you can while at Holbrook and at the Ranch too and
the Lord will bless you for it. I went and spent one night and day with
Uncle Laurence [Mariger]'s folks. Dagmar and husband live across
the street east. They all treated me so nicely, then they took me to
Saltair one day and we had a lovely time. Erma [Udall] can tell you
all about that. The bathing in Salt Lake is delightful. All the family
went bathing but Maty who took care of Dagmars boy. Tell Erma
that Laurence still goes with "his widow" he calls her. Vivian has
now gone out to work for the Wimmers on a ranch and they think
that will be better for him. I was going to see her Aunt Mary but she
has moved to another part of town and I will try and see them before I come home. I also went to Saltair as the guest of Sister [Maria]
Winder and to Calders Park as a guest of Sister [Clara?] Cannon and
went with Sister [Emma S.] Woodruff in an automobile to visit all
her daughters and to the theatre as the guest of Sr [Heber J.] Grant
besides Sister [Julia] Farnsworth took me all over the city. I did not go
out of the house on the 4th but the day before I went to a reception
at the Bee Hive house with Sr Farnsworth and heard all the grand
musicians and singers of the city. Now Grover I feel that all these
pleasures and honors have come to me as a reward for faithful labor at
home for many years, and they will surely come to you boys and girls
if you wait patiently and do your duty. I am thankful indeed our boys
are not being raised in a city. I hope you will be kind and obedient
to your papa for boys you have one father among a *thousand*. That's
what Pearl says and she is making quite a study of human nature,
living around as she has. God bless you always.

Your loving Mother   Ida H. Udall

Love to Aunt Ella and the girls and boys. Kiss little Don for me when
you go home. He will be eight years old this month and I am so
hungry to see you all.

Tell me how you enjoyed the 4th. People here are all so good to me. Have been visiting and buggy riding nearly everyday. Aunt Alice [Udall Edgehill] has a fine horse and buggy.[3]

Letter 25: To David, 28 August 1905

Beaver, Utah, Aug 28, 1905

My Best Beloved:

Your precious letter written at conference time in St. Johns has been received since coming to Beaver, and dear to say that it gave me the deepest joy, is too tame. To know that you never felt better in health and spirits, that you are loved and honored by all the dear ones at home, that our children are well and happy and obedient, and that I might hope to meet you face to face in a little more than a month now—what more could a loving wife ask!

The most of my old friends and classmates say that I have'nt grown older and they cannot believe I am married and have a family. How I wish you were all here with me to convince them. My old friend and beau, Johnnie Murdock looked at me in the same old tantalizing way and he didn't believe I had had a care or done a lick of work since I left Beaver so long ago. So my dear you are vindicated as a husband! X X X X X Kiss our boys and girls for me

Ida

Letter 56: To Pauline Udall, 23 August 1907

Hunt, Ariz   Aug 23rd 1907

My Darling Daughter,

It is after 9:30 and I am very tired, but I must drop you a line. We got home last Tues night quite late. We had an enjoyable trip. Nothing but pleasant memories of it. Will tell you all when I see you. Maud was the life of the party with her happy remeniscences of every little town and ranche.[4] She sent you a pair of lace stockings which I have in my trunk till you come. We found Aunt Mary [Morgan] nearly worked to death, as she had a steady run of customers while we were gone and it has kept it up since. We have never rested, but I am so glad you are enjoying yourself and having such an opportunity to study.[5] I pray constantly that you may be blessed with strength and wisdom, to keep the friendship and esteem of all your associates. If some from St J. do act unwisely don't you say any thing. Bro [Andrew] Gibbons was telling me he did not know whether you signed the contract & returned it as Julia had not notified him. I told him you surely had. Have you decided to try for first grade?[6] If so where? Dr Waite & wife were here yesterday, stayed two hours. He was the dentist who treated the girls so nicely in Winslow. Has wife and one little daughter. They are lovely. We gave their horses lunch and treated them the best we could for the girls sake. He said he would be pleased to fill your tooth and would guarantee it to *stay* if you would drop him a line. You could stop off on the morning train, wait till evening or if you would consent to they would be pleased to entertain you over night. That is the place to get your work done as he is a resident of Winslow, never leaves there only for a summer out, and the girls are well satisfied with his work.

Aug 24th   I am glad you are having such good times with Jesse,[7] for I imagine he has a lonely life, but be careful dear that he does not spend too much money on you individually. It is all right when he takes the crowd. But I have full confidence that you understand J. C's [Crosby's] turn of mind and will govern yourself accordingly. God bless you always. I hunger & thirst to see you. The boys and papa are getting anxious too. Grover would have written you today but said you would soon be home. He and Harold [Morgan] are hauling wheat. The others, Lin [Morgan], H [John H.], and Jesse cutting & raking lucern. David [Ella's son] is at St Johns putting up hay. We have had such heavy rain it hinders the harvest so. I have not seen Sr Farr since I returned. Poor folks their wheat is badly shrunken with rust, I expect she has the blues.

Well Arthur Tenney was here last night so I could not finish. He was telling papa all his sorrows. I guess there is bound to be a separation between him and his wife. Grace & Sue stopped with us the night before. Poor folks. Yesterday was H's birthday. I gave him a heifer and Aunt Mary a knife. I would like you to take time to purchase us a good cupboard in Holbrook and get some freighter to bring it up. Go to every store in town and see where the best washers and cupboards, chairs etc. are. Now goodbye for a short time. One more week and then—

Love to all your family in which I am joined by all

Your mother   Ida H. Udall

When does the Dist school start in St Johns. Papa says boys can't go from here till corn is up and crop thrashed.

Letter 69: To Ann Louisa Pratt Willis, 22 December 1914

St Johns, Ariz.   Dec 22nd 1914

My Dear Aunt Louisa:

As Christmas time draws near, how my heart goes out to you Auntie, the only person living besides Pa, who knew us or was intimately associated with us in our childhood. How cruel it seems that the few of the Pratt blood who are left on earth cannot be together at Xmas time. If I had the money and the health and strength, you and dear coz Nellie [McGary Jones] would come to us or we would go to you, and spend the coldest months of winter including the Holiday season together. Then would'ent we have a good time talking over our Christmases in dear old Beaver. I still remember the gingerbread boys and girls you used to make to help fill our gaping stockings, and other surprises you helped Santa Claus to carry out. If we were to have a new dress for any occasion *You* were the one to help get it done on time. (until dear little Aunt Kit [Conover Hunt] came to live near us.) How good you were to our dear mother, and how devoted she was to you in return. O Aunty to renew the beautiful associations with dear old Grandma and her girls is something to look forward to is it not? May we be worthy of each other is my constant prayer. Do you remember the "Star of Bethlehem" Grandma used to make and set out on her roof on Xmas Eve? Truly it beckons us on. As the nights begin to get so cold I have hard work to sleep warm in my cozy warm room with the sun beating thro south windows by day and a good stove and plenty of wood at night, then I think of you living away up in that cold snowy country perhaps with out plenty of wood and coal, and no one living with you, and I feel so worried about you I cannot sleep when I wake and get to thinking about you in the night.[8] I wonder how you get along for food and clothes. Are your little grand *children* Robert and Louesa thoughtful to come and see you every day, and could they go out in the snow and get your supplies if you had the money to purchase with? All these things I think & wonder about, and it would be such a joy to me if I only had a $10.00 or $20.00 bill to send you for Christmas. But to tell you the truth, dear Aunty, finances have been very close with us for the last few months   I have not had the heart to mention money for any thing, but we hope for better times in the near future, as we have lately been awarded third interest in a mail contract from Holbrook to Eagar, to begin running in Feb. so that gives us a little hope, and my son John H. has been elected clerk of the Superior Court of

Apache Co. which is a four years job at a good salary. Of course he is married & lives away from me 4 blocks but then I know as long as he has money his mother will never want. It is the same with all my children, and I realize that altho I am so helpless myself, I am rich in having *six* children. If I only knew that you had Tylman[9] at home with you I should not worry for if Tym as a man is anything like he was as a boy he would see that his mother did not need for any good thing. If you could have your lost boy home you would scarcely need a pension, but I hope and pray with all my heart that the year 1915 may bring both your boy and a pension both of which you richly deserve.

Jan 4th, 1915   Dear Aunty you will see how long I have been writing the foregoing and yet I have not said half I wish to. I hope May told you about our three weeks visit to Snowflake about Thanksgiving time. We did have a good time but O when I went to Bells I did miss you, and it seemed so strange to see so many pretty babies at Bells home, so long without any.[10] Marion & Cynthia surely make ideal parents for twins.[11] She has plenty of nurse for both babes. Never has had to feed them once, and Bell is indeed a happy grandma. I made my home with Aunt Hap while there   I had a good visit with Pa who seems quite smart for one of his age. He eats well and sleeps well and is able to ride horseback every day up to see Uncle Marsh who seems to be very near the end of his earthly career.[12] May writes that he is too weak to talk now which is something that never happened tho he is 87 years old. Dear old Aunt Sarah is just as faithful to him as she always was.

We passed the Holidays very pleasantly. We have two teachers boarding with us, also Levi and his young wife Louise Lee, grand daughter to Louesa Benalla whom you used to know. Then our English cousin,[13] besides Luella and her husband who have come to practice in St Johns and have 2 rooms in our house. So we have a jolly crowd of young people for Xmas times. Write and tell me how you passed the Holidays and all about yourself. Every detail is of interest. I am sure I have answered your letters but you have failed to receive them. I think I must have your number wrong so please give me your address every time you write. Accept the love and good wishes of our entire family for a Happy New Year.

Your loving neice   Ida Udall

NOTES

Abbreviations

Names

Ida	Ida Franccs Hunt Udall (second wife of David K. Udall)
David	David King Udall (married Ella and Ida)
Ella	Eliza Luella ("Ella") Stewart Udall (first wife of David K. Udall)
Pauline	Pauline Udall Smith (Ida's daughter, married Asahel H. Smith)
Pearl	Pearl Udall Nelson (Ella's daughter, married Joseph Nelson)
Annie	Annella Hunt Kartchner (Ida's sister, married Orrin Kartchner)
Bell	Christabell Hunt (Ida's sister, married Charles L. Flake)
May	May Louise Hunt Larson (Ida's sister, married Alof Larson)
Nettie	Nettie Hunt Rencher (Ida's sister, married Joseph A. Rencher)
Lois, Loie	Lois Hunt West (Ida's sister, married Joseph A. West)

Books and Depository

David King Udall	David King Udall, in collaboration with Pearl Udall Nelson, *Arizona Pioneer Mormon: David King Udall, His Story and His Family, 1851–1938* (Tucson: Arizona Silhouettes, 1959).
Jesse N. Smith	Jesse N. Smith, *Journal of Jesse Nathaniel Smith: The Life Story of a Mormon Pioneer, 1834–1906* (Salt Lake City: Jesse N. Smith Family Association, 1953).
Joseph Fish	Joseph Fish, *The Life and Times of Joseph Fish*, ed. John H. Krenkel (Danville, Ill.: Interstate Printers and Publishing, 1970). The journals of Joseph Fish.
AJ, LDSBE	Andrew Jenson, *Latter-day Saint Biographical Encyclopedia*, 4 vols. (Salt Lake City: Andrew Jenson History Co., 1901–36).
AJ, EH	Andrew Jenson, *Encyclopedic History of the Church* (Salt Lake City: Deseret News, 1941).

AJ, CC   Andrew Jenson, *Church Chronology* (Salt Lake City: Deseret News, 1899).

CHD Archives   The Church of Jesus Christ of Latter-day Saints, Historical Department, Archives. Salt Lake City.

Introduction

1. Orson F. Whitney, *History of Utah* (Salt Lake City, Utah: George Q. Cannon and Sons, 1904), 4:580.

2. "David K. Udall," AJ, LDSBE, 1:328.

Ida's Memoirs to 1874

1. Pauline Udall Smith, *Captain Jefferson Hunt of the Mormon Battalion* (Salt Lake City: Nicholas G. Morgan, Sr., Foundation, 1958), treats ancestry and family relations. See also Nettie Hunt Rencher, *John Hunt—Frontiersman* (Salt Lake City: Privately printed, 1966).

2. Ida's father, John Hunt, then fourteen years old, and Ida's grandmother, Celia Mounts Hunt, reached Salt Lake Valley 27 July 1847 with the sick detachment of the Mormon Battalion.

3. See biographical chapters in S. George Ellsworth, ed., *The Journals of Addison Pratt* (Salt Lake City: University of Utah Press, 1990); "Journal of Louisa Barnes Pratt," in *Heart Throbs of the West*, ed. Kate Carter (Salt Lake City, Utah: Daughters of Utah Pioneers, 1947), 8:189–400; and the holograph journals of Louisa Barnes Pratt and her sister Caroline Barnes Crosby in CHD Archives and Utah State Historical Society, respectively.

4. The breakup of the Mormon colony at San Bernardino as it related to the Pratt family is told in Ellsworth, *Addison Pratt;* the journals of Louisa Barnes Pratt and Caroline Barnes Crosby; and George William Beattie and Helen Pruitt Beattie, *Heritage of the Valley: San Bernardino's First Century* (Oakland, Calif.: Biobooks, 1951).

5. Ephraim Pratt, adopted by the Pratt family, was the son of Benjamin F. Grouard and Tearo, a native of the island of Anaa, Tuamotu Group, of the Society Islands. He ran away from home, was captured and held by the Sioux Indians for years, escaped, and turned guide to Captain Crook in the Indian wars. He took his brother's name of Frank and his father's surname Grouard. Joe DeBarthe, *The Life and Adventures of Frank Grouard* (St. Joseph, Mo.: Come Printing, 1894).

6. In preparing the journals of Louisa Barnes Pratt for publication by the Daughters of Utah Pioneers, Nettie Hunt Rencher inserted a story ("At that time . . . photographed together," pp. 353–54) to the effect that it was on this trip (when Ida was eight) that she had her hair cut and sold to a wife of Brigham Young. This is the only place where the story is told. Louisa's original journal does not mention such an event in Salt Lake City. When Ida's sister

May filled out Ida's memoir for her, she wrote, "She omitted the sale of hair, when she was 12. She had such heavy, lovely hair—too heavy for her head, which caused headaches, and good old Dr. Christian advised cutting it off, which nearly broke her heart, also the hearts of the rest of the family. I do not remember who cut it, but think it was Aunt Ellen, but how well I remember how she looked with it off. Grandma Pratt found a chance to sell it in Salt Lake City, to Aunty Twiss, a wife of Prest. B. Young, whose hair it exactly matched. She paid $8.00 in cash, and cloth in the amount of four dollars. $12.00." Photographs of Ida with the hair cut support May's account.

7. Latter-day Saints also used the word *Aunt* to designate a plural wife other than the natural mother. Aunt Matilda was Jefferson Hunt's plural wife.

8. Lucinda Lee (later Mrs. Charles W. Dalton), one of Utah's distinguished women, was noted as a teacher and a leader in women's rights movements in Utah. Her "Autobiography," written at Circle Valley, Piute County, Utah Territory, in 1876, is in the Bancroft Library, University of California, Berkeley, MS. P-F 20.

9. Thomas Willis had little education and poor eyesight, making it difficult for him to find employment. See Ida's journal entry for 27 August 1885. Ellen and her husband William McGary had been living in Ogden when he divorced her to marry a younger woman. Ellen returned to Beaver to live with her mother.

10. Louisa Barnes Pratt, Journal, typescript in possession of Maria S. Ellsworth, 363–76 (all page numbers refer to typescript version).

11. Aunt Mary was the daughter of Jefferson Hunt and his first wife, Celia, and a sister of John Hunt, Ida's father.

12. Professor Richard S. Horne of Salt Lake City, one of Utah's leading pioneer educators, came to Beaver and established a school of high ethical and educational standing. Students received a foundation seldom secured outside of colleges during that period. After the departure of Professor Horne for Salt Lake City, the school did not recover its high academic standards until the arrival of Professor R. Maeser in 1881. J. F. Tolton, *History of Beaver* (N.p., n.d.), chapters 8 and 13.

13. Hattie Shepherd was the daughter of Marcus Lafayette Shepherd, bishop of the Beaver First Ward. She married William Farnsworth.

14. The Young Ladies' Mutual Improvement Association (Y.L.M.I.A.) was founded by Brigham Young in November 1869 and the Young Men's Mutual Improvement Association (Y.M.M.I.A.) followed in June 1875. In those days, these organizations met weekly in ward meetings and sponsored intellectual, cultural, and spiritual activities, religious and moral lessons, and social and recreational activities, which served to encourage a love of music, public speaking, and social graces.

15. John R. Murdock was president of the Beaver Stake from 1877 to 1891. He served eight terms in the territorial legislature, was later a member of the state constitutional convention, and served one term in the state legislature. He was the father of Johnny Murdock, who had a romantic interest in Ida. AJ, LDSBE, 1:304.

16. With the coming of the transcontinental railroad to Utah in 1869, the mining frontier opened up rapidly, including west of Beaver, where successful mines were developed at Frisco, and mining towns like Minersville and Milford boomed. The mining frontier in Beaver County was based on earlier, successful lead mining at the Lincoln mine site.

Ida's Birthday Book, 1873 to 1905

1. At the celebration, Ida read a "Sketch of the Lives of My Grandparents Jefferson and Celia Hunt" (in Ida Hunt Udall Papers), which she had written in 1893 while her Grandmother Hunt was in Snowflake.

From Youth to Marriage, 1874 to 1882

1. Louisa Barnes Pratt, Journal, 422–23, typescript in possession of Maria S. Ellsworth.
2. Beaver Ward, Literary Society, minutes, CHD Archives.
3. Annie, Journal, 1, typed extracts in possession of Maria S. Ellsworth; May, Journal, 16, CHD Archives.
4. May, Journal, n.d. December 1876.
5. Louisa Barnes Pratt, Journal, 513.
6. Copy of blessing in Ida Hunt Udall Papers, in possession of Maria S. Ellsworth.
7. The endowment refers to certain temple ordinances wherein persons covenant obedience to the gospel and are promised special spiritual blessings.
8. Ida, Ledger Book, diary of trip, Ida Hunt Udall Papers. See also Annie, Journal; May, diary of the trip; George S. Tanner, "As It Was? or As You Like It?" 1987, typescript in possession of Maria S. Ellsworth; and George S. Tanner and J. Morris Richards, *Colonization on the Little Colorado: The Joseph City Region* (Flagstaff: Northland Press, 1977), 26–28, 175.
9. Tanner, "As It Was? or As You Like It?" 1.
10. Ibid.; Annie, Journal, 2.
11. Annie, Journal, 2.
12. Ibid.
13. Louisa Barnes Pratt, Journal, 521. The family pronounced her given name as Low-wise-uh, while her daughter's name was pronounced Lew-weez.
14. Caroline Barnes Crosby, Journal, 1247, typescript in possession of Maria S. Ellsworth.
15. Louisa Barnes Pratt, Journal, 521.
16. Beaver Stake, Young Ladies' Mutual Improvement Association, records, CHD Archives.
17. Caroline Barnes Crosby, Journal, 1262–63.
18. Louisa Barnes Pratt, Journal, 526.
19. Caroline Barnes Crosby, Journal, 1310.

20. Ibid., 1323, 1298.

21. Ibid., 1264.

22. Ibid., 1279.

23. Ibid., 1288.

24. Louisa Barnes Pratt, Journal, 524.

25. Ida to her parents, Beaver, Utah, 8 September 1879.

26. Caroline Barnes Crosby, Journal, 1309, 1310.

27. Louisa Barnes Pratt, Journal, 526.

28. Caroline Barnes Crosby, Journal, 1318–19.

29. Ibid., 1317.

30. Ibid., 1320.

31. Louisa Barnes Pratt, Journal, 526–27.

32. Ibid., 527.

33. Henry Pratt (1771–1841) of Winchester, New Hampshire, began making organs in 1792 and became one of America's first native organ builders. His instruments are museum pieces today and may be seen in Old Sturbridge Village, Sturbridge, Massachusetts; Storrowton Village Museum, West Springfield, Massachusetts; the Conant Library, Winchester, New Hampshire; and elsewhere. "Organ-Building in New England," *New England Magazine* 6 (January and March 1834), 25–44, 205–15.

34. This rich heritage was shared by word of mouth and in the journals of Louisa Barnes Pratt. Ida held the journals, and upon her death David K. Udall took them to her sister Nettie H. Rencher, who had them published by the Daughters of Utah Pioneers in 1947 and later put them into the hands of S. George and Maria S. Ellsworth for use in connection with the publication of the Addison Pratt journals and other projects. On 2 April 1987 they were deposited in the Church Historical Department Archives in the name of Nettie Hunt Rencher.

35. *Jesse N. Smith*, 239.

36. Louisa Barnes Pratt, Journal, 529–30.

37. *Jesse N. Smith*, 242–43.

38. The story of Ida's conversion to polygamy while traveling with Jesse N. Smith's families was told repeatedly to me by her daughter Pauline, my mother.

39. Eastern Arizona Stake, Young Ladies' Mutual Improvement Association, History, CHD Archives; Susa Young Gates, *History of the Young Ladies' Mutual Improvement Association* (Salt Lake City: General Board of the Y.L.M.I.A., 1911), 426–30.

40. Eastern Arizona Stake, Stake Relief Society, History, CHD Archives.

41. Annie, Journal, 3.

42. May completed Ida's memoirs by writing in Ida's journal, 34–35.

43. Folder 12, no. 23, Addison Pratt Family Papers, in possession of Maria S. Ellsworth.

44. Annie, Journal, 3.

45. Pauline, "A Life Sketch of Ida Hunt Udall," July 1941, typescript, Pauline Udall Smith Papers, in possession of Maria S. Ellsworth.

46. *David King Udall*; Pearl, "Synopsis of Sketch of Mother's Life," 12 May 1933, typescript in possession of Maria S. Ellsworth; "David A. Udall" and "David K. Udall," in AJ, LDSBE, 2:112–13 and 1:325–38, respectively.

47. Annie, Journal, 3.

48. *David King Udall*, 97.

49. Ibid., 97–98.

50. Ibid., 99–101.

51. Ibid.

52. Annie, Journal, 3.

53. *David King Udall*, 97; family stories maintained that David did not like the discord between his father's two wives.

54. Witness the experiences of Hiram B. and Ellen S. Clawson, in Salt Lake City, where financial security was assured, as told in letters and poems by Ellen Clawson. S. George Ellsworth, ed., *Dear Ellen: Two Mormon Women and Their Letters* (Salt Lake City: University of Utah Library, 1974).

55. The best introduction now to the vast literature on the Mormon experience with "celestial marriage," the "plurality system," or "polygamy," is Davis Bitton, "Mormon Polygamy: A Review Article," *Journal of Mormon History* 4 (1977), 101–18. Richard S. Van Wagoner, *Mormon Polygamy: A History* (Salt Lake City: Signature Books, 1989), covers the subject rather well. See also Lawrence Foster, "'Reluctant Polygamists': The Strains and Challenges of the Transition to Polygamy in a Prominent Mormon Family," in *Religion and Society in the American West: Historical Essays*, ed. Carl Guarneri and David Alvarez (New York: University Press of America, 1988); and Lowell ("Ben") Bennion, "The Incidence of Mormon Polygamy in 1880: 'Dixie' versus Davis Stake," *Journal of Mormon History* 11 (1984), 27–42.

56. Jane Snyder Richards, "The Inner Facts of Social Life in Utah," San Francisco, 1880, Bancroft MS. P-F 2, Bancroft Library, University of California, Berkeley.

57. *David King Udall*, 98.

58. The history of St. Johns may be traced in *Joseph Fish*; Joseph Fish, "History of Arizona Territory," typescript, CHD Archives; Charles S. Peterson, *Take Up Your Mission: Mormon Colonizing along the Little Colorado River, 1870–1900* (Tucson: University of Arizona Press, 1973); and *David King Udall*.

Just two months before the wedding trip, Congress passed the Edmunds Act of 1882, amending the 1862 antibigamy act, the first major anti-Mormon, antipolygamy legislation. Upheld by the U.S. Supreme Court, the law was the basis for the judicial crusade against the Mormons in the coming years. Polygamists would be sought out, caught, tried, and, if proven guilty, fined and imprisoned. If they were found guilty of polygamy, they could be fined up to $500 and imprisoned for five years; for "unlawful cohabitation," they could be fined up to $300 and imprisoned for six months. The threat of prosecution hung over David and Ida from the first day of their marriage. Although David suffered greatly from prosecutions, he was not tried for polygamy until

1905, when times had changed and the matter was resolved by his pleading guilty and paying the fine.

59. *David K. Udall,* 101.

Ida's Journal, 1882 to 1886

Ida used the following to indicate she was omitting a passage from the quoted letters: xxx.

1. The route taken by David's family was that of settlers going to Arizona and those going back to Utah, including wedding parties en route to the St. George Temple. See H. Dean Garrett, "The Honeymoon Trail," *Ensign* 19 (July 1989), 23–27; and Constance Brown, "Wagons Ho!: Retracing the Honeymoon Trail," *Americana* 8 (September/October 1980), 48–53.

2. Lot Smith was one of the pioneer leaders of the settlement along the Little Colorado River. He settled Sunset, where he served as president of the Little Colorado Stake from 1878. The history of Mormon settlement is traced in Charles S. Peterson, *Take Up Your Mission: Mormon Colonizing along the Little Colorado River, 1870–1900* (Tucson: University of Arizona Press, 1973). See also his " 'A Mighty Man Was Brother Lot': A Portrait of Lot Smith—Mormon Frontiersman," *Western Historical Quarterly* 1 (October 1970), 393–414.

3. Mary Udall, David's sister, married Ella's brother William Thomas (Tommy) Stewart.

4. "Between Mt. Carmel and Kanab, US 89 passes through Three Lakes Canyon, with its cave lakes and vari-colored, wind-blown sandstone formations. . . ." *Utah: A Guide to the State* (New York: Hastings House, 1941), 344.

5. Ammon M. Tenney married David's sister Eliza. Born in 1844, in Lee County, Iowa, he went to Utah in 1848 with his family and on to San Bernardino. In California he learned Spanish, which served him well on his missions among the Indians.

6. The incident is detailed in Joseph Fish, "History of Arizona Territory," typescript, 629–30, CHD Archives: "On June 24, 1882, Saint John's Day, the Mexicans were having a bull fight and celebration in St. Johns, Apache County. The Mexicans had ill feelings toward the Greers on account of their running off and scattering their sheep herds. The Greers were advised not to go to St. Johns upon this occasion as the Mexicans would make them trouble. They, however, with a few of their friends, eight in number decided to go. They were requested while in the store to give up their firearms which they refused to do. As they went from the store across the street the Mexicans to the number of about sixty who were secreted on top and behind buildings opened fire upon them. Four of the party escaped, one being wounded. The other four ran into an unfinished house near by, where a shower of bullets was poured in upon them, one man was killed and the other three finally surrendered to the Sheriff and were disarmed and put in jail where they were

guarded by citizens from this and other places to keep them from being lynched. Nathan C. Tenney, an old man, (one of the first settlers at Woodruff) went to stop the fight while it was going on and was shot through the head and killed instantly, while on his mission of peace. The arms that Sheriff Stover took from the three Greer boys were never returned, but were given to the Mexicans who carried them for years afterwards. After some expensive legal proceedings the boys were finally released. . . ."

7. Ida asked David and Ella to send bed ticking from the St. Johns store. Ida to David and Ella, Snowflake, Arizona, 4 July 1882, David K. Udall Papers, Special Collections, University Library, University of Arizona, Tucson.

8. Frances Stevens Pratt Dyer, third daughter of Addison Pratt and Louisa Barnes Pratt and sister of Lois (Mrs. John) Hunt, lived in Anaheim, Orange County, California, with her husband and child.

9. Meadows Ward included those Saints residing in The Meadows, about seven miles northwest of St. Johns, a valley about two miles wide and four miles long, watered by the Little Colorado River. First settled in November 1879, it flourished only a few years. AJ, EH, 486.

10. Miles P. Romney had two wives with him in St. Johns: Catherine Cottam Romney (married 15 September 1873) and Annie Maria Woodbury Romney (married 1 August 1877).

11. At year's end, Latter-day Saints were encouraged to examine for correctness the bishop's record of their voluntary contributions and if need be make up that which might be due, in cash or in kind.

12. Apostles Brigham Young, Jr., and Heber J. Grant were often assigned to visit these Arizona settlements, give instructions, and take messages to church headquarters.

13. Apparently the bargain was that May, Ida's sister, would take minutes for her, which she did. The sisters presided at and conducted these Sisters Conferences.

14. Round Valley, about thirty miles south of St. Johns, sustained two towns, Springerville and Eagar. The Udall family later lived there.

15. See note 21.

16. Ida's son-in-law, Asahel Smith, wrote that David told him that while Ida was teaching school, he would go to the schoolhouse after school for private moments with Ida that he could not have at home. Pauline Udall Smith Papers, in possession of Maria S. Ellsworth.

17. Andrew S. Gibbons and his son William H. Gibbons had pioneered southern Utah and Arizona: the Iron Mission, St. George, the Muddy, and then Arizona. In 1879 William H. Gibbons was called to St. Johns, where he served as counselor to David K. Udall in both the bishopric and stake presidency. AJ, LDSBE, 2:194; 4:704; 1:328.

The William A. Moffetts were called to Arizona in 1884 and remained two years, after which he was released to return to Utah to care for his aged parents. AJ, LDSBE, 2:673.

18. The newspaper, *Apache Chief*, edited by George A. McCarter, inflamed public anti-Mormon feelings and encouraged the people to follow the

example of Missouri and Illinois and expel the Mormons. *Joseph Fish*, 254; *David K. Udall*, 115–16.

19. Joseph Fish recorded that "everything was done to annoy and harrass the people that it was possible for them to do. The Board of Supervisors laid out a road through the center of three or four city lots belonging to these people and they also attached the school district of the Mormons to that of the Mexicans. The way for getting the certificates for Mormon school teachers was hedged up. The jumping of their lands was another great source of annoyance to the Mormons. Louie Trauer, a clerk of Sol. [Solomon] Barth's, and another man started the jumping of streets and erected a cabin in the center of one of them. Vacant city lots were jumped and held by force of arms. At the jumping of one of these lots David K. Udall and some others went to try to settle the matter and to avert the shedding of blood of which there was danger. For this act of peace making they were arrested." Fish, "History of Arizona Territory," 630.

20. Francis M. Lyman, son of Amasa M. Lyman, had lived in the San Bernardino colony. He was ordained an apostle in 1880. Thereafter he was often on visits to Arizona. With other leaders he was in Arizona and Mexico in January 1885, when so many Mormons were forced to leave St. Johns and move to Mexico. He was on the "underground" from 19 January 1886 to December 1888. He served time in the penitentiary.

21. C. G. W. French had served as chief justice and as judge in the First Judicial District from 1876 to 1884. Sumner Howard was chief justice of the Arizona Supreme Court, 1884–85. He had served in the judiciary in Utah and was famous for his harsh treatment of the Mormons. J. Jay Wagoner, *Arizona Territory, 1863–1912: A Political History* (Tucson: University of Arizona Press, 1970), 497–98, 504.

22. Joseph Udall married Emma Goldsbrough of Nephi, Utah.

23. Nettie Hunt Rencher wrote of her mother's illness: "A few years after Mother's last child was born, she had had a very serious miscarriage, with no doctor or nurse to attend her. Not long after this she started having fainting spells." Nettie Hunt Rencher, *John Hunt—Frontiersman* (Salt Lake City: Privately printed, 1966), 59–105, 96.

24. Ida was pregnant at the time she left St. Johns.

25. Willford, in the mountains near Round Valley.

26. Ida was in the best of company for her. Joseph F. Smith was a member of the First Presidency of the church and as a polygamist himself was most sympathetic to her situation. Apostle Erastus Snow and Ida would have many friends in common. John Morgan took special interest in her. Note their relations hereafter. Lorenzo H. Hatch was first counselor to Jesse N. Smith, president of the Snowflake Stake. He had come to the Little Colorado in 1878 and settled at Woodruff.

27. The Morgan Academy was on South Main Street.

28. The Groesbeck and Morgan families were related by marriage. Nicholas Groesbeck resided in Salt Lake City from 1856 till his death in 1884. With the coming of the railroad, he turned to mining in Little Cottonwood Canyon,

opening the Flagstaff Mine and coal and iron mines in Summit and Iron counties. John Morgan, who was married to Mellie Groesbeck, had served missions to the southern states and in October 1884 was ordained one of the First Seven Presidents of Seventies, a quorum ranking next to the Quorum of the Twelve. He traveled widely, devoted much time to church affairs, but was not particularly successful financially. He died in 1894 in Preston, Idaho. AJ, LDSBE, 1:204; Arthur M. Richardson and Nicholas G. Morgan, Sr., *The Life and Ministry of John Morgan* (Salt Lake City: Nicholas G. Morgan, Sr., 1965).

29. Dolman is a woman's coat with tapered sleeves.

30. David Udall was born in Kent, England, in 1829, joined the church and emigrated to Utah in 1852, and settled in Nephi, where he spent his life except for the years 1870–75, when he answered the call to settle in Kanab. He was bishop of the Nephi Second Ward from 1883 to 1891. He had three wives: Eliza King (married 2 December 1850), Elizabeth Rowley (married 5 April 1857), and Rebecca May (married 2 July 1864). Elizabeth and Rebecca, at different times, served in the presidency of the Relief Society. AJ, EH, 568; AJ, LDSBE, 2:112; *David King Udall*, 275–87.

31. George Washington Bean was a civic and church leader, who became first counselor in the Sevier Stake presidency from 1888 to 1894. AJ, LDSBE, 4:611.

32. Emmeline B. Wells, one of Utah's most distinguished women, was at this time editor and publisher of the *Woman's Exponent*. She had assisted in founding the Women's Relief Society in Utah and was active in women's rights movements. She was married to Daniel H. Wells, prominent church and civic leader. AJ, LDSBE, 2:731, 4:199, 586.

John Q. Cannon, a son of George Q. Cannon and a church and business leader, was likely there on business. He was in the printing business and was second counselor to William B. Preston, presiding bishop of the church from 1884 to 1886. AJ, LDSBE, 1:243, 4:387.

33. Helen Mar Whitney wrote *Plural Marriage, as Taught by the Prophet Joseph Smith* (Salt Lake City: Juvenile Instructor Office, 1882) and *Why We Practice Plural Marriage* (Salt Lake City: Juvenile Instructor Office, 1884).

34. John R. Murdock was president of the Beaver Stake. See Ida's memoirs, note 15.

35. Ida was to have close associations with the Pitchforths, Bryans, and Teasdales. Samuel and Mary Pitchforth came to Utah in 1847. Besides Mary, Samuel had a wife named Nora.

In December 1872, Brigham Young took Colonel Thomas L. Kane and his wife Elizabeth on a tour to St. George, stopping at Mormon homes en route. At Nephi they stopped at the Pitchforth home. Elizabeth Wood Kane described the household in her *Twelve Mormon Homes Visited in Succession on a Journey through Utah to Arizona* (Salt Lake City: University of Utah Library, 1974), 25–50.

36. W. A. C. Bryan, Juab County recorder from 1886 to 1888, hired Ida to copy court records. His wife Lizzie was a beautiful woman and an actress with many contacts in Salt Lake City.

o AJ, LDSBE, 1:629; and S. George Ellsworth, ed., *Dear Women and Their Letters* (Salt Lake City: University 4), which provides insight into the Hiram B. Clawson

parently did not survive.
op of the Salt Lake City Twentieth Ward, one of Utah's fluential men, and a polygamist, was arraigned 18 Sepird District Court for "unlawful cohabitation." Conactice of not admitting guilt, he pleaded guilty to the obey the law in the future. He was fined $300 and eated a sensation and was deplored by faithful Latterntained that "it was evident that Bishop Sharp had no wives, disown his children, or renounce his religion; rtheless, he was criticized for the example he was of Utah, 3:420–23; James B. Allen, " 'Good Guys' arp and Civil Disobedience in Nineteenth-century uarterly 48 (Spring 1980), 148–74.

widow of Gilbert Hunt, John Hunt's brother.
was bishop of the Joseph City, Utah, Ward from , LDSBE, 2:39; AJ, EH, 378.
sby family went by nicknames: Sarah was called am, Billy; and Jacob, Jake. Rencher, *John Hunt—*

with Ida's use of her mother's name in order to

Brigham Young, had extensive business interth the Atlantic and Pacific Road in Arizona, Colorado settlements. He traveled much. "Durh time in the East assisting in efforts of the endence for Utah and freedom from oppressive an C. Jessee, ed., *Letters of Brigham Young to* ret Book, 1974), 93.
aunched in 1850, was the church's daily newsedited by church people, was published beile Instructor, started in 1866, was published d members generally. Founded in 1840 and Latter-day Saints' Millennial Star reported eral news from Utah and the church.
the son of Apostle Franklin D. Richards udied law and was admitted to the Utah ar in 1881. During the 1880s he was emiser and general attorney. In Washington, tial in negotiations for the benefit of the courage and dignity and yet was affable 59; Whitney, *History of Utah*, 4:532–37;

37. Apostles Wilford Woodruff and George Teasdale, who was a resident apostle in Nephi. Born in London in 1831, Teasdale devoted full time to the ministry until he came to Utah in 1861. He was called to take charge of the Juab Stake, managing tithing resources and other programs. He was ordained an apostle in 1880 and from his Nephi base visited Mormon settlements from Idaho to Mexico. His wives were M. E., Etta Picton, and Tillie. AJ, LDSBE, 1:144, 3:790, 4:320, 345; Orson F. Whitney, *History of Utah* (Salt Lake City: George Q. Cannon and Sons, 1892–1904), 4:272.

38. William Paxman, an English convert, came to Utah in 1861 and settled in Nephi. He succeeded George Teasdale as stake president on 28 January 1883. The people loved him and held him in high esteem, erecting a monument to him honoring his life. He had three wives and twenty-two children. AJ, LDSBE, 1:515, 517; 4:308, 497, 498, 594.

39. Aunt Kit was Catherine Conover Hunt, wife of Joseph Hunt. See Appendix 1, the last paragraph of Ida's memoirs, and "From Youth to Marriage," herein.

40. Kit's daughters Celia and Ina married George F. Bean and Epaminondas Bean, respectively, sons of George W. Bean. The husbands were called Tank and Pam.

41. Ammon M. Tenney was David's brother-in-law. Christopher J. Kemp was later bishop of Concho Ward from 1886 to 1895. Peter J. Christoffersen was bishop of Eagar Ward, 1880–83. William J. Flake was the pioneer founder of Snowflake. All were polygamists, not necessarily church officers. AJ, LDSBE, 4:596, 597.

42. Seymour B. Young was one of the Seven Presidents of Seventies.

43. The St. Johns "Ring" was headed by Solomon Barth, a founder of the city who had come to St. Johns in 1873. He had business interests in mail contracts, merchandising, land, and cattle. Other Ring leaders included E. S. Stover, J. L. Hubbell, C. L. Gutterson, George Creigh, Charles Kenner, Henry Huning, and a Mr. Lopez. *Joseph Fish*, 247–48.

44. Mary Linton was the daughter of Nephi pioneer Samuel Linton and was a neighbor of David Udall. Mary became closely identified with Ida and her life.

45. John Bushman was the bishop of the St. Joseph (Joseph City, Arizona) Ward. He had come to Arizona with some two hundred others in 1876 to settle along the Little Colorado. See "From Youth to Marriage," herein; and AJ, LDSBE, 1:553.

John Henry Standifird was a pioneer settler of Taylor in 1878 and the first bishop of Taylor, Arizona Ward. He was succeeded by Bishop Merrill E. Willis in 1885. AJ, EH, 863; Bess Ericksen, ed., *Snowflake Stake, 1887–1987: 100 Years of Faith and Service* ([Snowflake, Ariz.: Snowflake Stake, 1987]).

46. Goldsbrough was the father of Emma (Mrs. Joseph) Udall.

47. Kate Love had recently become the plural wife of President William Paxman. She had been the president of the highly successful Young Ladies' Mutual Improvement Association in Nephi. She was the daughter of Andrew Love, pioneer of 1847 and one of Nephi's leading citizens. Keith Worthing-

ton, Sadie H. Greenhalgh, and Fred J. Chapman, *They Left A Record: A Comprehensive History of Nephi, Utah, 1851–1978* (N.p., 1979), 24.

48. Willard Farr was the son of Lorin Farr, a founder of Ogden, Utah. On 13 October 1877 he married Mary E. Ballantyne and in 1881 arrived at St. Johns with Elijah N. Freeman. He was a bookkeeper, clerk, and schoolteacher. David K. Udall selected him as a counselor in the bishopric, and Farr succeeded Udall as bishop. On 29 April 1886, he married Mary Ann ("Minnie") Romney, Miles P. and Hannah Romney's daughter, whom Ida refers to in her journal on 31 March 1886. AJ, LDSBE, 1:555.

John T. Lesueur, was born on the Isle of Jersey in 1852, emigrated to Utah in 1855, and in 1880 went to St. Johns, where he entered the mercantile business. He was elected county treasurer, probate judge, and a member of the Arizona legislature. He served on the high council and in the stake presidency after 1900. AJ, LDSBE, 1:330.

49. Early in 1885 Mormon leadership looked to Mexico as a refuge for polygamists who were liable to arrest in the United States. Companies of Latter-day Saints, led by Jesse N. Smith and Lot Smith, went into the state of Chihuahua, Mexico, and made permanent settlements of Colonia Juarez and Colonia Diaz, followed in the late 1880s by Colonia Dublan and Colonia Pacheco. Apostles Francis M. Lyman and George Teasdale directed the operations. At first lands were rented, but then the church purchased extensive tracts of land. Church organization was effected, and all features of Mormon village life were established. Polygamist men, sometimes with families, went from Mormon settlements in Arizona and Utah. B. H. Roberts, *The Life of John Taylor* (Salt Lake City: George Q. Cannon and Sons, 1892), 380–84; AJ, EH, a sketch on each colony; *Jesse N. Smith*, 296–321.

50. Ida here mentions some of the leading church and civic families in Nephi: Pitchforth, Bryan, Linton, Neff, Sparks, Paxman, Teasdale, and Millard.

51. William Ashworth had taken a new plural wife, Emma. Sade Maeser was a longtime friend of Ida's sister May. They carried on a lifelong correspondence.

52. Mary Jane (Mrs. John) West had taught school and studied organ before going to Arizona in 1879. On 12 July 1880, shortly after going to Snowflake, she became president of the Relief Society. Roberta Flake Clayton, ed., *Pioneer Women of Arizona* (n.p., n.d.), 655–60.

53. David Cazier was a pioneer leader in Nephi. Charles Sperry was bishop of Nephi North (or Second) Ward, 1877–83. Later he was counselor in the Juab Stake presidency, 1900–1904. AJ, LDSBE, 4:498.

54. Zion's Central Board of Trade was a new economic organization that President John Taylor established in 1878 as his answer to failing United Orders. Stake boards of trade promoted cooperative economic activities under a general coordinating agency. James B. Allen and Glen M. Leonard, *The Story of the Latter-day Saints* (Salt Lake City: Deseret Book, 1976), 383–85.

55. The autograph album is among the Ida Hunt Udall Papers. There a

some seventy aut
Forty-six were w
twenty-four wer
in 1894 and 189
56. There is
make his escar
was prompted
that the hors
therefore wo
57. Davic
28 April 18
tion claim
land office
residence
constitu
58. "(
mount;
palisac
preser
enl. e
On F
maj

m
w
c

Utah, 4:201. See als
Ellen: Two Mormon
of Utah Library, 197
family experience.
63. The picture ap
64. John Sharp, bish
wealthiest and most in
tember 1885 in the Th
trary to the Mormon pi
charge and promised to
went free. His action cr
day Saints. Whitney mai
intention to cast off his
and he never did." Neve
setting. Whitney, *History*
vs. 'Good Guys,' John Sh
Utah," *Utah Historical Q*
65. Aunt Lydia was the
66. Gideon A. Murdoch
15 July 1877 until 1893. A
67. Members of the Cro
Sade; Taylor, Jr., Bud; Willi
Frontiersman, 97.
68. David is going along
divert any possible attention
69. John W. Young, son o
ests, including contracts wi
which took him to the Little
ing the 1880s he spent muc
Church to gain political indep
anti-polygamy legislation." D
His Sons (Salt Lake City: D
70. *Deseret Evening News*, I
paper. *The Salt Lake Herald*,
tween 1870 and 1896. The *Juve*
especially for Sunday schools a
published from Liverpool, the
sermons, mission news, and ger
71. Franklin S. Richards was
and Jane Snyder Richards. He s
bar in 1874 and the California b
ployed by the church as legal ad
D.C., he was particularly influen
church. He exhibited great moral
and entertaining. AJ, LDSBE, 4:55

Edward W. Tullidge, *History of Salt Lake City and Its Founders* (Salt Lake City: Edward W. Tullidge, Publisher, c. 1886), 132–40.

72. The guitar is a Bruno and is a prized possession of Pauline's son Richard A. Smith of Provo, Utah.

73. The baby was Luella.

74. George Q. Cannon, a leading power in the church, was counselor in the First Presidency of John Taylor, Wilford Woodruff, and Lorenzo Snow, successively. He was Utah Territory's elected delegate to Congress. In 1885 he went into seclusion with President Taylor and there directed the church in secrecy. He took a train for California but was arrested at Humboldt Wells on 13 February 1886. On his way back to Utah he fell from the train and was hurt, but the marshal suspected an escape attempt and placed him under heavy guard. He was placed under a $45,000 bond. He forfeited the bail and went into hiding until 17 September 1888, when he surrendered. He was tried, found guilty, sentenced to prison for 175 days, and fined $450. He served in the Utah Penitentiary until his release on 21 February 1889. AJ, LDSBE, 1:42; Whitney, *History of Utah*, 3:478 ff., 634 ff.

75. William Thomas (Tommy) Stewart served as president of the Australian Mission from 1883 to 1886. He was succeeded by William Paxman, who served from 1886 to 1889. Lanny Britsch, historian of the church in the Pacific, estimated that "President Stewart was probably the most successful missionary at this time." R. Lanier Britsch, *Unto the Islands of the Sea: A History of the Latter-day Saints in the Pacific* (Salt Lake City: Deseret Book, 1986), 278–80.

President Paxman witnessed the translation of the Book of Mormon into Maori and printed it in April 1889, whereupon he returned to his home in Nephi. Ida could not help but compare her situation with that of her close friend Kate, a young plural wife who went with her husband on the three year mission to New Zealand. AJ, EH, 581. During the "underground" years, many men went on missions away from Utah, to spend their time more profitably for the Kingdom out of the reach of the marshals.

76. The McCune family, prominent in Nephi history, came to Utah in 1856–57. The father, Matthew, had been an officer in the British army in India when the family joined the church. A son, Henry F., and his wife Elizabeth Grace were well known to Ida. AJ, LDSBE, 3:160–61; Susa Young Gates, *Memorial to Elizabeth Claridge McCune: Missionary, Philanthropist, Architect* (Salt Lake City: Privately printed, 1924).

77. The ill treatment of wives of polygamists before the courts so enraged Latter-day Saint women that a mass meeting of Mormon women convened at the Salt Lake Theatre on 6 March 1886. A memorial was written, protesting the treatment of women, and ordered taken to Washington, D.C. Whitney, *History of Utah*, 3:492 ff.

78. The Deseret Hospital opened its doors for the reception of patients on 17 July 1882. It was located on Fifth East Street, between East South Temple and First South. AJ, EH, 184.

79. William B. Preston was presiding bishop of the church, 6 April 1884 to 5 December 1907.

80. St. Johns Stake was organized 23 July 1887 by the division of Eastern Arizona Stake into the St. Johns and Snowflake stakes. David K. Udall was the first president. See "Pioneering in Eastern Arizona," herein.

81. At this time, Pearl was four and a half and Erma was two and a half.

82. This pen picture of Pauline was included in Ida's letter to David, Nephi, Juab County, Utah, 26 March 1886 (see Letter 10, Appendix 2).

83. John Henry Smith, an apostle since 1880, was the son of pioneer leader George A. Smith and was prominent in both church and civic affairs. He often came to visit the Arizona settlements. AJ, LDSBE, 1:141; Merlo J. Pusey, *Builders of the Kingdom: George A. Smith, John Henry Smith, and George Albert Smith* (Provo, Utah: Brigham Young University Press, 1981), part 2. John Nicholson was a prominent writer and editor. AJ, LDSBE, 4:684.

84. As James R. Clark explained, the First Presidency, all in hiding on the "underground," chose to have their message printed, distributed, and read in absentia to the Saints assembled in regional tabernacles during these years: "The Presidency were safeguarded, their messages put before the people, and gentile merchants who had joined the anti-Mormon crusade lost the usual lucrative conference business in Salt Lake City." James R. Clark, ed., *Messages of the First Presidency* (Salt Lake City: Bookcraft, 1965–75), 3:45–73; B. H. Roberts, *Comprehensive History of the Church* (Salt Lake City: Deseret News Press, 1930), 6:168–69.

85. George Q. Cannon was in prison. See note 74.

86. Bishop William M. Bromley, American Fork Ward, 1883–89, did go to prison and serve his time. AJ, EH, 19–20; AJ, CC, 127, 131, 135, 143.

87. Co-ops had been established in most of the Little Colorado Mormon settlements. They were all part of the Arizona Cooperative Mercantile Institution (A.C.M.I.), which was patterned after the Utah Zions Cooperative Mercantile Institution (Z.C.M.I.). Apparently Ida had acquired stock by putting in cash or cattle while teaching school before her marriage. Peterson, *Take Up Your Mission*, 136–53, discusses these cooperatives.

88. The baby was Nicholas G. Morgan, Sr., son of John and Mellie Groesbeck Morgan.

89. The Sunset United Order, founded when Sunset was settled in 1876, had its successes and failures, but many people left in the years 1882–84, and dissolution soon followed, requiring a settlement with all members. A committee was appointed to conduct a full-scale investigation and effect an honorable and equitable settlement. David K. Udall was named chairman by the apostles. All properties had to be inventoried: livestock, real estate, ranch properties, A.C.M.I. assets and debts, and personal accounts. A fiscal history was constructed to distribute the assets equitably to individual families. The enormous task required much attention during 1886 and 1887. Peterson, *Take Up Your Mission*, 112–22.

90. On 7 October 1886 John Q. Cannon was arrested for polygamy and

placed under bond. AJ, LDSBE, 1:243; 4:387; Joseph Fielding Smith, *Essentials in Church History*, 24th ed. (Salt Lake City: Deseret Book, 1971), 596.

91. His two wives did not get along. See "Pioneering in Eastern Arizona," herein.

92. A "recommend" that a person be admitted to the Endowment House or temple, and was worthy to do so, had to be signed by that person's bishop and stake president.

93. Ann Louisa Pratt Willis had moved to Eagle Rock (Idaho Falls), Idaho, where she died many years later.

Pioneering Eastern Arizona, 1887 to 1905

1. This account of Ida's life during these years is based chiefly on her letters, the memoirs of her daughter Pauline, the personal records of her sisters May, Annie, Lois, and Nettie, and oral history passed on to Maria S. Ellsworth.

2. Annie, Journal, 1 December 1886, typed extracts in possession of Maria S. Ellsworth; May, Journal, 52, CHD Archives. Ida, May, Annie, Bell, Lewis, and John were all sealed to their parents.

3. Ida to Nellie Jones, Nephi, Utah, 5 February 1887.

4. Ibid. Obviously Ida had her grandmother's journal at this time, but the journal must have been returned to Ida's aunt, Frances P. Dyer. In the summer of 1906 Ida's sisters, May Larson and Bell Flake, visited their aunts, Frances and Ann Louisa, in Anaheim, California, and as they were leaving, Aunt Frances gave them her mother's journal. Later, Frances realized she still had part of it and sent it registered mail to Snowflake. She wrote Bell, "Ellen and I had talked it over and we had decided that we would leave it with yours and Lois's daughters. The night before Ellen died, she told me to leave it with Ida." Fragment of letter, Addison Pratt Family Papers, in possession of Maria S. Ellsworth.

5. Ida, Birthday Book, 1887.

6. Pauline, Memoirs, 2, Pauline Udall Smith Papers, in possession of Maria S. Ellsworth.

7. Annie, Journal, March 1888; Lois, Journal, 6–8, typescript in possession of Maria S. Ellsworth.

8. Lois, Journal, 6–8. Songs sung by the Hunt sisters, according to Annie Kartchner's daughters, Jennie K. Morris, Thalia K. Butler, and Leon K. Fulton, included the following: "'Tis the Valley of Custer," "Sweet Birds," "When the Little Birds Begin to Sing," "When the Leaves Begin to Turn," "God Plans It All," "Pass Under the Rod," "Blanch Alpine," "I Dreamed I Dwelt in Marble Halls," "This Evening Brings My Heart to Thee," "He Only Did His Duty," "Murmuring Sea," "Oh, Little Shining Silver Thread, Shining upon My Dear One's Head," "What Shall the Harvest Be?" (before it was in the church hymnal), "Ben Bolt," "Hard Times Come Again No More," "I'll Take You to Your

Home Kathleen," "In the Gloaming," "Listen to the Mocking Bird," "Silver Threads among the Gold," "Silver Bells of Memory," "Juanita," and "The Spanish Cavalier."

In the back of Ida's account book were written the words to new songs she learned that were sung to music fitting the versing. The songs include "Stick to Your Mother, Tom," "Bring Back the Old Folks," "Pretty Pond Lillies," "Queen of the West," "Why Do Summer Roses Fade," "The Bridge," "Who's on the Lord's Side," "Days that Are Gone," and "Darling Chloe."

May's readings included "Whistling in Heaven," "De Fust Banjo," and "Uncle Dan's Confession."

9. *David King Udall*, 149, 147–59.

10. Ibid., 160 ff.; Annie, Journal, March 1888; David K. Udall Papers, Special Collections, University Library, University of Arizona, Tucson; Lois, Journal, 9.

11. Annie, Journal, July 1888.

12. Pearl to Pauline, Los Angeles, California, 28 March 1909, Pauline Udall Smith Papers; Pauline, statement to Maria S. Ellsworth.

13. *David King Udall*, 160–93; Pauline, Memoirs, 16.

14. Pauline, statement to Maria S. Ellsworth.

15. Ida, Birthday Book, 1889; Pauline, statement to Maria S. Ellsworth.

.16. Ida to Ella, Snowflake, Arizona, 14 April 1889.

17. Ibid.

18. Ida, Birthday Book, 1890.

19. Ibid., 1890 and 1891.

20. Ibid., 1891.

21. Ibid., 1892.

22. Ida to Ella, [Round Valley], June 1891, David K. Udall Papers.

23. Ida, Birthday Book, 1892.

24. Ibid.

25. The meaning of the Manifesto was debated in and out of the church. Some held it meant only the end of contracting additional plural marriages, while others contended it also meant the cessation of continued cohabitation with plural wives. B. H. Roberts, a member of the First Council of Seventy, thought it meant both: "In effect, though not in express terms, the Manifesto went to the matter of polygamous living in violation of the law, as well as to the contracting of plural marriages. . . ." B. H. Roberts, *Comprehensive History of the Church* (Salt Lake City: Deseret News Press, 1930), 6:210–29. Frank J. Cannon, son of George Q. Cannon and political negotiator, insisted church leadership meant both, but, as historian Gustive O. Larson pointed out, "If . . . the church leaders included giving up their polygamous wives in their acceptance of the Manifesto, they soon reconsidered their position." Gustive O. Larson, *The "Americanization" of Utah for Statehood* (San Marino, Calif.: Huntington Library, 1971), chapter 13, especially p. 265, n. 1. The contest between these two interpretations is seen in various treatments of these events. See, for example, Edward Leo Lyman, *Political Deliverance: The Mormon Quest for Utah Statehood* (Urbana: University

of Illinois Press, 1986); and Richard S. Van Wagoner, *Mormon Polygamy: A History* (Salt Lake City: Signature Books, 1989), chapter 14.

26. Pauline, Memoirs, 27; Ida, Birthday Book, 1893.

27. Lois, Journal, 11; May, Journal, 2–5 July 1892. *Jesse N. Smith*, 3 and 4 July 1892, 388, described the Pinetop Conference. Publicly the chief purpose of the conference was political—dividing Mormon votes between the Democratic and Republican parties. John Smith, clerk of the conference, reported it in *Graham County Bulletin*, 22 July 1892.

28. Ida, Birthday Book, 1893; Lois, Journal, 12; May, Journal, mid-November 1892.

29. Ida, Birthday Book, 1893.

30. Pauline, Memoirs, 13.

31. Ida, Birthday Book, 1894. There are almost four years difference in the ages of John H. and Jesse. Most of Ida's children were born two years apart.

32. Pauline, Memoirs, 21; Ida, Birthday Book, 1899; Nettie Hunt Rencher, *John Hunt—Frontiersman* (Salt Lake City: Privately printed, 1966), 145; Eagar Ward, Relief Society and Y.L.M.I.A. records, CHD Archives.

33. Pauline, Memoirs, 35.

34. Ida to Nettie, Springerville, Arizona, 26 April 1896.

35. Pauline, Memoirs, 23; May, Journal, 44.

36. Pauline, "Ida Frances Hunt Udall," in *Pioneer Women of Arizona*, ed. Roberta Flake Clayton (N.p., n.d.), 638.

37. Poem-letter to Ida, Snowflake, Arizona, 8 March 1898, Ida Hunt Udall Papers, in possession of Maria S. Ellsworth.

38. Pauline, statement to Maria S. Ellsworth; Pauline, Memoirs, 32.

39. May, Journal, 14 November 1905.

40. Pauline, Memoirs, 18; Pauline, stories told to Maria S. Ellsworth.

41. Ida, Birthday Book, 1894; Ida, "Student's Notebook," Ida Hunt Udall Papers.

42. Annie, Journal, 2 September 1899; Pauline, Memoirs, 22.

43. Pearl to Pauline, Los Angeles, California, 28 March 1909, Pauline Udall Smith Papers.

44. Pauline, Memoirs, 8, 16, 30.

45. David K. Udall Papers.

46. *David King Udall*, 163 ff.; Ida, Birthday Book, 1900 and 1901. At David's fiftieth birthday party, Annie read from a bit of her doggerel:

> "When Alas! one dark day, it is found, though too late,
> Creditors have become anxious, are not willing to wait.
> The belongings held dear, are all rudely snatched,
> The home and the farm, everything is attached.
> 'This trial seems the greatest of all we have borne
> After all our hard labor to be thus rudely shorn. . . .' "

MS, Pauline Udall Smith Papers.

47. Keith Udall, St. Johns, Arizona, statement to Maria S. Ellsworth; Ida, Birthday Book, 1900.

48. May, Journal, 6 September to October 1901.

49. Pauline, Memoirs, 36–37.

50. Ida, Birthday Book, 1903; *David King Udall,* 171.

On 20 May 1908, Ida made application for land under Desert Land Entry No. 04607 (old No. 188), as follows: N 1/2 of NW 1/4, SW 1/4 of NW 1/4, and NW 1/4 of SW 1/4, Sec. 18, Township 14N, Range 26E, Gila and Salt River Meridian, Phoenix Land Office. Annually she had to file proof of improvements, which consisted mainly of surveys, fences, canal work, water development, and ditch and levy work for flood protection. She frequently sought extensions, pleading the forthcoming completion of the Udall Reservoir, but she was often denied. Final proofs were extended to 20 May 1915. Homestead Application Files, Bureau of Land Management, Department of the Interior, Washington, D.C. Her sister May noted Ida's filing on 18 May 1909: "Ida made proof on the land claim she is entering."

51. Ida, Birthday Book, 1904.

52. Ibid., 1903 and 1904; Pauline, Memoirs, 38–40.

53. Arthur M. Richardson and Nicholas G. Morgan, Sr., *The Life and Ministry of John Morgan* (Salt Lake City: Nicholas G. Morgan, Sr., 1965), 455, 465. David's marriage to Mary Linton Morgan was likely negotiated in October 1903. David invited his father and his father's wife, Aunt Rebecca, to accompany them back to Arizona. Ida recorded their arrival in her Birthday Book, 1904: "During the winter we were visited by dear Father Udall and Aunt Rebecca from Nephi and Sister Eliza [Udall Tenney] from Mexico, remaining with us some months. Sister Mary Linton Morgan with her three sons came with father arriving Dec 23rd 1903 where they expect to make their home, and share our fortunes as a family." See also Pauline, Memoirs, 49; May, Journal, February 1904. "Aunt Mary" is often mentioned hereafter in family letters and journals. She and her boys made their home with Ida until the spring of 1906, when Mary purchased a nearby house, vacated by a family moving from Hunt.

Confronted with charges of continuing plural marriages after the Manifesto, President Joseph F. Smith in the April 1904 General Conference called a halt to future marriages: "if any officer or member of the church shall assume to solemnize or enter into any such marriage he will be deemed in transgression against the church. . . ." Roberts, *Comprehensive History,* 6:401. Elders John W. Taylor and Matthias F. Cowley persisted, and they resigned from the apostleship in 1905. Later Elder Taylor was excommunicated, and Elder Cowley was disfellowshipped. Joseph Fielding Smith, *Essentials in Church History,* 24th ed. (Salt Lake City: Deseret Book, 1971), 575–76. The closeness of the time of this plural marriage to the prohibition may have been a factor in the family's saying little about the relationship.

54. This description of Ida's early life at Hunt is drawn from her letters; the birthday book; Pauline's memoirs, 45 ff.; and Pauline's statements to Maria S. Ellsworth. For background, see *David King Udall.*

55. Pauline, statement to Maria S. Ellsworth, and folk memory. See also Ida's birthday book, 1905, which tells of the devastations.

56. The Pearl Udall-Rudger Clawson marriage relationship was a closely guarded secret in the Udall family through the years and was not known at all among members of the Clawson family, until a grandson of Rudger Clawson established the marriage while researching the Clawson papers and writing the biography. Roy Hoopes, "My Grandfather, the Mormon Apostle," *American Heritage* 41 (February 1990), 82–92, and David S. Hoopes and Roy Hoopes, *The Making of a Mormon Apostle: The Story of Rudger Clawson* (New York: Madison Books, 1990), treat the marriage rather completely. The marriage is mentioned in the Pearl Udall Nelson letters in the David K. Udall Papers and in letters in the possession of Mrs. Louis O. (Jeanie) Glazier, Rialto, California. One can trace parts of the story in a number of other sources: Papers of Rudger Clawson, Special Collections, University of Utah, and in CHD Archives; Pearl Udall Nelson letters, Pauline Udall Smith Papers; AJ, LDSBE, 1:174–78; 4:313; *Jesse N. Smith*; St. Johns Stake Historical Record, CHD Archives; Church Temple Records, Index Bureau, card on Pearl Udall; *Graham Guardian* (Thatcher, Arizona), 16 October and 4, 11, 25 December 1903, 12 August and 2 September 1910, 16 June 1911; European Emigration Card Index, Church Family History Division, GS film #298, 438; and *Latter-day Saints' Millennial Star*, vols. 73–75 (1911–13).

57. Pauline, statements to Maria S. Ellsworth; Church Temple Records, Index Bureau.

58. Hoopes and Hoopes, *The Making of a Mormon Apostle*, 227–28.

59. Pearl to Ella, Eagar, Arizona, 1 February 1905, in possession of Mrs. Louis O. (Jeanie) Glazier, Rialto, California.

60. Pauline, Memoirs, 52; Pearl to Ella, Eagar, Arizona, 1 Feburary 1905.

61. Ida's six-month visit to Utah is told in her letters, chiefly to Pauline, dated 24 and 30 May, 15 July, 28 August, 6, 11, and 20 September, and 10 October, all 1905. Pearl also wrote valued letters to her mother of her experiences. See her letters in David K. Udall Papers and those in the possession of Mrs. Louis O. (Jeanie) Glazier. See especially Ida to David, Beaver, 28 August 1905; Ida to Pauline, Nephi, 6 September 1905; Pearl to Ella, Salt Lake City, 11 August 1905; and Ida to Pauline, Salt Lake City, 20 September 1905.

62. Pearl to Ella, Salt Lake City, 25 June 1905, in possession of Mrs. Louis O. (Jeanie) Glazier.

63. Ibid., 11 August 1905, in possession of Mrs. Louis O. (Jeanie) Glazier.

64. Ida to Pauline, Salt Lake City, 30 May 1905. The Philo T. Farnsworth home was one of Salt Lake City's most pretentious. Situated on the north side of Brigham Street (East South Temple Street), just east of Eagle Gate, it overlooked the city. Farnsworth purchased it from Priscilla Jennings in 1896.

65. Ibid., Ida to Pauline, Salt Lake City, 20 September 1905.

66. Ida to Pauline, Salt Lake City, [n.d. July 1905].

67. Ibid.

68. David to Pauline, Hunt, Arizona, 19 October 1905, Pauline Udall Smith Papers; Rencher, *John Hunt—Frontiersman*, 81.

69. *Joseph Fish*, 5 October 1905, 467. See also AJ, LDSBE, 2:215; May, Journal, 8 and 12 July 1905; David to Pauline, Hunt, Arizona, 31 October

1905, Pauline Udall Smith Papers; Joseph W. Smith, Journal, July 1905, CHD Archives.

70. David to Pauline, Hunt, Arizona, 31 October 1905, Pauline Udall Smith Papers.

The Ranch at Hunt and Ida's Last
Years, 1905 to 1915

1. Ida to Pauline, Hunt, Arizona, 24 October 1905.

2. Ibid.

3. Ibid., 24 December 1905.

4. Luella to Pauline, Hunt, Arizona, 1 April 1906, Pauline Udall Smith Papers, in possession of Maria S. Ellsworth.

5. Pauline, statement to Maria S. Ellsworth.

6. Ida to Pauline, Hunt, Arizona, 23 August 1907.

7. Ibid., n.d. October 1905.

8. Ibid., 23 November and 24 December 1905.

9. Ibid., 30 December 1905.

10. Ibid., 7 January and 13 January 1906; Ida to Nellie Jones, Hunt, Arizona, 26 January 1906.

11. Ida, Birthday Book, 1906, complete version in possession of Maria S. Ellsworth.

12. Don T. Udall, statement to Maria S. Ellsworth.

13. Ida to Mary Morgan and boys, Salt Lake City, 10 October 1905.

14. Ida to Pauline, Hunt, Arizona, 30 December 1905.

15. Ibid., 16 March, 21 March, and n.d. April 1906.

16. Ida to Pauline, St. Johns, Arizona, 5 January 1907; Pauline, Memoirs, 57, Pauline Udall Smith Papers.

17. Purchase of the Air Castle property in St. Johns was effected 8 February 1907. Book of Deeds, Recorder's Office, Apache County, St. Johns, Arizona. The instrument notes that $300 had been paid on the purchase price. Pauline, Memoirs, 64; Pauline, statements to Maria S. Ellsworth. See also, May, Journal, 14 February 1907, CHD Archives, for a reference to "the house Pauline was buying for her mother."

18. Pauline, Memoirs, 51, 52, 58.

19. St. Johns Stake, minutes of stake conferences and Relief Society meetings, CHD Archives.

20. Ida to Pauline, St. Johns, Arizona, 5 January 1907.

21. Ida to Pauline, Hunt, Arizona, 23 August 1907; Pauline, Memoirs, 59–65.

22. Pauline, Memoirs, 66–68; David King Udall, 266. They left Holbrook on 19 June 1908 and were gone just over a month. May, Journal, 13–19 June 1908. May had a communication from Los Angeles on 2 July.

It has generally been held in the family that Rudger Clawson paid for Pearl's medical training.

23. Pauline to David, Los Angeles, California, [July 1908], Pauline Udall Smith Papers: "These doctor bills and extra expense calls for more money than I have with me. In the morning I am going down and rent an invalid's chair which will be $1 per week. It will do mama so much good to ride and see and hear something. I am doing anything that will build her up if it does cost. I can't get my money out of Coop without a notice sixty days before hand so maybe you can send me about forty dollars before long and when I get home I can settle with you."

24. Ibid.

25. Pauline, Memoirs, 68–69; Pauline, statement to Maria S. Ellsworth.

26. Ida to Pauline, Snowflake, Arizona, 31 March, 7 April, and 15 April 1909; Pauline, Memoirs, 82. From Snowflake, 7 April 1909, Ida confided to Pauline this experience: "I was up to Aunt Mays all day yesterday the 6th and sister [Mary] West and Sister Nellie Smith came down in the p.m. and they three washed, annointed and blessed me in such a sincere humble way that I feel almost as tho I had been to the Temple and feel sure that I have already been greatly benefitted and blessed by it."

27. Pauline, Memoirs, 82.

28. "Hunt Ward," AJ, EH, 346; "Asahel Henry Smith," AJ, LDSBE, 4:598.

29. Pauline, Memoirs, 89; Pauline, "Life Sketch of Ida Frances Hunt Udall," July 1941, Pauline Udall Smith Papers.

30. Pauline to Asahel Smith, St. Johns, Arizona, 16 November 1908; ibid., n.d. November 1910.

31. Pauline, Memoirs, 91; Jesse A. Udall and Pauline, statements to Maria S. Ellsworth.

32. Ida to Nellie Jones, Snowflake, Arizona, 12 August 1910.

33. *David King Udall*, 176–79.

34. Ida to Ella and Pearl, St. Johns, Arizona, 28 November 1911, David K. Udall Papers, Special Collections, University Library, University of Arizona, Tucson.

35. Ibid., 7 December 1911.

36. Ida to Pauline, St. Johns, Arizona, 7 January 1912.

37. Ibid.

38. Ibid.; Jesse Addison Udall, *Jesse Addison Udall*, compiled by Lela Lee Flaherty, David K. Udall, and Louise Udall (Orem, Utah: Remember When, c. 1981), 13–15.

39. David S. Hoopes and Roy Hoopes, *The Making of a Mormon Apostle: The Story of Rudger Clawson* (New York: Madison Books, 1990), 279.

40. Ibid. See also Pearl's letters from England, David K. Udall Papers.

41. Ida's 1907 purchase instrument was not recorded until 1 March 1912. The 1912 deed was recorded 26 September 1913. Book of Deeds, Recorder's Office, Apache County, St. Johns, Arizona.

42. *David King Udall*, 178–79. David to Ella, Hunt, Arizona, 20 November 1911, Correspondence, David K. Udall, 1895–1911, David K. Udall Papers.

43. While living in the big home, the married children paid board and room. They were expected to help out with the work of keeping house and

cooking meals when visitors came. It is said that Levi's wife Louise objected to having to help out in the kitchen and refused to return to St. Johns after the birth of Inez, until they had a place of their own. They purchased the Air Castle and lived there a number of years. Elma Udall, statement to Maria S. Ellsworth.

44. Adele Hunt Ballard, statement to Maria S. Ellsworth.

45. When David, Jr., returned home from his mission to England, Alice White accompanied him, and she lived with the Udall family until about 1920, when she returned to England. Alice White told about her reception at the Udall home in 1913 in a letter to Pearl, Thornton Heath, Surrey, England, 3 December 1937, David K. Udall Papers. See also a 1912 letter from Alice to Pearl; Ida to Ella, St. Johns, 5 April 1914; and Ida to Luella and Garl, St. Johns, 14 May 1914. Pauline, Memoirs, 102–3, tells of Alice's association with the family.

46. Pauline, statement to Maria S. Ellsworth; Pauline, Memoirs, 91.

47. May's journal notes Ida's visits to Snowflake.

48. Ida to Nellie Jones, St. Johns, Arizona, 12 August 1910; Ida to Ella, St. Johns, Arizona, n.d. April 1914; Ida to Luella and Garland Pace, St. Johns, Arizona, 14 May 1914.

49. Ida to Pauline, St. Johns, Arizona, 27 December 1914.

50. *David King Udall*, 179.

51. Ida to Louisa Pratt Willis, St. Johns, Arizona, 22 December 1914. See Appendix 2 for the entire letter.

52. On 19 January 1915 her Aunt Louisa answered her, thanking her for her letter and telling of her own struggles to keep warm in her little house in Idaho Falls. She told Ida that her only surviving son, Tillman, had come from Jackson, Montana, to see her in October, and that if his copper and gold mine was successful, she would not lack for anything. Folder 12, Addison Pratt Family Papers, in possession of Maria S. Ellsworth.

53. Pauline, Memoirs, 110.

54. Pauline to Pearl, Hunt, Arizona, 2 May 1915.

55. Ibid.

56. Ibid., describes in detail the events surrounding Ida's death and funeral.

57. Ibid.

58. Ibid.

59. "Funeral Services," Ida Hunt Udall Papers.

60. Ibid.

61. Ibid.

The Legacy

1. Pauline, Memoirs, 119, Pauline Udall Smith Papers, in possession of Maria S. Ellsworth.

2. Pauline gave in, prompted partly by her concern for the "welfare of my

own soul, next for the memory of my angel mother." Pauline to Louella, 28 June and 22 July 1915, Hunt, Arizona, Pauline Udall Smith Papers.

3. *Graham Guardian* (Thatcher, Arizona), 1 October 1915.

4. Pauline, statement to Maria S. Ellsworth.

5. Pearl to Pauline, Los Angeles, California, 28 March 1909, Pauline Udall Smith Papers.

6. Pearl met Joseph Nelson while attending his sick wife and children. They were married 17 September 1919, and Pearl took into her care his children, ages thirteen to nineteen. *David King Udall*, 253–54. On 14 June 1893 Joseph Nelson had married Leonora Smith, the daughter of church president Joseph F. Smith, but she died 23 December 1907; on 7 February 1917 he married Edith Miller, who died in 1918.

7. The settlement of properties held in a polygamous family could be complicated, though in the Udall family it was fairly simple. First, re Ida's ranch at Hunt. Though Ida occupied the land from 1902, made a Desert Land Entry application for 160 acres on 20 May 1908, and made her three annual proofs, she failed to receive patent for the land. Her investments, mostly in labor, surveys, fences, irrigation works, canals, and flood control measures, failed to meet the requirements. Technicalities had to be overcome. She repeatedly appealed for extensions, based usually on the expectation that the Udall reservoir would soon be completed. Her last extension was to 20 May 1915, a month after her death. U.S. Department of the Interior, Bureau of Land Management, Branch of Records, supplied a copy of Ida's file: Phoenix DLE file 04607; copy of file in Ida Hunt Udall Papers. As late as 1920 David was working to obtain title to the land. On 28 February 1920 he wrote Pauline: "As yet I have not come into legal possession of our Hunt property, but I am looking to do so any day. As it stands now, I am not permitted to rent the house or property, as much as I would like to see the place making some interest." Letter, Pauline Udall Smith Papers.

Second, re the Air Castle, purchased by Pauline for her mother. The residence was in Ida's name until 19 March 1912, when she signed it over to David. It was later purchased by Ella's son Levi. See "The Ranch at Hunt and Ida's Last Years," herein, notes 17, 41, and 43.

Upon David's death, the pattern of making peace remained with Ida's children through the settlement of the estate and years thereafter. The will provided that his children were "to share and share alike in the division" of the property, and so it was. But Pauline felt slighted on one point, though she said nothing. The estate paid $839 to Erma for her months of caring for her father after her mother's death, and $1,061 was paid to Pearl for services rendered, including compensation for closing her medical practice and returning home to cook for the builders of the big house in 1911–12 and for taking care of her mother in Los Angeles when Ella had a serious operation. All this was approved, but no mention was made of Pauline's five years of teaching, with her earnings going to help the Udall enterprise at Hunt, or her purchase of the Air Castle for Ida, or her payment of all her mother's medical and other expenses after her stroke. As a result of these hurts, Pauline made a practice in her own family of keeping accounts of her children's contributions to and withdrawals from mission and college "funds." The will and related papers are contained in Probate file No. 300, Superior Court, Apache County, St. Johns, Arizona, filed 21 March 1938. The will was drawn up 15 January 1926 in Holbrook, Arizona.

8. Quoted in *David King Udall*, 208. See also David to Pauline, St. Johns, Arizona, 28 February 1920, David K. Udall Papers, Special Collections, University Library, University of Arizona, Tucson.

Appendix 2

1. Grover had red hair and fair skin, making him susceptible to sunburns. He had suffered a sunstroke two years earlier.

2. Ella, her son Levi, and her daughters Erma and Louella were keeping a hotel in Holbrook, where the mail drivers could stay overnight.

3. Aunt Alice was David's half-sister, Alice Udall Edgehill, the daughter of his father's second wife, Elizabeth.

4. Maud Pace was Pearl Udall's friend from Thatcher, Arizona, who was visiting the Udalls.

5. Caroline Smith, Pauline's friend from Snowflake, had invited Pauline to join her and Rebecca and Leonora Smith in a living arrangement while attending eight weeks of summer school at Northern Arizona Normal at Flagstaff. They were to live with Caroline's brother, Hyrum, and her nephew, Silas Fish, in the janitor's house while he and his family were on vacation. The men would do the janitorial work, and the women would keep house and prepare the meals.

6. After school was out, Pauline planned to take the county school-board exam in St. Johns. She wanted to pass the requirements for a first grade certificate, which required a knowledge of math and was good for four years, instead of the second grade certificate she now had that had to be renewed every two years. Pauline had studied math on her own at Hunt. At Flagstaff she took classes in algebra and physics.

When Pauline finished her work, she rushed to get home to take the exam on Monday morning. Floods had washed out the bridges between Holbrook and St. Johns, making it necessary for her to go by way of Snowflake, then to ride horseback thirty miles to Hunt, and to take the mail rig to St. Johns that arrived Sunday. On Monday she took the exam. When the grades were published in the Phoenix newspaper, friends wrote their congratulations, for she had earned 90 percent in algebra and 95 percent in physics. Pauline, Memoirs, 59–65.

7. Jesse A. Crosby was an older man working in his brother's law office in Flagstaff. He had access to a three-seated carriage that he used to take Pauline and her friends on excursions around Flagstaff. He was interested in her, as he proved the following summer when he proposed marriage.

8. Ida's Aunt Louisa was living alone in Eagle Rock, Idaho.

9. Tylman, or Tillman, her only surviving son and his wife were living in Jackson, Montana. Louisa was trying to get a government pension to help take care of her needs.

10. Louisa had lived in Snowflake with Bell Hunt Flake in 1913, but she had gone back to Idaho.

11. Marion and Cynthia Flake had twin girls named Maurine and Marvine, who were Bell's first grandchildren.

12. Uncle Marsh was John Hunt's older brother, who lived in Taylor, four miles south of Snowflake.

13. The English cousin was Alice White, who came to the United States for an extended visit with the Udalls.

BIBLIOGRAPHY

Unpublished Family Sources

Ida Hunt Udall Papers

Central to this work are the writings of Ida Frances Hunt Udall. Her writings were inherited by her daughter, Pauline Udall Smith, who bequeathed them to her daughter, Maria Smith Ellsworth. They include the following:

Autograph Book, 1885–98. 7½" x 4½" floral album containing messages and signatures of friends (most in 1885 and 1886). Entries usually record place and date.

Birthday Book, 1873–1905. 5½" x 7⅝" book given to Ida by her mother and grandmother, Louisa Barnes Pratt, on her birthday, 8 March 1872, Beaver, Utah, in which she annually recorded where she was on her birthday and, in later years, what she had done during the year.

"Funeral Services Held over the Remains of Sister Ida Hunt Udall, at St. Johns, Arizona, April 27th, 1915, in the Academy Building. Died 26 April 1915." Six typewritten leaves, 8½" x 11", containing minutes and summary of her funeral.

Journal of Ida Frances Hunt. 7½" x 9½" bound record book containing the memoirs she wrote to 8 March 1874 (pp. 1–9) and her journal from 6 May 1882 to 8 November 1886 (pp. 22–222). It also contains May Hunt Larson's continuation of the memoirs after 8 March 1874 (pp. 9–21), and "Memoirs of Pauline Udall Smith, Mesa, Ariz. 9 May 1951," penned into Ida's journal (pp. 222–30).

Ledger Book, 1875–1877. 3½" x 5¾", containing "I. Hunt's Account Book, March 25th 1875, Beaver City" (account with students, April 1875), words to songs, and "Ida F. Hunt's Diary, during Journey to New Mexico," 21 February 1877 to 13 March 1877.

Letters. Some seventy-four letters Ida sent from September 1879 to January 1915. An additional six letters are in the David K. Udall Papers, Special

Collections, Library, University of Arizona, Tucson, and two are in the Addison Pratt Family Papers in possession of Maria S. Ellsworth.

Poem-letter to Ida Hunt Udall, from Snowflake, Arizona, 8 March 1898. Two leaves, 8½" x 14", containing a birthday greeting recounting and naming Ida's suitors. Signed by Alof Larson, May H. Larson, Orrin Kartchner, Anne H. Kartchner, Bell H. Flake, Lewis Hunt, Della Hunt, John Hunt, Nellie Hunt, and Nettie Hunt.

"Sketch of the Lives of My Grandparents Jefferson and Celia Hunt, Read at the Birthday Celebration of Bishop John Hunt Held in Snowflake Stake House March 9th 1905, by Ida Hunt Udall." Five leaves, 7¾" x 10¼", written on both sides.

Student's Notebook. 5¾" x 8¾" notebook filled with her writing. Contains her notes taken in February 1894 at the women's physiological, hygienic reform class taught by Ruth Hatch in Snowflake, Arizona.

Pauline Udall Smith Papers

Preserved by Pauline Udall (Mrs. Asahel Henry) Smith, of Snowflake and Mesa, Arizona, consisting mainly of letters sent and letters received. In the custody of Maria S. Ellsworth. Included in the collection of her papers are these biographical writings:

Pauline Udall Smith. "Ida Frances Hunt Udall." In *Pioneer Women of Arizona*, edited by Roberta Flake Clayton. Mesa, Arizona: N.p., n.d.
———. *Memoirs of Pauline Udall Smith*. Logan, Utah: Privately printed, 1976. Typewritten, 568 pp. Limited edition of twelve copies, distributed among her children. A careful transcription of the holograph, filed among the Pauline Udall Smith Papers.

David K. Udall Papers

Collected by Elma Udall and presented to Special Collections, University Library, University of Arizona, Tucson. This research studied mainly the following:

"Correspondence—Ida Hunt Udall, 1889–1911." Copies of six Ida letters, holographs in this collection, have been placed in the Ida Hunt Udall Papers.

"Correspondence—Pauline Udall Smith."

Journal, 1898.

Other Family Papers

In addition to Ida's documents, unpublished materials for her life story include the personal records of her immediate family listed below. Unless otherwise mentioned, these (as described) are all in the possession of Maria S. Ellsworth.

Crosby, Caroline Barnes (Mrs. Jonathan). Memoirs and Journal. Thirty-six signatures or sections grouped into ten folders. Memoirs to September 1846; journal-memoir, 10 May 1848 to 7 February 1853; journal to 2 December 1882. Holograph in Utah State Historical Society; typescript in possession of Maria S. Ellsworth. Cited as Caroline Barnes Crosby, Journal.

Kartchner, Annella ("Annie") Hunt (Mrs. Orrin). "Excerpts from the Journal of My Mother Annella Hunt Kartchner, Which Mention Aunt Ida Hunt Udall, Mother's Oldest Sister. Copied by Thalia K. Butler." Four leaves, 8½" x 14", typewritten on both sides. Cited as Annie, Journal.

Larson, May Hunt (Mrs. Alof). A continuation of Ida Hunt Udall's memoirs, after 8 March 1874, written in Ida's journal, pp. 9–21.

———. "A Continuation of Sister Ida F. Hunt Udall's Birthdays, by May Hunt Larson." Six leaves, 5" x 8", beginning 8 March 1906 and concluding with an entry treating her funeral on 27 April 1915.

———. Journals, May 1894 to April 1943. Six volumes, including reminiscences of her life until May 1894. Holograph in CHD Archives; microfilm copy in possession of Maria S. Ellsworth. Cited as May, Journal.

Nelson, Pearl Udall (Mrs. Joseph). Letters in David K. Udall Papers and other letters in possession of Jeanie (Mrs. Louis O.) Glazier, Rialto, California.

———. "Synopsis of Sketch of Mother's Life—For D.U.P. Camp," Salt Lake City, 12 May 1933. Biography of Eliza Luella Stewart Udall. Three typewritten leaves, 8½" x 11", on four sides.

Pratt, Louisa Barnes (Mrs. Addison). Journal-Memoir to 1880. Eleven signatures rewritten from earlier drafts. Holographs in CHD Archives; typescript in possession of Maria S. Ellsworth. Cited as Louisa Barnes Pratt, Journal, with page numbers of typescript. The journal-memoir was published, reduced about one-third, as the "Journal of Louisa Barnes Pratt." In *Heart Throbs of the West*, vol. 8, edited by Kate Carter. Salt Lake City, Utah: Daughters of Utah Pioneers, 1947.

Pratt family. Addison Pratt Family Papers. Documents, letters sent, letters received, and mementos.

West, Lois ("Loie") Hunt (Mrs. Joseph A.). "The Journal of Lois Hunt West." Typescript by Jack H. West. Cited as Lois, Journal.

Other Manuscripts and Documents

Dalton, Lucinda Lee. "Autobiography," Circle Valley, Piute County, Utah Territory, 1876. Bancroft MS. P-F 20, Bancroft Library, University of California, Berkeley.

Fish, Joseph. "History of Arizona Territory." Typescript. Microfilm copy, JP 532, CHD Archives.

Richards, Jane Snyder. "The Inner Facts of Social Life in Utah," San Francisco, 1880. Bancroft MS. P-F 2, Bancroft Library, University of California, Berkeley.

Smith, Joseph W. Journal, 1859–1939. Holograph, CHD Archives.

Tanner, George S. "As It Was? or As You Like It?" 1987. Three-page, typewritten account of the trip Ida took from Beaver, Utah, to Snowflake, Arizona, in 1877. Copy in possession of Maria S. Ellsworth.

Ward and Stake Records in the Archives of the Church of Jesus Christ of Latter-day Saints, Salt Lake City, Utah. A variety of records were kept in the wards and stakes during the pioneer period, including historical records, minute books, and roll books of the Relief Society, Sunday School, Y.M.M.I.A., Y.L.M.I.A., and special programs. Extant records from Beaver, Utah, and Eagar, Snowflake, and St. Johns, Arizona, have been searched for reference to Ida Hunt Udall.

Published Primary Sources

Ellsworth, S. George, ed. *The Journals of Addison Pratt, Being a Narrative of Yankee Whaling in the Eighteen Twenties, a Mormon Mission to the Society Islands, and of Early California and Utah in the Eighteen Forties and Fifties.* Salt Lake City: University of Utah Press, 1990.

Fish, Joseph. *The Life and Times of Joseph Fish, Mormon Pioneer.* Journal edited by John H. Krenkel. Danville, Ill.: Interstate Printers and Publishers, 1970.

Pratt, Louisa Barnes. "Journal of Louisa Barnes Pratt." In *Heart Throbs of the West*, vol. 8, edited by Kate B. Carter. Salt Lake City: Daughters of Utah Pioneers, 1947.

Smith, Jesse Nathaniel. *Journal of Jesse Nathaniel Smith: The Life Story of a Mormon Pioneer, 1834–1906.* Salt Lake City: Jesse N. Smith Family Association, 1953.

Smith, Pauline Udall. See Pauline Udall Smith Papers.

Udall, David King, in collaboration with his daughter Pearl Udall Nelson. *Arizona Pioneer Mormon: David King Udall, His Story and His Family, 1851–1938.* Tucson: Arizona Silhouettes, 1959.

Udall, Jesse Addison. *Jesse Addison Udall, 1893–1980.* Compiled by Lela Lee Flaherty, David K. Udall, and Louise Udall. Orem, Utah: Remember When, c. 1981.

Secondary Sources

Allen, James B. " 'Good Guys' vs. 'Good Guys,' John Sharp and Civil Disobedience in Nineteenth-century Utah." *Utah Historical Quarterly* 48 (Spring 1980), 148–74.

Allen, James B., and Glen M. Leonard. *The Story of the Latter-day Saints.* Salt Lake City: Deseret Book, 1976.

Anderson, Nels. *Desert Saints: The Mormon Frontier in Utah.* Chicago: University of Chicago Press, 1966.

Beattie, George William, and Helen Pruitt Beattie. *Heritage of the Valley: San Bernardino's First Century.* Oakland, Calif.: Biobooks, 1951.

Bennion, Lowell ("Ben"). "The Incidence of Mormon Polygamy in 1880: 'Dixie' versus Davis Stake." *Journal of Mormon History* 11 (1984), 27–42.

Bitton, Davis. *Guide to Mormon Diaries and Autobiographies.* Provo, Utah: Brigham Young University Press, 1977.

———. "Mormon Polygamy: A Review Article." *Journal of Mormon History* 4 (1977), 101–18.

Britsch, R. Lanier. *Unto the Islands of the Sea: A History of the Latter-day Saints in the Pacific.* Salt Lake City: Deseret Book, 1986.

Brown, Constance. "Wagons Ho!: Retracing the Honeymoon Trail." *Americana* 8 (September/October 1980), 48–53.

Clark, James R., ed. *Messages of the First Presidency of the Church of Jesus Christ of Latter-day Saints, 1833–1951.* 6 vols. Salt Lake City: Bookcraft, 1965–75.

Clayton, Roberta Flake, ed. *Pioneer Women of Arizona.* N.p., n.d.

DeBarthe, Joe. *The Life and Adventures of Frank Grouard.* St. Joseph, Mo.: Come Printing, 1894.

Ellsworth, S. George, ed. *Dear Ellen: Two Mormon Women and Their Letters.* Salt Lake City: University of Utah Library, 1974.

Embry, Jessie L. *Mormon Polygamous Families: Life in the Principle.* Salt Lake City: University of Utah Press, 1987.

Ericksen, Bess, ed. *Snowflake Stake, 1887–1987: 100 Years of Faith and Service.* [Snowflake, Ariz.: Snowflake Stake, 1987.]

Flake, Chad J. *A Mormon Bibliography, 1830–1930.* Salt Lake City: University of Utah Press, 1978.

Foster, Lawrence. " 'Reluctant Polygamists': The Strains and Challenges of the Transition to Polygamy in a Prominent Mormon Family." In *Religion and Society in the American West: Historical Essays,* edited by Carl Guarneri and David Alvarez. New York: University Press of America, 1988.

Garrett, H. Dean. "The Honeymoon Trail." *Ensign* 19 (July 1989), 23–27.

Gates, Susa Young. *Memorial to Elizabeth Claridge McCune: Missionary, Philanthropist, Architect.* Salt Lake City: Privately printed, 1924.

———. *History of the Young Ladies' Mutual Improvement Association of the Church of Jesus Christ of Latter-day Saints from November 1869 to June 1910.* Salt Lake City: General Board of the Y.L.M.I.A., 1911.

Hoopes, David S., and Roy Hoopes. *The Making of a Mormon Apostle: The Story of Rudger Clawson.* New York: Madison Books, 1990.

Hoopes, Roy. "My Grandfather, the Mormon Apostle." *American Heritage* 41 (February 1990), 82–92.

Jenson, Andrew. *Church Chronology: A Record of Important Events, Per-*

taining to the History of the Church of Jesus Christ of Latter-day Saints.
2d ed., rev. and enl. Salt Lake City: Deseret News, 1899.

——. *Encyclopedic History of the Church of Jesus Christ of Latter-day Saints.* Salt Lake City: Deseret News, 1941.

——. *Latter-day Saint Biographical Encyclopedia.* 4 vols. Salt Lake City: Andrew Jenson History Co., 1901–36.

Jessee, Dean C., ed. *Letters of Brigham Young to His Sons.* Salt Lake City: Deseret Book, 1974.

Kane, Elizabeth Wood. *Twelve Mormon Homes Visited in Succession on a Journey through Utah to Arizona.* Salt Lake City: University of Utah Library, 1974.

Larson, Gustive O. *The "Americanization" of Utah for Statehood.* San Marino, Calif.: Huntington Library, 1971.

Levine, Albert J. *From Indian Trails to Jet Trails: Snowflake's Centennial History.* Snowflake, Ariz.: Snowflake Historical Society, 1977.

——. *Snowflake: A Pictorial Review, 1878–1964.* N.p., [1964?].

Lyman, Edward Leo. *Political Deliverance: The Mormon Quest for Utah Statehood.* Urbana: University of Illinois Press, 1986.

McClintock, James H. *Mormon Settlement in Arizona: A Record of Peaceful Conquest of the Desert.* Phoenix: N.p., 1925.

Merkley, Aird G. *Monuments to Courage: A History of Beaver County.* Beaver, Utah: Daughters of Utah Pioneers of Beaver County, Utah, 1948.

"Organ-Building in New England." *New England Magazine* 6 (January and March 1834), 25–44, 205–15.

Peterson, Charles S. " 'A Mighty Man Was Brother Lot': A Portrait of Lot Smith—Mormon Frontiersman." *Western Historical Quarterly* 1 (October 1970), 393–414.

——. *Take Up Your Mission: Mormon Colonizing along the Little Colorado River, 1870–1900.* Tucson: University of Arizona Press, 1973.

Pusey, Merlo J. *Builders of the Kingdom: George A. Smith, John Henry Smith, and George Albert Smith.* Provo, Utah: Brigham Young University Press, 1981.

Rencher, Nettie Hunt. *John Hunt—Frontiersman.* Salt Lake City: Privately printed, 1966.

Richardson, Arthur M., and Nicholas G. Morgan, Sr. *The Life and Ministry of John Morgan.* Salt Lake City: Nicholas G. Morgan, Sr., 1965.

Roberts, B. H. *A Comprehensive History of the Church of Jesus Christ of Latter-day Saints, Century I.* 6 vols. Salt Lake City: Deseret News Press, 1930.

——. *The Life of John Taylor: Third President of the Church of Jesus Christ of Latter-day Saints.* Salt Lake City: George Q. Cannon and Sons, 1892.

Romney, Thomas C. *Life Story of Miles P. Romney.* Independence, Mo.: Zion's Printing and Publishing, 1948.

Roylance, Ward. *Utah: A Guide to the State.* Rev. and enl. ed. Sponsored

by the Utah Arts Council. Salt Lake City: Utah, a Guide to the State
  Foundation, 1982.

Smith, Joseph Fielding. *Essentials in Church History.* 24th ed. Salt Lake
  City: Deseret Book, 1971.

Smith, Pauline Udall. *Captain Jefferson Hunt of the Mormon Battalion.* Salt
  Lake City: Nicholas G. Morgan, Sr., Foundation, 1958.

Tanner, George S., and J. Morris Richards. *Colonization on the Little Colorado: The Joseph City Region.* Flagstaff: Northland Press, 1977.

Thomas, Estelle Webb. *Uncertain Sanctuary: A Story of Mormon Pioneering
  in Mexico.* Salt Lake City: Westwater Press, 1980.

Tolton, J. F. *History of Beaver: Dating from the Founding of the City to the
  Time of Admittance to Statehood.* N.p., n.d. Copy in CHD Archives.

Tullidge, Edward W. *The History of Salt Lake City and Its Founders.* Salt
  Lake City: Edward W. Tullidge, Publisher, c. 1886.

Utah: a Guide to the State. Compiled by Workers of the Writers' Program of
  the Work Projects Administration for the State of Utah. American Guide
  Series. Sponsored by the Utah State Institute of Fine Arts, co-sponsored
  by the Salt Lake County Commission. New York: Hastings House, 1941.
  See Ward Roylance for rev. and enl. ed.

Van Wagoner, Richard S. *Mormon Polygamy: A History.* Salt Lake City:
  Signature Books, 1989.

Wagoner, J. Jay. *Arizona Territory, 1863–1912: A Political History.* Tucson:
  University of Arizona Press, 1970.

Whitney, Orson F. *History of Utah.* 4 vols. Salt Lake City: George Q. Cannon
  and Sons, 1892–1904.

Worthington, Keith N., Sadie H. Greenhalgh, and Fred J. Chapman. *They
  Left a Record: A Comprehensive History of Nephi, Utah, 1851–1978.*
  N.p., 1979.

Young, Karl E. *Ordeal in Mexico: Tales of Danger and Hardship Collected
  from Mormon Colonists.* Retold by Karl E. Young. Salt Lake City: Deseret
  Book, 1968.

Recommended Background Reading

Since much of our story took place against the background of the church's
struggle to maintain its peculiar institutions against the prosecutions of the
federal judiciary for disobedience to specially enacted laws, general histories
of Utah and the church will provide some background. Orson F. Whitney,
History of Utah, volume 3, covers the years 1877 to 1890, with empha-
sis on political affairs and the antipolygamy crusade. B. H. Roberts in his
Comprehensive History, volumes 5 (pp. 539 ff) and 6 (pp. 1–229), covers
much the same subjects. Nels Anderson's *Desert Saints* treats the political
struggle much more succinctly in chapter 12 and has a chapter on "Social
Implications of Polygamy." As to the practice of polygamy, Richard S. Van

Wagoner has written *Mormon Polygamy: A History*, and Jessie L. Embry has a wide-ranging report in her *Mormon Polygamous Families: Life in the Principle*. The more recent accounts of Utah's struggle for statehood include Gustive O. Larson, *The "Americanization" of Utah for Statehood*, and Leo Edward Lyman, *Political Deliverance: The Mormon Quest for Utah Statehood*. These works represent most recent scholarship making the best use of the greatest variety of sources. The Arizona part of the anti-Mormon crusade has yet to be told altogether, but the general background for the story told here in this book may be gleaned from old and newer works. James H. McClintock, *Mormon Settlement in Arizona*, is basic, though old. The contemporary Joseph Fish not only left a fine journal, edited by John H. Krenkel, but a "History of Arizona" that has gone by largely unappreciated. An able and prodigious scholar, he has left excellent works. The most recent to survey the history is Charles S. Peterson in *Take Up Your Mission*, the work most likely to give a good, quick background on the history of the region. George S. Tanner and J. Morris Richards portray life in the Joseph City area.

INDEX

Note: Ida Frances Hunt Udall is indexed under Udall. Her Hunt sisters and the Udall sisters are indexed by their maiden names.